# THE LAND OF
# JOURNEYS' ENDING

AGAINST THE EVENING LIGHT THE SAHUAROS HAVE **A**
STATELY LOOK

# THE LAND OF JOURNEYS' ENDING

MARY AUSTIN

With an Introductory Essay by
LARRY EVERS

Illustrations by
JOHN EDWIN JACKSON

THE UNIVERSITY OF ARIZONA PRESS
Tucson, Arizona

*About the Author...*

MARY HUNTER AUSTIN (1868–1934) was the author of twenty-seven books and more than 250 articles, essays, short stories, and poems on subjects ranging from anthropology and folklore to metaphysics, the fine arts, and poetics. A precursor of feminism and environmentalism, Austin worked tirelessly to advance those causes long before they became publicly prominent. Born in Carlinville, Illinois, Mary Austin moved as a girl to the eastern slopes of California's Sierra Nevada; later events in her life, as recounted by Augusta Fink in the biography *I-Mary* (The University of Arizona Press, 1983), took Austin to New York, Europe, and Santa Fe, New Mexico, where she wrote *The Land of Journey's Ending* and many other works on the American West.

*Second printing 1985*

THE UNIVERSITY OF ARIZONA PRESS

Copyright © 1983
The Arizona Board of Regents
All Rights Reserved
Manufactured in the U.S.A.

The text of *The Land of Journeys' Ending* is a facsimile of the first edition, published in 1924 by George Allen & Unwin, Ltd., London.

**Library of Congress Cataloging in Publication Data**

Austin, Mary Hunter, 1868–1934.
  The land of journeys' ending.

    Originally published: New York & London: Century Co., c1924.
    1. Southwest, New—History.   2. Southwest, New—Description and travel.   I. Title.
F786.A928 1983        979        83-1217

ISBN 0-8165-0807-0
ISBN 0-8165-0808-9 (pbk.)

To
DANIEL T. MacDOUGAL
OF THE CACTUS COUNTRY

# CONTENTS

# ILLUSTRATIONS

# MARY AUSTIN AND
# THE SPIRIT OF THE LAND

WHEN MARY HUNTER AUSTIN left Santa Fe, New Mexico, on the third of April, 1923, to begin a 2,500-mile journey "between the Rio Colorado and the upper course of the Rio Grande," she knew what she wanted to find. Out to the south and west lay the lodestone of all her wanderings, a place she was already calling The Land of Journeys' Ending. Austin undertook the passage with great anticipation and not a little apprehension. It was to be for her a journey of return, an opportunity to recover a sense of place in her writing that had slipped away over the twenty years since the publication of her first and most successful book, *The Land of Little Rain.* "I see now," she wrote in 1920, looking back as she readied herself, "that where I came wholly into the presence of the Land, there was a third thing came into being, the sum of what passed between me and the Land which has not, perhaps never could, come into being with anyone else." That "third thing," that "transaction" between her "spirit and the spirit of the Land" is what Austin

ix

sought as she motored into the Sonoran desert to meet her guide and confidant Professor Daniel Trembly MacDougal in Tucson in the spring of 1923.[1] *The Land of Journeys' Ending*, dedicated to MacDougal, tells us what she found. It is a book about a place, reflecting the common denominator which Augusta Fink identifies in Austin's finest writing: "the awareness of presences and powers unsensed by the casual observer."[2] A book, too, about a relationship to a place and the history of that relationship, a history through which "men felt...the nameless content of creative spirit in the presence of its proper instrument."

Born in 1868 in Carlinville, Illinois, Mary Austin's first glimpse at the arid lands of the American West came in 1888 as she migrated by train with her widowed mother and an older brother to homestead in southern California. "All that long stretch between Salt Lake and Sacramento Pass," Austin later wrote of the experience in her autobiography *Earth Horizon*, "the realization of presence which the desert was ever after to have for her, grew upon her mind...something brooding and aloof,

1. Mary Austin to Daniel Trembly MacDougal, July 5, 1920, The Carnegie Desert Laboratory Collection, Special Collections, University of Arizona Library.

2. Augusta Fink, *I-Mary: A Biography of Mary Austin* (Tucson: The University of Arizona Press, 1983), p. 42.

charged with a dire indifference, of which she was never for an instant afraid."[3] The next twelve years of struggle confirmed these perceptions. The Hunter family filed on three homesteads in the southern part of the San Joaquin Valley near Bakersfield. There, without irrigation and in the middle of a drought, Mary began to experience the harsh realities of desert living. The homesteads failed; the family fought; marriage to would-be vineyardist Stafford Wallace Austin floundered; the birth of a retarded child added a heavy and constant burden.

Despite these trials, perhaps because of them, Mary Austin turned for relief to the natural world around her. Early on in her residence she met General Edward Beale, the man she remembers in *The Land of Journeys' Ending* for bringing camels into the American Southwest. Beale gave Mary Austin the run of his 200,000-acre Tejon Ranch and his foreman as a guide. Austin's wanderings about the Tejon laid a foundation for the intimate knowledge she came to have not only of the flora and fauna

---

3. *Earth Horizon: An Autobiography* (Boston: Houghton Mifflin Company, 1932), p. 182. I rely on this work, Augusta Fink's fine biography *I-Mary,* and T. M. Pearce's two works on Austin, *The Beloved House* (Caldwell, Idaho: The Caxton Printers, Ltd., 1940) and *Mary Hunter Austin* (New York: Twayne Publishers, Inc., 1965) for most of the biographical information which follows.

of the California deserts, but of its native cultural life as well. As she moved around the area, finally settling with Stafford at Inyo in the Owens River Valley, Mary continued to absorb the lifeways around her and the land that supported them. Out of this lengthy tenure in the desert came her first publications and the finest writing of a long literary career.

Although Austin thought of herself as a writer from a very early age, it took the encouragement and sponsorship of Western editor and publisher Charles Lummis to get her to begin to sell stories and essays. The first appeared in the *Overland Monthly* in 1893, and others followed in such national magazines as *The Atlantic Monthly* and *Cosmopolitan*. But it was the publication of a collection of sketches of the southern California deserts in 1903, titled *The Land of Little Rain* to echo her mentor Lummis's very successful book *The Land of Poco Tiempo* (1893), that seems to have provided Austin with the confidence that she could make a living with her writing. Armed with favorable reviews and the promise of more book contracts, she left her husband behind in Inyo and moved north, first to San Francisco and then on to Carmel. There a lively bohemian community of artists and writers was settling in around George Sterling and Jack London.

A mystic from childhood, eccentric, and opinionated in an age when women were not permitted
opinions, the experience of Carmel set Austin free.
There she could do or say whatever she wanted,
even set up her writing studio in a tree house. From
Carmel, Austin launched a whirlwind literary
career that by 1918 included publication of a dozen
books and over a hundred short pieces, as well as
continuous lecture tours throughout the United
States with forays into the literary communities of
Italy, France, and England. The power of Austin's
work, backed by her forceful presence, her eccen-
tricities, and her ambition, carried her during the
same times in and out of relationships with an
amazing range of literary and political celebrities.
On the European tours Austin managed to sit with
H. G. Wells, Joseph Conrad, Hilaire Belloc,
William Butler Yeats, George Bernard Shaw,
Henry James, G. K. Chesterton, and the Herbert
Hoovers. Back in Carmel, Ambrose Bierce and
Robinson Jeffers joined Sterling, London, and
others in exchanging ideas with her. And in New
York City, where Austin kept her writing table most
of this time, she held forth with William Dean
Howells, Sinclair Lewis, Vachel Lindsay, Carl
Sandburg, Robert Frost, Carl Van Doren, and,
inevitably, in Mabel Dodge's famous literary salon.
Although Austin remained tethered to an abiding

concern with Western American lands, she wished to address the whole of the nation's experience in her writing and in her talk during these prolific years. The world war, Washington politics, women's rights, mysticism, religion, American Indian affairs, the world food supply, and of course the flourishing world of the American arts: Mary Austin had something to say about everything and a market for what she said. But by the early 1920s the exhilaration had worn thin, and Austin began to question what she was doing and how far she had drifted from the California deserts. "I am writing and writing the same kind of hack work," she complained in a letter, "liking it less everyday, and not yet seeing any way out of it."[4] Austin's correspondent was Dr. Daniel Trembly MacDougal, naturalist and director of field laboratories sponsored by the Carnegie Institution in Carmel and on Tumamoc Hill in Tucson. It was MacDougal who helped Mary Austin remember the Land of Little Rain and to imagine a Land of Journeys' Ending.

Friend, neighbor, and long-time admirer of Austin's writings about arid lands, MacDougal took it upon himself to renew Mary Austin's early love

4. Mary Austin to D. T. MacDougal, Feb. 2, 1923, Austin Collection, The Huntington Library.

for the Western deserts. "I am concerned that you keep in touch with your subject matter," he chided her in a letter from Tucson dated March 16, 1918, "and that you will not, as did Bret Harte, go off with some impressions...and then write and re-write about them the rest of your life."[5] MacDougal urged Austin to get out of New York City and to come to the Sonoran Desert "as early as you can in April," for "life at that time of year would be very interesting and there would be enough taste of the desert weather to help your impressions without it being unbearably hot."

Austin accepted the challenge and the invitation, and after a short visit to Tucson in November 1919 began writing sketches for *The Land of Journeys' Ending*. It is very clear that from the outset Austin relied heavily on MacDougal's knowledge in composing the book. On March 13, 1920, she wrote from New York back to him in Tucson that she was having no trouble selling the writing spawned by the trip, but that she regretted "not keeping fuller notes in Tucson." She continued, "For instance, is there a name for that gap by which we left the main road to turn in toward Papaguería and what were the names of those distant mountains we looked at

5. D. T. MacDougal to Mary Austin, March 16, 1918, Austin Collection, The Huntington Library.

the first day you took me in?"[6] MacDougal dutifully
answered Robles Pass, Baboquívari, and the Coyote
Mountains, and even sent along a list of possibilities
in response to Austin's request for "the name of
some remote and romantic sounding Papago village." The pattern for the collaborative project
which was to become *The Land of Journeys' Ending*
was set. "I can take from you," Austin wrote Mac-
Dougal a few months later, "I can use your experiences exactly as freely as I use my own."[7] And by
October 11, 1922, as she made arrangements for
the second journey into the Sonoran Desert which
gave the book its final form, Austin wrote Mac-
Dougal to suggest that he "set aside some pages in
his notebook" for material that might be helpful in
writing it. Austin concludes in the same letter that
"this book must be in a sense, a monument to our
common delight in the Southwest."[8]

For all the planning, the trip fell short of Mary
Austin's high expectations. As traveling companions she recruited Gerald and Ina Sizer Cassidy, a

6. Mary Austin to D. T. MacDougal, March 13, 1920, The Carnegie Desert Laboratory Collection, Special Collections, University
of Arizona Library.

7. Mary Austin to D. T. MacDougal, July 5, 1920, Austin Collection, The Huntington Library.

8. Mary Austin to D. T. MacDougal, October 11, 1922, Austin
Collection, The Huntington Library.

young couple she had met some years before at a suffragettes' convention. The three of them left Santa Fe by automobile on April 3, 1923, and two days later met their guide MacDougal in Tucson. "The place I shall take you to is the place which I take all distinguished artists," he promised. "You haven't seen the beauties of the Tucson desert if you haven't been to this spot."[9]

The only published record we have of the journey the four took out across the Altar Valley and over to the children's shrine near Santa Rosa on the Papago Reservation is Ina Sizer Cassidy's brief memoir "I-Mary and Me: The Chronicle of a Friendship." As she tells it, the trip was one of those rare times when the human world and the natural world began to converge into meaning. The Sonoran Desert was in full bloom, washed clean by recent rains. MacDougal, who probably knew more about it than any non-Papago scientist in the world, shared his knowledge with an easy magnanimity. He proved, too, an expert camp cook, barbecuing ribs over a mesquite fire as Gerald Cassidy prepared delicate pencil sketches of the magnificent vistas. Ina Cassidy pictures herself as an eager ingénue, ready to give full audience to Mary Austin.

9. Ina Sizer Cassidy, "I-Mary and Me: The Chronicle of a Friendship," *The New Mexico Quarterly,* 9 (1939), pp. 208–9.

The setting seemed perfect for the "transaction" Austin was seeking between her "spirit and the spirit of the land."

You must decide for yourself how well Austin succeeded as you read the sketches that make this book. The prose is surely as expansive and perceptive as any Mary Austin wrote, and there is a stylistic confidence that could have come only at this point in her career. As we have seen, however, Mary Austin set out to the Land of Journeys' Ending to recover the relation to the natural world that she had known during the days in the California deserts, that direct, personal, and intimate relation she had captured in *The Land of Little Rain*. Her biographer Augusta Fink reports that in writing *The Land of Journeys' Ending* Mary wished to lose the "sophistication" she had acquired in the years since she left the desert. An impossible goal. Measured against the writing in *The Land of Little Rain*, these sketches in *The Land of Journeys' Ending* too often fall into a magisterial tone which works against the "transaction" Austin sought. The problem, no doubt, was the role of the eccentric, opinionated writer to which Austin had become so accustomed over the years that there was no shedding it for a trip or two into the desert. Ina Cassidy reports that all the way out of Tucson, before she ever set foot on Papago lands or in a Papago community, Mary Austin lectured the three of them on Papago history and culture. Cassidy writes: "The role of mentor is a favorite of I-Mary's, and, with her remarkable memory for the printed word, she really is a rich source of information. Whether this role is prompted by a spirit of generosity, a desire to share her knowledge, a subconscious prompting of her old 'teacher' habit, or an exposition of egotism, one is never sure. Her friends commend her for it; her enemies condemn."[10]

Back in New York again after the trip into the heart of the Southwest, Mary Austin found herself besieged by the very pressures she sought to escape. There were the magazine articles to write to meet the rent. She had committed herself to two other book contracts in addition to the one with Century for *The Land of Journeys' Ending.* The sustaining relationship with MacDougal strained and began to fade. Augusta Fink writes that "the book begun as a labor of love had become an intolerable burden." Austin's old friend Mabel Dodge Lujan, now firmly established in Taos, wrote to give support, certain that what Mary was going through was "a recapitulation—a cleaning up period...a metamorphosis—a kind of rebirth."[11] Perhaps. Not long

10. Cassidy, p. 205.

11. Mabel Dodge Lujan to Mary Austin, May 28, 1923 (?), in T. M. Pearce, ed., *Literary America 1903–1934: The Mary Austin Letters* (Westport, Connecticut: Greenwood Press, 1979), p. 174.

after *The Land of Journeys' Ending* finally appeared
in the fall of 1924 to favorable reviews, Mary Austin
left New York City for good and moved to Santa
Fe. There she built the house she called Casa
Querida. Into that "beloved house," until her death
in 1934, the literati in the area clustered around her
to work for the rise "of the *next* great and fructifying world culture" which she predicted in this book
would appear in the American Southwest.

*The Land of Little Rain* and *The Land of Journeys'
Ending* are Mary Austin's best books. Both find
their strength in their common subject: man's relation to a particular landscape. Yet they are very
different books. Read against Austin's biography,
they make a frame for the whole of her work, a
frame that marks her extraordinary achievement as
a professional writer even as it reminds us of what
she lost in the distance of that achievement. *The
Land of Little Rain* was the result of a long, day-to-
day engagement between an unfamiliar landscape
and a student eager to find meaning in all its individual parts. Austin's patient portrayal of all the
journeys that can be made into the California deserts, whether following the faintest animal trails
or well-defined "streets of the mountains," are all
distinguished by a sharp and loving attention to
particular detail. It is the kind of book that N. Scott

Momaday must have had in mind when he wrote in *The Way To Rainy Mountain:* "Once in his life a man ought to concentrate his mind upon the remembered earth, I believe. He ought to give himself up to a particular landscape in his experience, to look at it from as many angles as he can, to wonder about it, to dwell upon it. He ought to imagine that he touches it with his hands at every season and listens to the sounds that are made upon it. He ought to imagine the creatures there and all the faintest motions of the wind. He ought to recollect the glare of noon and all the colors of the dawn and dusk."[12] Out of just such a concentration *The Land of Little Rain* was made.

*The Land of Journeys' Ending*, by contrast, is the result of an even grander impulse and a grandiose sensibility. "Anyone can write fact about a country," Mary Austin tells us early on, and, as specialists from every cubbyhole in academia will testify, she pays precious little attention to them here. She is, rather, concerned with representing the "presence," the larger patterns and pulses of the Land which, in the immensity of their reality, go unremarked and even unnoticed.

12. N. Scott Momaday, *The Way To Rainy Mountain* (Albuquerque: University of New Mexico Press, 1969), p. 83.

By the time she wrote *The Land of Journeys' Ending,* Mary Austin was ready and able to open her vision to an astonishing scale. "By Land," she writes here, "I mean all those things common to a given region...the flow of prevailing winds, the succession of vegetal cover, the legend of ancient life, and the scene, above everything the magnificently shaped and colored scene." Much of the prose in this book proceeds directly from this breadth of vision:

> Thus the march of the tall trees is with the wind along the trend of the tall mountains striking diagonally across from the turn of the Rio Grande to the Grand Cañon, with scattered patches wherever the cumbres are high enough to drag down the clouds as snow, and hold it as a mulch for the pines.
>
> A little to the west of the Continental Divide, from the Fort Apache Reservation to the country of the Hualapai along the Colorado, the land drops off in broken ranges, along the Rim of the Mogollon Mesa. North of the Rim it lifts in alternate patches of grasslands and forest which exhibit the wide spacing and monotony of type characteristic of arid regions. Both the grass and the trees run with the wind in patterns that on a European map would measure states and empires, reduced by the whole scale of the country to intimacy. Once you have accepted the scale, it is as easy to be familiar with a grass-plot the size of Rhode Island or a plantation of yellow pines half as big as Belgium, as with the posy-plots of your garden.

In passages such as this Mary Austin increased the scale of nature-writing to the measure of the continent. As Henry Smith puts it "she has taken the unisonal melody of a Muir and scored it for full orchestra."[13]

For the sharpness of focus in *The Land of Little Rain* and the breadth of vision of *The Land of Journeys' Ending*, it is among the naturalists that Austin will find her most comfortable place in American literary history. Her fiction works when the land is a central presence, as it is in the stories in *Lost Borders* (1909) and the novel *The Ford* (1917); her theorizing about the influence of landscapes on poetic forms in *The American Rhythm* (1923) might stimulate further work if it were better known;[14] her own poems and "re-expressions" of American Indian songs seem locked in time-bound clichés; and her social theories, derivative as they are of a Victorian evolutionary view of culture, are probably best forgotten. When they surface here in characterizations of Indians and Negros, contemporary readers rightfully wince. It is in the tradition of Thoreau, Burroughs, and Muir that her

13. Henry Smith, "The Feel of the Purposeful Earth: Mary Austin's Prophecy," *The New Mexico Quarterly*, 1 (1931), p. 21.

14. James Ruppert makes a beginning in "Mary Austin's Concept of the Landscape Line," *Southwest Review* (1983).

achievement is most secure. She looked back to them, as Peter Wild observes, even as she "prepared the way for such as Aldo Leopold, Joseph Wood Krutch, Edward Abbey, and others."[15] Before Annie Dillard wished she could talk to stones, Mary Austin held whole conversations with the land; before Frank Waters found a mystical center in the Four Corners area, Mary Austin had felt it and named it; and long before Barry Lopez published his remarkable story "The Orrery," Mary Austin had let her imagination play with the desert winds in the saguaro forests out beyond the last spur of the Santa Catalina Mountains.

The most distinguished of Southwestern readers, Lawrence Clark Powell, calls this "the book that best embodies the essences of the region whose heartland is Arizona and New Mexico. It was written in her prime by a wise and indomitable woman who synthesized history, anthropology, mythology and religion, flora and fauna, the seasons and the weathers, in strong and poetic prose...the ripest, richest book of all the many that she wrote."[16] Those of us who come now again from all around

15. Peter Wild, *Pioneer Conservationists of Western America* (Missoula, Montana: Mountain Press Publishing Company, 1979), p. 91.

16. Lawrence Clark Powell, *Southwest Classics* (1974; rpt., Tucson: The University of Arizona Press, 1982), p. 95.

the continent to make this our land of journeys' ending need desperately to attend to those who have traveled here before us. Mary Austin knew that sixty years ago, and with this book she made a place for us to begin.

LARRY EVERS

# AUTHOR'S PREFACE

This being a book of prophecy, a certain appreciation of the ritualistic approach is assumed for the
reader. The function of all prophecy is to discern
truth and declare it, and the only restriction on the
prophet is that his means shall be at all points capable
of sustaining what he discovers. Anybody can write
fact about a country, but nobody can write truth who
does not take into account the sounds and swings of
its native nomenclature.

There is a peculiar flourish to the names of distinctive places, as of eminent men, proceeding out of
the heart of their life. Who would have the most
revered President called anything but Abraham? And
who would not readily pick up the tune to which New
Mexico was settled, from the exactly sounded rhythms
of Don Juan de Oñate, Gobernador, Capitan Generale
y Adelantado de Nueve Mexico?—not one syllable of
which is pronounced in English as it is spelled. You
would know at once that such a founder would choose
his capital badly and move it two or three times. Thus
you will save yourself much time by consulting the
glossary at the back whenever in these pages you strike
the Spanish trail.

Not that even a glossary can achieve perfection. For the Land of Journeys' Ending—is it not appropriate that it should do so!—has dragged and elided the sixteenth-century Spanish in which the journey began, almost to the softness of aboriginal name words, which are spelled in Spanish but in pronouncing are pushed back upon the palate like ripe fruit. Still, you will get a great deal more out of my book by attending to the Spanish accents and vowels, since there are aspects of every country impossible satisfactorily to describe except in rhythms that have a derivative relation to the impression the land makes on its inhabitants.

Being a book of prophecy of the progressive acculturation of the land's people, this is also a book of topography. And the topography of the country between the Colorado and the Rio Grande cannot be expressed in terms invented for such purpose in a low green island by the North Sea. A *barranca* is terrifyingly more than an English bank on which the wild thyme grows; an *arroyo* resembles a gully only in being likewise a water gouge in the earth's surface, and we have no word at all for *cañada,* half-way between an *arroyo* and a *cañon,* which—though, naturally, you have been accenting the syllable that best expresses the trail of the white man across the Southwest—is really pronounced can-*yon.*

There are also terms such as *abra, playa, encerro,* which cannot be Englished at all except by the use of more words than you will have time for when you attempt to inquire your way about that country. You might, indeed, without some acquaintance with them, be looking for a mechanician unexpectedly, and be told to "keep right along this road, here, until you come to an *arroyo,*—not one of these little *arroyos,* but a regular *hondo,*—then you keep up along the foot of the *barranca* until you come to a *cienaga,* then you go up along the *loma* until you come to a *cienaguilla,* and you find a *placita* . . ." but if you read my book conscientiously, you will have nothing to fear.

If, elsewhere, I have been less explicit topographically, in an attempt to describe the country by the effect it produces on the author, that also is within the province of a prophet of human nature, which lives so much more by effects produced than by facts described. Also, if you find holes in my book that you could drive a car through, do not be too sure they were not left there for that express purpose.

# JOURNEYS' BEGINNING

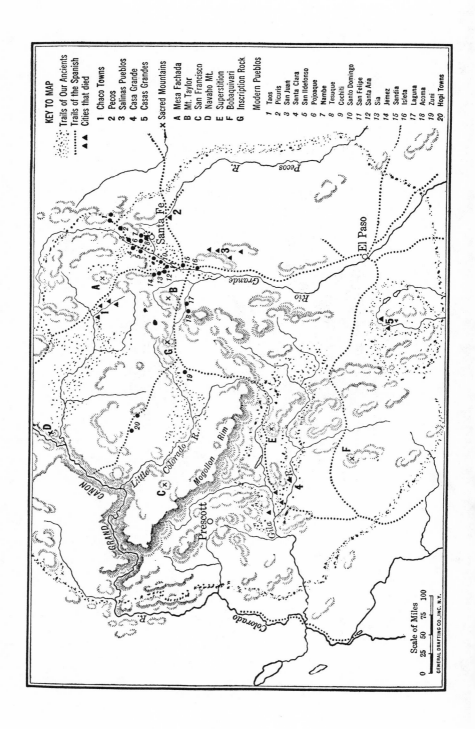

KEY TO MAP

· · · · Trails of Our Ancients
· · · · Trails of the Spanish
▲ ▲ Cities that died

1 Chaco Towns
2 Pecos
3 Salinas Pueblos
4 Casa Grande
5 Casas Grandes

× Sacred Mountains

A Mesa Fachada
B Mt. Taylor
C San Francisco
D Navaho Mt.
E Superstition
F Bobaquivari
G Inscription Rock

Modern Pueblos

1 Taos
2 Picuris
3 San Juan
4 Santa Clara
6 San Ildefonso
6 Pojoaque
7 Nambe
8 Tesuque
9 Cochiti
10 Santo Domingo
11 San Felipe
12 Santa Ana
13 Sia
14 Jemez
15 Sandia
16 Isleta
17 Laguna
18 Acoma
19 Zuni
20 Hopi Towns

Scale of Miles

0  25  50  75  100

GENERAL DRAFTING CO., INC., N.Y.

# THE LAND OF JOURNEYS' ENDING

## JOURNEYS' BEGINNING

BETWEEN the Rio Colorado and the upper course of the Rio Grande lies the Land of Journeys' Ending.

No such natural boundaries, but the limits of habitableness, define it north and south. About the sources of its inclosing rivers the ranges of the continental axis draw to a head in the Colorado Rockies. Southward they scatter, like travelers who have lost their heads in terror of desertness, among the vast unwatered plateaus of Old Mexico. But all the country east of the Grand Cañon, west and north of the Jornada del Muerto, is like the middle life of a strong man, splendidly ordered. This is the first sense of the land striking home to the traveler who gives himself up to it. Go far enough on any of its trails, and you begin to see how the world was made. In such a manner mountains are thrust up; there stands the cone from which this river of black rock was cast out; around this moon-colored *playa,* rises the rim of its ancient lake; by this earthquake rent, the torrent was led that drained it. What man in some measure understands, he is no longer afraid of; the next step is mastery.

That this is the first and the lasting effect of the country comprised in the western half of New Mexico and the whole of Arizona, may be discovered, if from no other source, from the faces of the men who first made it habitable. In any collection of pioneer portraits you will find one type of physiognomy predominating—full-browed, wide between the eyes, and, in spite of the fierce mustachios and long curls of the period, with a look of mildness. Superior to the immediate fear of great space, of the lack of water or the raiding savage, there was a subtle content at work. Seeing ever so short a way into the method of the land's making, men became reconciled to its nature.

There can be no adequate discussion of a country, any more than there can be of a woman, which leaves out this inexplicable effect produced by it on the people who live there. To say that the Southwest has had a significant past, and will have a magnificent future, because it is a superb wealth-breeder, is to miss the fact that several generations of men wasted themselves upon it happily, without taking any measure of its vast material resources. The nineteenth-century assault which found California a lady of comparatively easy virtue, quailed before the austere virginity of Arizona; but the better men among them served her without recompense. If the Southwest is becoming known as an unrivaled food-producer, still, food-producing is one of the things man has taught the land to do since he has lived in it. There was nothing that betrayed its crop capacity to the untutored sense of the Amerind savage and the unlettered American pioneer. Both of these married the land because they loved it, and afterward made it bear. If more lines of natural development converged here, between the bracketing rivers, more streams of human energy came to rest than anywhere else within what is now the United States, it was because men felt here the nameless content of the creative spirit in the presence of its proper instrument.

Such a country as this, calls its own from the four world quarters. It had called many known and some forgotten peoples before any European, just to hear of it, had been afoot, in that neighborhood, and that not of his own wish, for seven years.

In April of 1536, when San Miguel de Culiacan in Sinaloa was the northernmost outpost of Spanish settlement in the New World, and Diego de Alcaráz with twenty soldiers had pushed as far as he dared toward the frontiers of Sonora, on a slave-hunting foray, he met with a most deplorable spectacle. A man clad, so far as he was clad at all, in the feathers and amulets of an Indian shaman, twirling a painted gourd and followed by a negro and a handful of the natives of that region, burst, running, toward him, crying thanks to the mercy of God, in the Spanish tongue.

It was not until Maldonado and Dorantes, plainly Europeans, came up with them, that Alcaráz was convinced that the four were survivors of the party of Pánfilo de Narvaez, who, seven years earlier, had touched Florida and been forced to sea with all his company in open boats, hoping to drift along the gulf coast to ports of Mexico, all perishing except this Cabeza de Vaca, treasurer of the expedition, and his three companions. Now, whether, in their long walk from the coast of Texas, where their boat struck, to Sonora, the party of Cabeza de Vaca had heard anything of the terraced-house culture of the north, or learned that there was gold there, is a matter over which scholars to whom evidence, until it is printed in a book, scarcely exists, are still exercised. By Cabeza de Vaca's own published account, they came no nearer to what almost at once began to be known as the Seven Cities of Cibola, than the Sierra Madre, among whose somber pines he heard the green-plumed sititch scold. But there was also a private report whispered into the ear of the King of Spain, and why private if all was told in the *"Naufragios y Jornada"?* Gold, I am certain he did not hear of; for he was, after all, a Spanish gentleman, and if he had believed that there was gold in the north, he would hardly on his return have become the Adelantado of Paraguay as soon as the post was offered him.

But that he may have heard of large settled populations in the north, from speaking of which publicly he refrained, seems more than likely. There was, first of all, the trade in turquoises by which he had partly maintained himself in the latter half of his wanderings, to be accounted for; there were also the five emerald arrows which were given to Dorantes. If Cabeza de Vaca had inquired concerning the peoples from whom these things were purchased, and not heard of any other good reason for speaking of them, he would have found reason enough in what happened to himself and his companions on meeting with Alcaráz, who took them prisoners because they refused to betray their Indian companions to slavery. The wanderers themselves had been slaves to the wild tribes, and may have modified their account of the peoples of the north on the same principle that made them hold out against Alcaráz. But the negro, Esteván, whom the viceroy Mendoza bought from Dorantes, did not hold out.

Whatever was lacking from Cabeza de Vaca's account to make a good story of it, he seems to have added; and he was perfectly willing to return to the scene of his wanderings to search for the Seven Cities of Cibola, rumor of which sprang up too suddenly, in all the ports of New Spain, not to have received considerable augmentation from the survivors of Narvaez's expedition.

Of the stuff of which such rumors are made as presently set the whole tide of Spanish interest toward the territory that is now the United States, there was more than a little lying at hand in the popular report. There was first of all, among the Spaniards, the story of the Bishop of Lisbon, who, fleeing before the Arabs, had founded seven settlements in the islands of Antilla, lying *ante insular* before some fabled *tierra* to the west.   There was also a tradition current, among the Nahuatl tribes of Old Mexico, of seven caves in which their legendary Ancients had rested in their wanderings, easy to reduce to Seven Cities in a land where, as was afterward proved, whole cities may be built in caves and flourish there.   It was said of the Aztecs, who appeared on the great central plateau of Mexico about the twelfth century of our era, that they came out of the north.

And in the north, among the pueblos of the Rio Grande, which even at that date had a trade in feathers and turquoise and cotton cloth south into Chihuahua, there was a tradition of Poseyemo or Poseueve, a culture hero who, after being stoned out of the pueblos, in the manner of prophets had departed south, drawing after him the most revolutionary of their young men. Do they not dance yearly in the terraced-house country for his return? Whenever, as the Spanish conquistadores led them back and forth, there was mixing of the native tribes, and exchange of histories, it was inevitable that there should be surmises and identifications of their legendary great. Montezuma was Poseyemo; and Poseyemo, Montezuma. Thus, the tradition of a many-citied culture to the north, capable of having produced the founder of the Nahuatl nation, grew apace.

That the legend of Poseyemo should have become identified with the local prayer rites for the return of the rainy season, as is indicated by the local names for him, He-that-Scattereth-Moisture, or Finely-Divided-Rain, does not disprove him as the prophet and leader of young rebellion. And since the revolt of youth against the despotic communism of the pueblos —more strangling to individual genius than the less happy tyrannies of kings—must be led, why not by Poseyemo, who was born at that ruined pueblo above Ojo Caliente, as you go toward Tierra Amarilla?

Is it any the less likely that New Mexico should have produced the founder of a veritable line of kings, than that the whole of that territory from which they sprang should have been rediscovered through the combined activities of a Spanish adventurer called Head-of-a-Cow, a negro slave, and a Frenchman— a Savoyard, to be exact—in the habit of a Franciscan?

At any rate, the swift rise of a belief in Seven Cities having their doorways crowned with turquoise, and whole streets of gold- and silver-workers, must have had more confirmation than appears in documentary evidence, since it attracted the interest of the viceroy Don Antonio de Mendoza, one of the greatest administrative minds of the time. Pedro de Castañeda, who wrote an account of the expedition of Coronado, says that as early as 1530 Nuño de Guzman, at that time President of New Spain, had an Indian slave who told of trading with his father as far north as the streets of the silver-workers of Cibola, from which they had brought away good metal. But Guzman could hardly have believed it, or he would not have kept so long from the field. Even after the report of the Narvaez survivors, it was three years before anything happened.

There was, first of all, a tedious business of royal patents to make discoveries, and much politics. The wild tribes lying between New Spain and the Seven Cities were to be pacified by the revocation of the order reducing them to slavery; guides and interpreters must be found and trained. The choice of captains fell upon Francisco Vasquez de Coronado, who seems not to have had any particular qualifications for this business, except that of being a courageous gentleman with an expensive wife and a credulous disposition. But before Coronado's time there were exploratory sallies. Even Dorantes seems to have wished to have a try at the Seven Cities, which is another reason for thinking that his party knew more of the country north than appears in any report. Mendoza spent money in outfitting him, but nothing seems to have come of it. Finally the Franciscan Fray Marcos de Niza, the negro Estevánico, two Castilian greyhounds, and a handful of Indians set out for Cibola, arriving somewhere in the wilderness of Arizona about the time that Fernando de Soto sailed from Habana de Cuba to the conquest of Florida.

This was in March of the year 1539, and by the time the finely divided foliage of the mesquite began to gather like mist across the llanos, Fray Marcos and the slave had reached farthest north of the white man in New Spain. This would have been about the northern limit of the sahuaro in Arizona; but if our travelers made no mention of it, that was because they had seen cacti taller, in the place of their setting out. The *fraile,* while he paused to make the topographical observations required of every Spanish explorer, sent the negro on ahead, with instructions to send back crosses, beginning with a palm's span in size and increasing as the search for Cibola grew warm and warmer. In four days, came back a cross the size of a man. No doubt the confirmatory reports which the travelers began to hear on every side, of cities of stone houses four stories high, were magnified by contrast with the daub-and-wattle huts of the Pimas and Sobaipuris, which were all they had so far found.

What Fray Marcos could not guess was that the land had reached out and laid a hand on Estevánico. More a savage than the Indians who led him, the negro was the more sensitive to the concealed, pregnant powers of the land; like all lovers of the Southwest, he translated his subconscious impression of it into the certainty of success. From the first, in imitation of Cabeza de Vaca, he had adopted the rôle of the medicine-man. One sees him going north by trails the Indians showed him, his greyhounds well in leash; clad, you may be sure, in as much magnificence, Spanish and aboriginal, as the exigencies of the trail permitted, gathering goods and women at the villages that entertained him. Rumor ran before him that a god-man, one of Those Above, was passing. Such attention as this belief evoked, the Franciscan had borne with tact and modesty; but with every day's journey into the wilderness, Estevánico became less a slave and more a savage. He ended by disobeying the *fraile's* instructions to wait at the crossing of the Gila, and proceeded on his own account to the discovery of Cibola.

After him, through the country now known as White Mountain Apache, Fray Marcos came hurrying, finding huts prepared for him, and lacking neither

FRAY MARCOS AND ESTEVÁNICO . . GOING NORTH BY TRAILS THE INDIANS SHOWED HIM . . .
HIS GREYHOUNDS WELL IN LEASH

13

food nor water. Everywhere his inquiries were met with that pleasant disposition of the primitive to tell to those whom he would please, the thing they wish to hear. Great cities? Yes! Gold? Surely! Even the name Cibola, or Shivola, which appears to be a twice-corrupted version of Shiwina, by which name the Zuñi know themselves, was confirmed. It was with great surprise, therefore, that Fray Marcos met, on the last day of May, fugitives of the negro's band reporting the killing of Estevánico at the first of the Seven Cities.

It must be borne in mind that the negro is in most respects inferior to the Amerind, and the people of Zuñi are of particular astuteness. At Hawikuh, this side of Thunder Mountain, where Estevánico presented his trumpery claims to medicine power, the caciques were offended. They resented the boldness of his demands for women and turquoises; and when told of the numbers and might of his white brothers, they thought him a spy and a liar. For why should a white people have a black man to represent them? So that is the last we see of Estevánico, going into a city of Zuñi in his faked medicine trappings, with his greyhounds and his concubines, plumes on his arms and on his ankles; then confused rumor of flight and wounding.

Fray Marcos, to whom these things were told, was clear as to his duty. With two or three of the least timorous of his following he stole up to the heavily wooded southwestern rim of the valley of the Shiwina. Here he saw the red plain with the red river winding through it, and the flat roofs of Hawikuh crowning a brown, rocky promontory. He perceived that this was indeed a city, judging it larger than the City of Mexico. Having set up a wooden cross as a token of possession, he returned, according to his own account, with "more fright than food," to Mendoza. In this fashion was our Southwest made part of the known world.

Concerning the exploratory expedition of Francisco Vasquez de Coronado to the country so reported upon, which took place as speedily as possible after the return of Fray Marcos, there is this to say: it was undertaken at his own expense, and cost in the neighborhood of a quarter of a million dollars.

The charge that Fray Marcos magnified his report for the viceroy's ear, cannot be justified from documentary evidence. It has been naïvely recorded by a chronicler of that time that he produced the effect of having more to report than proved the case, by *not* talking about the Seven Cities to anybody except in strictest confidence. The fact is that Mexico City had filled up with young Spanish bloods, sharp for adventure. Word had already reached them, about the time of Fray Marcos's return, that De Soto had landed in Florida, and might, for all they could guess of geography at that time, be making for the self-same gold- and silver-workers' streets of the Seven Cities.   Men talked of little else; traded and gambled in Spanish ports of the New World for royal licenses to explore the country of Cibola.

Finally, in the latter part of February, in 1540, Francisco Vasquez de Coronado got off, with three hundred Spanish companions, most of whom were well horsed; about a thousand Indians, and four Franciscans in orders, including Fray Marcos.   Besides food and goods for barter, they were provided with droves of sheep and swine, and half a dozen pieces of light artillery.   The viceroy Mendoza saw them off from Compostela in four companies, in full military order.   Fine-sounding names their captains had: Don Tristan de Arellano; Don Pedro de Guevara, nephew to the Count of Oñate; Don Garcia Lopez de Cárdenas; Don Rodrigo Maldonado, brother-in-law of the Duke of the Infantada, and, for ensign-general, young Don Pedro de Tovar, son of that Fernando de Tovar who was guardian and Lord High Steward to the Queen, Doña Juana.   Noble gentlemen as ever were got together for the exploration of new continents. *Caballos* pranked in brilliant horse-cloths sweeping to the ground; lances and long swords; coats of mail scarcely less shining than the gilded armor of the viceroy; many-colored Spanish sleeves and hose; visored head-pieces of Spanish bull's-hide; crossbows for the footmen, and for the wild allies, who neglected nothing of paint and plumes for the occasion, war-clubs and bows and arrows.

Thus, amid an immense throng of onlookers and with great noise of flocks and herds, the expedition was set in motion. It is hinted by historians of that period that Mendoza found its departure good riddance, for many of that company were freebooters, trouble-makers in the provinces, and every ship from home brought new scions of noble houses that must somehow be accommodated in a country already looted to the uttermost. There was also at least one honest woman; for we find her husband, Juan de Paladinas, in 1560 petitioning his Majesty for some slight favor on the ground of what his wife did, in nursing the sick and mending the soldiers' clothes; he having undertaken this expedition with arms, horses, and servants "at his own expense like a good soldier."

It is likely that the splendor of the company was considerably abated by the time the advance party under Francisco Vasquez de Coronado arrived at the region known, from the clusters of small springs there, as Arizonac. This was in May, when the sahuaro was in bloom, the sand already hot underfoot, and the only gold they had seen, the honey-scented bloom of the palo-verde. North from the Salt River was uninhabited country, sparsely forested, leagues of red clay and needle-grass, gray marl, and menacing high cones of waterless mountains. About the fourth of July, lacking food and somewhat diminished in numbers, the expedition sighted the first of the Seven Cities.

This Cibola, Shivola, *Shiwina,* Zuñi, is a red-and-yellow plain reaching away to undulating hills in the west, blue with piñon, cloud-shadowed, dim with mirage and the whirling of dust-cones that on the stillest days rise unaccountably and go spiring skyward. The valley wall is banded red and white, and near its eastern end rises a vast rocky island, flat-topped, wind-carved along its streaked edges into towers and pinnacles, Toyoállanne, sacred Thunder Mountain. Where the mesa rises flat beyond Thunder Mountain is Uhanami, Mount of the Beloved Twins, guardians of *Shiwina.* Down the valley winds a glittering red streak of river. Not too far from it at any point, rise brown hummocks, squaring into brown walls and flat roofs, bristling with ladder-poles and chimneys of bottomless brown pots stuck together with clay.

Out of the first brown mound, the Spaniards saw the people issue like ants from an ant-hill, making, between them and the strangers, sacred meal roads by which it was vainly hoped danger would be averted.

Coronado demanded the submission of the town,

in round Spanish fashion, promising amnesty. The Zuñi shut the town and defended it from the roofs, with arrows and throwing-stones by which the *comandante* himself was twice knocked from the saddle. Everywhere against the mud walls the crossbows were at a disadvantage, but superstition played on the side of the invaders. In the night, after the Spaniards had gained a few out-dwellings, the inhabitants fled to their stronghold on top of Toyoállanne. At Hawikuh, then, the advance party rested while the rest of the army could be brought up from the Valley of Hearts in Sonora.

Of how Coronado made terms with the inhabitants of Hawikuh; of Halona, and Matsaki, and other of the Seven Cities of the Zuñi; of how Don Pedro de Tovar subdued the cities of the Hopitu, chiefly through their fear of the horses which the natives believed to be man-eating; how Cárdenas was sent to discover the Great River of the West, which he did within the eighty days allotted, thus proving that California was not an island, must be left for another relation. What mattered most to the expedition was the rage of the young bloods over the way the land withheld its secret of the gold which they—rightly enough, as it proved in the long run—could not disbelieve in.

As for these Seven Cities of which the eager imagination of Fray Marcos had made marvels, they proved mere aggregations of mud huts, piled one upon the other, the whole aspect of them as pasteboard crumpled and thrown away. As for the turquoise over the doors; the Zuñi had no doors, but entered their dwellings through hatchways, by means of ladders, and though it was the custom to place blue stones there to put the dwellers under the protection of the Sky Powers, these were by no means so many nor so fine as had been reported. Silver there was none, gold not so much as heard of, and so loud were the cursings visited on Fray Marcos that Coronado found it expedient to send him south again with the detachment that brought up the rest of the army from the Valle de Corazones. While he waited, early in August, came the representatives from Cicuyé, most easterly of the Rio Grande pueblos, to make submission; and with them, rising as unaccountably as dust devils in the wind, new rumor of discoverable riches. Don Hernando Alvarado, being sent to reconnoiter, pushed as far beyond the last of the mud towns as the plains on which were first encountered the fabled humpbacked cows which had long figured in rumors of the north country. As a result of Alvarado's report, the winter quarters of the expedition were removed to Tiguex, near the site of what is now Bernalillo.

There they saw the quick snows of that region mantle and disappear, saw the poplars whiten before they broke into green flame, and the fragrant fire of the wild plums run in the underbrush. Here the gorge of the Rio Grande widens to a fertile intervale, and the basalt cliffs are modulated to low, breast-shaped hills. North and south on tributaries of the river, west about the skirts of Jemez, east on the Salinas between Sandia and Manzanos, and north on the upper Pecos, in high-piled, mud-walled towns, were gathered the sedentary tribes to the number of twenty thousand. But there was no gold at Tiguex, either. None, at least, that the expedition heard of; though whether or not its existence might, in time, have been brought to knowledge, was settled finally by the exorbitant demands of the *comandante* for food and blankets, and by the burning alive, though that was not directly chargeable to Coronado, of two hundred Indian hostages.

It seems certain that, as a thing of use and value, metal of any sort was unknown to the Pueblos until the Spaniards taught it to them. Of gold as a matter of secret superstitious reverence, it was impossible that, after the first three months of residence in the Pueblo country, the companions of Coronado should have heard anything. Only when the mud roofs are muffled in snow and the flames of cedar run up the walls of the three-cornered fireplaces, when the ceremonial cigarettes are lighted and the talk turns to the days of our Ancients, you may hear something of the Seed of the Sun which made sacred the places where it was found, known only to priests of the Sun and a few elders. At first it was not clearly understood that this gold for which the Spanish went everywhere peeking and prying, was the same sacred seed. But, say the old men, after the burning alive of the two hundred at Tiguex, out of every village one society was chosen, and of that society, two persons were made the keepers of the secret, no one knowing who they were, and each choosing his own successor.

Whether by this process the secret has altogether died out, or whether indeed the very Ancient who tells you this may himself be a keeper, there is no knowing; no knowing, in fact, if the legend of the Seed of the Sun may not be such a myth of the mystery of gold as all men who have once felt the power of gold love to make of it.

The conquistadores, if not myth-makers, proved most notable believers. There was at Pecos, then called Cicuyé, a slave taken in war, a high-nosed Pawnee nicknamed the Turk, who had probably acted as guide to Alvarado's excursion in search of buffalo, affording him ample opportunity to find out what the Spaniards wanted and what sort of stories they would believe about it. What he made them believe was that in his own country of Quivira, his people ate off golden plates, and their chief went to sleep to the sound of golden bells swung from the tree-tops over him. He confessed at the last, when the Spaniards were about to kill him, that the caciques of Pecos had persuaded him to this deception, in hopes that the Spaniards, drawn away from the pueblos, might perish utterly.

Perhaps he thought of it for himself, thinking only that as a slave he had little to lose, and if he died, at least it would be where a man most wishes to meet death, in his own country. Perhaps Coronado snatched at the story, finding no other way to restrain the disappointment of his men from breaking out against himself in default of other victim. At any rate, in April, when the willows redden and the land is full of the drip of snow-water, we find the whole expedition setting out, with the Turk chained to the *comandante's* saddle-bow, for Quivira, no one of them willing to be left behind, and all so full of this new fable that they could scarcely be persuaded to carry full horse-loads of food, for fear there would not be room for the gold they should bring returning.

North by west they went, across the short-grass country, where the moving horizon shut them in at the distance of a musket-shot, where the infrequent rivers hid themselves at the bottom of unsuspected ravines, and the treeless lakes, round as plates, gave back the color of the fleckless sky. Bison they saw, with Indians chasing them, white wolves following the bison, and gray deer pied with white, in great companies.  It seems certain, from all accounts, that the Turk tried desperately to lose them, and that the difficulties of the way proved so insurmountable that the main part of the expedition returned to Tiguex, to await the outcome of the adventure.  Somewhere en route they heard of the Father of Waters, which about this time—it was in July that the company parted—had been crossed by the desperate De Soto.

The buffalo-grass bleached and withered, wild grapes ripened along the creeks, wild plums bent over with sweet purple fruit.  But at Quivira, which seems to have been somewhere about Wichita, Kansas, even the rumor of gold ran out.  Accordingly, having heard the confession of the Turk, they strangled him, Jaramillo says at night, so that he never woke up, but by another account, at early morning as a way of beginning the day well, which I prefer to think was the case.  For, though you have only to look at the track of their wanderings on the map to see that the Pawnee purposely tried to mislead the expedition, I think there was much to be said on his side.  And if he was what we suppose him, he would have wished to die at the hour when the Morning Star, guardian of all the Pawnees, consoled him.

Of the final draggletail withdrawal of the expedition from New Mexico, and its reception in New Spain, but one thing concerns us.  This is the trap the land set, and the lure with which it was baited to draw to itself the sort of people to whom its treasures would finally be revealed. Not only did Coronado miss all the mineral wealth of the country visited, but there is not even a mention, in Castañeda's account, of the turquoise-mines which were at that time worked by the Indians, located within a day's ride of his permanent camp. The one thing, however, that the Franciscans would not let him miss, was that there were souls here to be saved. Fray Juan Padilla, with some acolytes he had trained and put into the Franciscan habit, asked leave, on the withdrawal of the expedition, to return to Quivira,  on that business which he judged more propitious than the search for gold. There was also Fray Luis de Escalona, who with a few sheep, an adze and a chisel to make crosses with, and a great zeal for God in his heart, remained at Pecos. Of whom no more is known than a rumor that they died as became them. From that slender point of attachment was to be spun the thread that bound New Mexico to the known world.

After Coronado, the land had rest for forty years. The conquistadores turned their attention to Central and South America as offering the richest reward to their military and picaresque ability. The people of the pueblos worked the episode of the Spanish *entrada* into their dance-dramas, and named the pale-gold-colored papooses born to their women, "Children of the Moon." Of what finally became of Francisco Vasquez, nothing is known, but the Franciscans, who went everywhere in the New World, would not let that world forget the martyrdom of Fray Luis and Fray Juan de Padilla, news of which brought the brown skirts humming about the doors of the civil authorities, demanding as reparation the right and opportunity to convert the whole of that country to Christianity. We who are at the diminished outer ripple of the rings of missionary impulse, estimate it too feebly as one of the driving forces of the middle ages. Put it that Spain had swarmed, as a little later the English. Whatever the urge that compels great populations to sow themselves to all four quarters of the earth, the desire to spread the blessings of Christianity was, in the sixteenth century, a popular way of rationalizing it.

In forty years the colonization of New Spain had proceeded northward from Mexico City as far as Chihuahua, where it touched the extreme southern end of the immemorial trade trail that connected Mexico with the country of the Rio Grande. Across the wastes it traversed, trickled a sense of the true nodality of the land of the pueblos. It began to be thought of as the seat of a considerable culture, a center of human activity and interest, a *new* Mexico.

In 1581 there was a sally in that direction led by Fray Agustin Rodriguez to whom Don Lorenzo Suarez de Mendoza, Conde de Coruña, Viceroy of Mexico, had given permission, with two companions of his order and a handful of soldiers, to go mission-arying among the Pueblos. There all three of the Franciscans met the supreme reward. The news of their killing aroused one Antonio de Espejo, a devout man of excellent repute and fortune, to undertake an expedition of inquiry and relief; for at the moment it was not certainly known that all three of the mis-sionaries had perished.

The trail, which is one of the oldest traffic routes in America, emerged from Chihuahua, followed the Conchos River to its junction with the Rio Grande, up along the south bank, to a ford at about the present location of the city of El Paso. It also crossed the track of Cabeza de Vaca, as Espejo discovered from Indians he met, affording grounds, for those who like to believe it, that the survivor of Narvaez touched New Mexico and knew more of the terraced-house country than appears in his published account. North of this point the trail continues for a bitter interval along what came to be known as La Jornada del Muerto.

Espejo, being a man of tact, and the Indians by this time better instructed in the nature of white people, succeeded in learning such things of the resources and topography of the country as made it from that time forth part of the known and familiar world. He lost no lives and provoked no wars with the inhabitants. He discovered the Salinas, and brought away specimens of rich ores and precious metals which he says he found in the Indians' houses. This is a matter which wants some explaining. Something is due to the displacement of the reckless, lustful hope of gold, free gold, ready worked to the conqueror's hand, which had been the mainspring of Coronado's expedition, by a soberer appreciation of the nature and values of raw ores. But if the Pueblos had had no metal at all before the coming of the Spaniards, they could hardly have arrived at such a use of it, in the forty years' interval, as enabled Espejo confidently to assert that the country was as rich in minerals as it was already known to be rich in corn. What he brought away with him was the profound desire for the material mastery of that country which it provokes to this day in those who know it.

Espejo immediately applied for leave to colonize in New Mexico, as did many other Spanish gentlemen. And while he was doing it the whole village of Almaden made an exploratory *pasear* across the Rio Bravo and up the Pecos from which they were brought back under arrest by the authorities. Finally, by the devious course of Spanish politics, the choice of adelantado fell upon Don Juan de Oñate. Now mark how the note of high romance holds throughout the history of the Southwest. Oñate was married to a granddaughter of Cortés and of Montezuma, and he came for the founding of his first city to the very walls of that pueblo in which the fabled Poseyemo had taken refuge when his own town of Poseunge had denied him, from which he was finally driven in turn, drawing off with him all those rebellious youths, to found —so the Indians there believe to this day—the line of Montezumas and the Aztec nation.

Whether, among the numbers of Indian slaves and servitors, Oñate brought any of that blood to the land of their cradling, you may believe or not according to your disposition, for it was more than likely. At any rate, he brought the author of what was quite certainly the first American drama, a comedy relative to the conquest of New Mexico which was written by Captain Farfan and performed on the south bank of the Rio on the evening of the day of Oñate's formal *entrada*. The expedition had likewise its poet, one Gaspar de Villagrá, also a captain, to whose execrable but accurate epic we are indebted for much we know of it. Believe me, nothing of significance had been done in the land of Journeys' Ending but with something of the poet's largeness and the dramatist's gesture. Don Juan, himself, was, in an age of flourishes, distinguished for the magnificence of his own postures.

Arriving at El Paso del Norte, he took possession ceremoniously of all the country north, "In the name of the Most Holy Trinity, and the Undivided Eternal Unity, Deity and Majesty, Father, Son, and Holy Ghost . . . and of his most sacred and blessed Mother, the Holy Virgin Mary . . . Mother of God, Sun, Moon, North Star, guide, and advocate of humanity; and in honor of the Seraphic Father, San Francisco . . . patriarch of the poor, whom I adopt as my patrons, advocates, guides, defenders, and intercessors . . . I, Don Juan de Oñate, Governor and Captain General and Adelantado of New Mexico, and of its kingdoms and provinces, as well as those in their vicinity and contiguous thereto, as settler, discoverer, and pacifier of them and of the said kingdoms, by order of the King our Lord." In this fashion, with a very large company of soldiers and settlers, with seven thousand head of live stock and eighty unwieldy, solid-wheeled carretas, Oñate made his *entrada* the thirtieth day of April, 1595, and the long journey of Spanish exploration in the New World came to rest.

# "WIND'S TRAIL I AM SEEKING"

# "WIND'S TRAIL I AM SEEKING!"

## THE TRAIL IN THE NORTH

THE location of forests in New Mexico and Arizona is largely a matter of the force and direction of prevailing winds. These tend to draw along the chutes prepared for them by the cumbres of the Continental Divide. From the gulfs of California and Mexico, great wind rivers go over with enormous freightage of sunlit cloud. Surcharged, they pile and topple and carom against the raking ranges and give down the precious ballast of the rain. Or the wind leaves them in fleets, like great barges becalmed in mid-air, until they darkle and run together and reveal the true nature of clouds. On the miraculous floor of the air the Rain stands upright between the mountains. In pure, shadowed grayness it stretches from cumbre to cumbre. "White blossom clouds, clouds like the plains!" says the Rain-song of the Sia.

Then the checked mass begins to bellow for the wind, *Thona! thona!* the voice of the Rain standing! Into its cavernous blueness the People of the Lightning send their serpent-darting arrows. Around the roots of the junipers the rain makes slithery yellow

33

runnels; it gurgles in the acequias.   The great Corn Plant rejoices.   From some far pasture of the sky the wind comes hurrying.   Oh, then, to see the Rain walking!

Trailing rainbow veils, it moves between the ranges, thundering and shining.   "It stands, the great bow stands on the summits of the mountains!" sings the Rain-cloud clan.

As the moving weight of moisture thins, the wind catches it again, rolls up the suspended particles as children roll snowballs, glistening, rounded.   As cloud it sails again the great wind rivers.

Thus the march of the tall trees is with the wind along the trend of the tall mountains striking diagonally across from the turn of the Rio Grande to the Grand Cañon, with scattered patches wherever the cumbres are high enough to drag down the clouds as snow, and hold it as a mulch for thé pines.

A little to the west of the Continental Divide, from the Fort Apache Reservation to the country of the Hualapai along the Colorado, the land drops off in broken ranges, along the Rim of the Mogollon Mesa. North of the Rim it lifts in alternate patches of grasslands and forest which exhibit the wide spacing and monotony of type characteristic of arid regions.   Both the grass and the trees run with the wind in patterns that on a European map would measure states and empires, reduced by the whole scale of the country to intimacy.  Once you have accepted the scale, it is as easy to be familiar with a grass-plot the size of Rhode Island or a plantation of yellow pines half as big as Belgium, as with the posy-plots of your garden.  This would be about the eight-thousand- or nine-thousand-foot levels, for above ten thousand feet there is little difference between the forest cover of New Mexico and that of the Colorado Rockies.  The Douglas spruce, by whose root, according to the Tewas, the first men climbed up from the under-world, flourishes on these altitude islands, manured by the lasting snows, and innumerable blossomy brush and herbs, accredited to New Mexico and Arizona but alien to the types of vegetative life that give character to the country north of the Rim.  For true mesa cover, one must keep to the coasts of the great wind rivers, and the region of uncertain rain.

Where the continental trails cross the National Forest Reserves of Tusayan and Coconino, regiments of yellow pine may be discovered deploying about the basins of "dry lakes" and holding the seven-thousand- and eight-thousand-foot levels without a break, except where occasionally, below some granitic outcrop, a seasonal spring makes footing for a clump of quaking aspens.  It is noticeable that the butts of arid-region pines are without the bulging curve toward the down-throw of the hills which, in the region of lasting snow, shows where the weight of the season's fall has been

supported.  Here the thin air and the coarse soil drink
the snow with such rapidity, that, even while it falls,
it may be seen disappearing around the pine-boles like
water lowering in the trough of a thirsty horse.  In
the yellow-pine regions the lift of the needle crown is
occasionally high enough to admit a scant carpeting
of grass on a patch of deciduous growth, but where
the volcanic drift runs out into whitish marl, the road
straightens through park-like intervals, in which
nothing is tolerated but the universal juniper of the
New Mexican highlands, fat pineapple shapes resting
on the swept marl.

At the turn of the two seasons, following the march
of the sun home from the north or up from the
south, a far-flung wing of storm sifts fine snow like
down, or finer rain, over the masked shapes that by a
solemn movement of their boughs give thanks.  In
May or April, in the storm-cleared space that no seedling has yet preëmpted for its own, white borage or
blue nemophila creeps low as a church mouse, and the
black-and-white flash of a magpie's wings startles like
the striking of a match.  Nothing else for a thousand
years.

East of the Rio Grande the junipers are small and
widely interspersed among the green rosettes of the
one-leaved piñon pines, with which the pale hills are
spotted like an ocelot.  The green of the junipers is
slightly yellower than the pines, which may also be

identified for the stranger by their tendency to run to
a true tree form with an upright stem, and by the
blue back and the white ellipse of the spread wings of
the piñonero, the piñon jay, whose winter pasturage
is extracted from small, globose cones.  From Raton
Pass, the gateway of New Mexico, juniper and piñon
hold steadily south and west until they give place, beyond Albuquerque, to mesquite and creosote and salt-
bush, each keeping to its kind, in open order on a
gravelly, grassless ground.

It is this prevalence of a single type of growth over
enormous areas, combined with the lack of surface
cover for the naked, fire-colored sands, that gives the
Southwest its undeserved reputation for desertness.
To most people a forest is a persisting communality
of tree and plant life, thought of in collective terms
as one thinks of a city.  What you have here is a pine
and another pine and another, mesquite and mesquite
and mesquite, each in its inviolate circle of bare earth,
bound together by not so much as the roots of grass.
And to many people grass is as indispensable an index
of fertility in the earth as long hair is of femininity
in a woman.  Actually, all that grass and other annual
cover afford to the casual observer, is evidence of the
quick, continuous rhythms of vegetating life.  But in
arid regions where the period of growth is confined
to the short season of maximum rainfall, the processes of foliation and floration are pushed almost to

explosion; followed by a long quiescence in which life merely persists.   To feel the growing pulse of the New Mexican forest, you must take to the trail weeks before the high passes are open, loitering about the Santa Fé highlands until you discover, in the leaning towers of the yellow pine along the lowest limit of summer waters, the magpie on whose wings are the footsteps of the morning.   If you see one, cross yourself and return to your home.   But two together are a fortunate omen.

The first sound of spring in the Rio Grande country is the sound of snow-water.   In the March-April Moon, the Moon of the Rabbit Brush Disappearing, when the Indians take down their wind-breaks and shelters, snow may still fall.   Lodging like fluffs of cloud on the flat roofs and the finely divided foliage of the piñon pines, it begins at once to sparkle with the dew of the drip.   The drip quickens to a gurgle.   Pools, yellow but mirror-bright, collect in the hollows of the road, so that your car seems every moment about to plunge into an abyss of basalt cliff and cambric sky. Lacy hummocks on the sage and the cedars are undercut by the warm breath of the earth, and the trickle of snow-water is intermittent with the swish of dropping wreaths and straightening boughs.

By this time the rabbit-brush has lost its veil of winter fluff; its pale stalks, passing insensibly into light along the banks of washes, are defined only by the green smudge at the base of its dry fascicles. Bluebirds flutter in the chaparral like flecks of falling sky; the willows are lacquered orange and vermilion. Now the wind has a growing smell, but along the wooded tops of the ranges snow still filters delicately through the rarefied air. The diffused, shut-in light of the snow is like the whiteness of rapid vibration, the earth envelop disappearing in a mist of its own motion. Farther south, where snow is made rain midway of the vault, the storm, seen moving across the *abras* from the inclosing hills, has the effect of emanating from the ground, as if the earth exhaled it, and, by a gentle, down-streaking motion, drew it to its breast again.

Between the last snows and the coming of the green, broken-winged cold winds play between the ranges. The dried watercourses are picked out by lifting veils of dust as the wind struggles woundedly with the returning sun. Around the Little Colorado, which was once called Rio de Lino because of the flax that grew there, and on the *plan del Zuñi* and all sandy washes toward the west, there is a Bigelovia which at this season gathers a silvery lint along stems that are milky blue with the cold, and on a day are suddenly, definitely green. About this time, walking among the junipers, still sticky yellow and friable like discarded Christmas trimmings, first one and then another pricks itself on your attention. As if all the vitality of the tree, which during the winter had been withdrawn to the seat of the life processes underground, had run up and shouted, "Here I am." Not one of all the ways by which a tree strikes freshly on your observation,—with a greener flush, with stiffened needles, or slight alterations of the axis of the growing shoots, accounts for this flash of mutual awareness. You walk a stranger in a vegetating world; then with an inward click the shutter of some profounder level of consciousness uncloses and admits you to sentience of the mounting sap.

But it is only in the low growths of the New Mexico highlands, where, as you walk, your head comes level with the forest crown, that it happens with authority. What can we know of trees whose processes of elongation toward the light go on a hundred feet or more overhead? Only occasionally, after a long time in the tall forest, doing nothing and thinking very little, a sense of the alien and deeply preoccupied life of the tree shakes our less experienced human consciousness with a touch called Panic.

There is an exceeding subtlety about the spring in New Mexico, at once virginal and experienced, like Mona Lisa's smile. The planted orchards hold aloof, the wild-plum thickets are tiptoe for flight. Suddenly at the end of May, from painted-cup and filmy cactus-flower blazons forth the secret of that country, the secret of fire that gave it birth.

Farther south, where there is more sun and all the rain is drunk by the sand, there is a briefer and more varied bloom, miles and miles of yellow poppies fluttering their cups an inch or two from the powdery earth, whole hill-slopes streaked along the stream-lines with nearly stemless, pale-gold cruciferæ. Later, two or three varieties of yucca and agave send up tall banners of whitish bloom in companies like marching men.

But across the Santa Fé highlands and the tall potreros of the Rio Grande, the local growth takes color of the dark conifers against the rose and ocher clays, black trap and dazzling pumice. Where the scant soil on the flat tops of the potreros thins out the conifers, blood-red flowers of nopál open delicately to the light, and from tuft to tuft of bunch-grass the young winds stalk one another.

At the bottoms of deep cañons hereabout, may be found willow and cottonwood, alder, chokecherry, mulberry, and aspen; and climbing up the steep cumbres, dwarfish oaks putting forth, about corn-planting time, red furry tips of leaves like a mouse's ears.

Anywhere in New Mexico, but especially along stream-sides, and even in the driest years, there is an unbelievable variety of herbaceous bloom forever underfoot. Anything that will grow at this latitude, grows here in its preferred setting, but according to the rhythms of the arid lands, which have been perfectly learned.  Dry years, familiar species will make seed so close to the ground, and with such economy of leaf and flower that you must get down and paw about in the loose gravel to find them.  Or, through successive seasons when the Rains walk not on earth, they will abide inert.  Then in a propitious spring they pattern the plains of Vegas and Cienaguilla like a Spanish dancer's shawl.

It must be the overwhelming scale of things in New Mexico which makes one heedless of the variety, the color, and the texture of the herbaceous bloom, tending as it does to produce a kind of twilight sleep of the sensuous faculties, under which the deep self expands to the measure of the horizon.  Often, walking for an hour on the Santa Fé highlands, I discover myself unmindfully treading down pale primroses, white forget-me-nots, crimson castellia, and lilac-tinted pentstemen; something that never happens to me in any other country.

And yet I always notice and remember any plants that the Indians tell me have use and virtues; as if from their long service to men they had acquired something of man's power of catching human attention.  I never ride in the Sangre de Cristo without looking for that unidentified *monardia* whose faint but distinct perfume is valued as an aphrodisiac, or for the soothing aromatic root osha, which for unknown centuries has been an article of commerce in the Rio Grande settlements; is there not a peak called Questa la Osha because of it? In the Carson and White Mountain forests I am quickest to note, in spite of the overgrowth, the peeled boles of the yellow pines, where roving bands of Apache once stripped them of the inner bark for bread. In the early summer, when the peeling is done, the cambium layer is sweet and nutritious, and only the modern timber-man complains to find the great butts "cat-faced" by the flow of resin to the ancient wound. Nor do I ever push back the springy boughs of the cedar without remembering that the best bows are made of it,—the next best being mulberry,—or that tinder is made of its powdered bark, and that the Spanish explorers first called the Colorado River "Rio del Tizon," from the brands of rolled cedar bark by which the Indians of that country carried fire from place to place. One sees them still, in that country, carrying small burning rolls of it to warm their hands; but the *tizon* carried on tribal migrations was half as long as a man.

This is the common "white" cedar. There is also a "red" cedar found only in Superstition Mountain, and a grove near Natural Bridge, from twenty to sixty miles from the cliff dwellings, in which it has had such general use for roof beams that it must at one time have been much more widely distributed than now.

It is a mistake, though, to imagine that the Indian in his use of things was influenced altogether by convenience. He is as much taken with the charm of rarity as any of us; like us, he prizes things for what they cost him, and loves them for their power of poetic suggestion. Thus to the Navajo the plumy styles of the mountain mahogany are associated with  the misty whiteness of the east, the blue berries of Foresterri are ritualistically assigned to the blue south, the dark fruit of the wild cherry to the storm-dark north, and the juniper, whose branches at most seasons have a yellowy tinge, to the sunset-colored west. So in his cosmogony they stand at the four quarters of the earth.

In all their life-invoking rites, the dancers of the pueblos wear wreaths and armlets of Douglas spruce, symbol of Life-Everliving. For certain of their ceremonies, young trees are brought down by the heads of the clan having jurisdiction over the rite, from days-distant ranges; and the children, pattering out on the terraces on the festival day at sunrise, find them growing at the ritual four world corners of the plaza, and are as enchanted as we once were by the starred and candle-lit Christmas fir. But you would have to go deeper than this simple doctrine of correspondences to appreciate the use of cottonwood and aspen boughs for the festival of Poseyemo Departing.

The aspen itself is the peculiar treasure of the upper watercourses; sparsely branched, delicately leaved, a lady tree, a fairy-lady tree forever ruffling her petticoats or washing her gold hair beside the dark duenna pines. High up, circling a mountain meadow, its white-limbed branchlets flow each to the other like Botticelli's nymphs. Thick ranked along the water-borders of the Rio Grande as it comes through the Culebra, the straight greenish boles carrying their thyrses of shifty, pattering pale leaves fifty or sixty feet above the stream-bed, it becomes mysterious, formidable as massed femininity. All summer the leaves of the quaking aspen are pale glaucous green, but in the Moon of the Cold Touching Mildly, which is also the month of the sun turning south, they are coined anew of glinting gold, making gold of all the air. The cottonwoods, stayed all summer along the lower river-bottoms and around solitary water-holes, like green umbrageous clouds, burn suddenly hot gold. . . . I remember, over Galisteo way, where the walls of the houses are all rosy from the rosy earth, one that cast a spell on me, burning solitary, in the clear yellow of every perfect leaf, in the hollow of a turquoise sky!

In the northern pueblos at the feast of Poseyemo, which has been approximated to the day of that Christian saint whose festival comes nearest the autumnal equinox, the dancers hold their bright aspen boughs toward the rays of departing Poseyemo, the legend of whose journey south was very early assimilated to the sun-myth.   But, in their ritual cosmogony, the aspen stands for the golden east from which, in the manner of all Great Ones, their Poseyemo is expected to return.   Thus by way of its evergreenness, its goldness, by white blossom styles, by pollen clouds such as the blue larkspur sheds to be the fertility-invoking medicine of the Navajo bride's marriage basket, the plant world begins to stand to man not for itself but for ideas.   And in this fashion begins the long process which leads from the thing to its idea, by way of its name and pictured shape, to the discovery of print. But few of *us* read the plant world as a book; by all our ways of speaking of it, denying the thing that happened.   Even I, saying that the best bows are made of juniper wood! when, in fact, before there could be a bent stick from which a pointed stick could be launched, there was the idea of the bow arching in the bough of the juniper, making itself known to man by springy branches, being drawn down and flying back, catapulting light weights; bending, not breaking.   By even more subtle ways of catching his attention, of which, after long uninterrupted hours with it, I have a hint, the juniper got itself made into bows. By such direct, dark paths, lost and only occasionally recovered, the wild grass and the tree on the mountain yearned toward and made themselves evident in man.

## II

### THE WIND IN THE SOUTH

The phrase that gives its title to this chapter, like that one about the magpie's wings, I have borrowed— as too often the most apt of my descriptions—from the native phrase-makers who have had several centuries more than I have for making them both apt and interpretative.  This one is from a myth of the Mojave-Apaches, who have their home in the Verde Valley of Arizona, from a song of the Deathless One, Sekala Ka'amja, whose wife, called Flower of the Maguey, the wind had stolen away.  This is the way of the Hot Wind in that country, to seduce the maiden bloom where he finds it dancing; and every year the Deathless One, following hard on the Wind's trail, brings it back.

Apache is merely a name of our giving to the fierce tribes living, since our knowledge, along the Mogollon Rim, and especially about the Chiricahua Mountains, and the myth of Sekala Ka'amja is only an Indian way of saying that the country that the Apaches chose for their own is the land of wind-sown life.  Their symbol of the Increase-giving Powers is the sacred *hoddentin,* the pollen of the reed become sacred, as the snake is sacred to the Pueblos, being found always in proximity to indispensable water-holes.  Every

Apache hunter carries a pinch of *hoddentin* in a pouch
at his belt, to be scattered in the path of the wounded
for their health's sake, or before distinguished guests;
loosed in the air to protect from lightning, blown to
the crescent moon for good fortune, or offered prayerfully to the dawn. . . . "O Dawn, let me live a long
time!"  For in the arid regions of southern Arizona,
not only the life-increase but the vegetative cover lies
largely at the mercy of the wind.

Here the llanos do not reach to more than two or
three thousand feet, falling seaward, and the cumbres
are seldom high enough to intercept the fleets of cumuli that go over them on the great wind river rising
out of the California Gulf.  Twice a year, when the
sun turns in its course, under changed conditions of
temperature, the wind drops, frets, and flounders,
stirring up a great dust, and bringing it down again
with an annual maximum of ten or twelve inches of
rain.  Thus the country below the Mogollon Rim is
redeemed from desertness only by the rivers that take
their rise in the broken ranges, along the edge of the
Mogollon Mesa.  Here lie the sources of the Gila and
the Mimbres, and the greater part of San Francisco
watershed, and in the sage- and cactus-covered highlands farther west, the streams that supply the Roose-
velt Dam.  Peaks that intercept the lower levels of
the cloud-flow are islands of Rocky Mountain growth,
whose coasts are lapped by interminable stretches of
social shrubs.

The choice of habitat among arid-region plants is governed by the nature of the adjustments they have learned to make to the restricted water-supply. In the country below the Rim there are three general types of adjustment, the first of which is the speeding up of the vegetating cycle of plants that elsewhere take the whole summer season for flower and fruit. Thus within a few days after the winter solstice, the borages begin to send up leafy spikes as thick as hairs, and within a few days have matured their white prickly burrs. Verbena flowers in the sand, and the decumbent Callindra cover the low hills with a delicate rosy fringe. Alfileria, a relative of our eastern cranes-bill, spreads in every available space its flat rosettes of lanceolate leaves and pinkish flowers, followed by the long-billed fruits that children stick in their stockings to tell them what o'clock it is.

Within the same few days, poisonous green plats of loco-weed widen along the washes, wither, and leave their pale, papery pods to rustle about the sand. But the very swiftness with which the reproductive cycle is accomplished, leaves the field of observation to be dominated by the second type of adjustment in which the life of the individual plant is infinitely prolonged, as in the creosote bush, which grows according to the rain, waits and grows and waits, for two or three hundred years, and with the flight of its delicate shadows on the swept sand makes an effect of motion without change or sound from which impressions of the country below the Rim are inseparable. Occupying the gravelly upper levels of the vast *abras,* the creosote is easily recognizable by its springy slender boughs, crowned with fine, sparse foliage, varnished until it gives back the light in a green sparkle.

After the winter solstice brings the first of the rains, the creosote covers itself with thin yellow corollas that detach themselves on the wind in flocks like butterflies, and within a week or two are followed by tiny cotton balls, bursting white and lining the runnels of the later rains with fluff. A little later, across the clayey *playas* the delicate feather-form foliage of the mesquite and the acacias blows under the green moons of summer twilights like green hair.

When the track of the sun behind the western ranges passes insensibly into bands of pale citron, half-way up the sky, which at this latitude holds on a deep liquid blue until midnight, the earth walks a virgin. From the tall peaks, one by one, the rosy light is let go like smiles she leaves behind her on the way to her devotions. Dark ranges fold about her as a cloak; there is no sound, nor any motion except the blowing of her hair.

Of other desert shrubs and trees which contribute to the effect of delicacy in the landscape of southern Arizona, the most important is the palo-verde, lifting its sharply etched, leafless brooms well above the mesquite, outlining the dry washes. In Papagueria, and

THE SMOKE BUSH DISAPPEARING INTO A MIST OF ITS OWN INFINITELY DIVIDED TIPS south into Sonora, the palo-verde becomes a veritable tree, "big bean tree," and in wet years its bright-green stems put forth minute scale-like leaves that vanish with the rains.  In May or June, between its wire-like twigs are caught swarms of delicate flowers of that lovely, lively color that painters call king's yellow, lining the streamways like the stroke of a loaded brush across the landscape.  Long after nightfall the palo-verde may be located by its honey-locust scent, carried by little fitful airs that play about the bolsons after the sun goes down, left in the warm hollows like a dropped handkerchief.

In that long dry wash which runs parallel to the Santa Fé railroad just east of the crossing of the Colorado, both the mesquite and the creosote may be observed, growing apart in the white dust, also the palo-verde, and that other fine-haired desert shrub, the Arizona smoke-bush, disappearing into a mist of its own infinitely divided tips.  Here, at the edge of the streamways, is Findler's rose, its furzy green starred with small, white, yellow-hearted bloom, between the dense, dusty globes of *garamboya*.

Farthest from the crossing where the wash begins, there is a plantation of shaggy tree yuccas, the Joshua-tree of the plainsman, and clusters of dead-looking long wands close-bundled at the root, which in May or June may be recognized by their scarlet tips, as ocotillo.  This is the only locality with which I am

familiar in which so many of the types of arid growth
may be found together. In the great *abras* farther
inland, they occupy uninterrupted miles of their
chosen levels, with scarcely any other company. Even
grass, if it grows at all in this country, prefers the
company of grass. High on the bajadas, slopes too
steep to hold the soil that even the humbler sort of
shrubs demand, or masking lava flows not yet worn
down to nourishing dust, great patches of *Hillaria*
make color splashes visible for miles.

Tufts of bunch-grass and bear's-grass, the tall
reed-like growth which furnishes the coil of Papago
basketry, may be found contesting the steep bajadas
with globose, downy-white brittle-brush, which in the
fore-summer makes a golden glow of bloom. About
this season, too, the crêpe-petaled thistle poppy, the
"fried-egg flower" of the cow-boy, makes a lovely
whiteness over sandy patches, persisting on into the
Inner Bone Month of the Papago winter. But none
of these things are on a scale to modify the effect of
monotony in the country of the social shrubs. It is
not until the lowest, most arid levels are reached that
the yellowish greens of the creosote, mesquite, and
palo-verde are relieved by the silvery-bluish grays of
the ironwood, hackberry, *hohoba,* and *garamboya.*
The ironwood you will know by its stiff upright
branching and its roundish, easily ruffled leaves, as
well as by the quality of its wood, for which a special

ax is sold in that region, called the ironwood ax.  The hackberry has a cleaner trunk and a brushier habit of branching, and the *garamboya* is that dense, rounded heap of brittle gray leaf and twig, frequently as large as a Papago house, from which at nightfall you may hear the twitter of the plumed quail seeking, in its impenetrable shelter, safety from their worst enemy, the coyote.  Perched on the low branches near the central stem, like some strange secret fruit, they spend the nights, and raise in perfect secrecy their young broods.

The *hohoba* is a shrub conspicuous in its dull-green leafage, but important not to be missed by the traveler unacquainted with the resources of the arid regions, since it produces an extremely palatable nut, to the quality of which its native name, *hohoba,* youth-maker, is a sufficient tribute.

All this is to be observed between the beginning of winter rains and the hot fore-summer when from bristling leaf clusters the yuccas and agaves send up tall stalks that break, often in a space of hours, into long panicles of waxen white and yellow bells.  Love-liest of all, the thousand-flowered maguey, wife of Sekala Ka'amja, whom the Hot Wind stole away.

It is not only the agaves and the yuccas that are wind-sown and wind-fertilized, but practically all the plants that give character to the arid region, the creo-sote, mesquite, acacia, palo-verde, the desert willow, the poplars lining the streamways, the walnuts at the bottoms of steep cañons, the batamote, whose surprising silver leafage, springing out of dead stems, betrays the presence of underground moisture, are raped of their virgin bloom by the seducing wind. Sometimes, when the rains have come quick and crowding under strong suns, streams of all but invisible pollen may be discovered on the moving air.

Later, the seed of wind-wrung bloom is blown about as down, or left rustling along the sand in dry pods and capsules, until in the Deathless Round of Life it comes to leaf and flower again. Long after the wind has passed, the tall flower-stalks of the yuccas and agaves remain upright, blanched white, and the Indians gather them to use for the pole-and-ring game, by the skilful playing of which, according to the later myth, Sekala Ka'amja won back the maiden flowers again. There is always a great dust raised by this seasonal chase of the Hot Wind, fine yellow dust of the *playas,* so that between the dust and the heat-quavers the whole landscape is veiled, and the mountains shadowed by the great fleeces of cumulus blown up from the California Gulf.

Thus the wind and the dust work together, for the fine silt of the wind rivers, when it falls, covers the seed the wind sows, and many of the winter-blooming varieties of flowering herbs, such as the cassia and verbena and the borages will make a second growth and bloom, following the summer solstice. If the *temporales* are heavy enough, seeds of the social shrubs will germinate and often make sufficient growth to enable them to maintain themselves through the autumn drought till the turn of the sun in the south. It is the summer rains that sweeten the mesquite pods and fill out the corn. They also bring to quick maturity plants that require much heat with their drink, such as the wild pumpkin, whose silvery pubescent leaves gathered in close plats, tips pointed resolutely at the sun, may be seen increasing hourly in the exposed sandy bottoms. At this season the gourd runs and climbs by ropy stems, from which, late in November, after the leaves are off, lovely golden balls may be seen swinging from branches of the mesquite and acacia.

The summer rainy season is seldom prolonged beyond the middle of August. Then the land assumes again that aspect of life defeated which is the accepted note of desertness. This, since it is the season at which the roads, no longer exposed to the ravages of summer torrents, are likely to be safest, is the time at which the desert is usually traversed. For this reason the casual traveler is likely to come away from the country below the Rim without learning that, to the initiate, the secret charm of the desert is the secret of life triumphant.

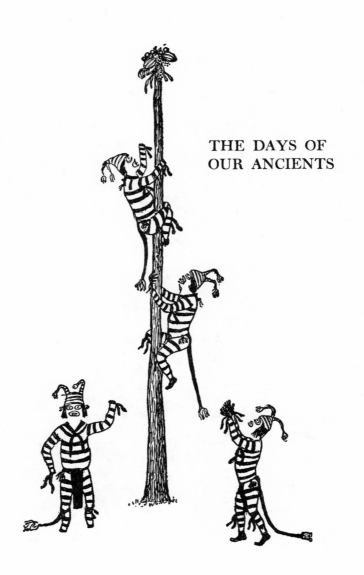

# THE DAYS OF
# OUR ANCIENTS

# THE DAYS OF OUR ANCIENTS

A T Halona, the Middle Ant-heap of the World, which is Zuñi, when the snow lies on the terraced houses like a summer cloud, when clear flame runs up the cedar logs in the three-cornered fireplaces and no one looks out of doors for fear of what may be roaming about there, under dim breasts of Thunder, "Come," say the Elders, "let us abide with our Ancients a while." Then you may hear, if you are so privileged and have the wit to disentangle it from the skein of tribal symbolism, the only account of early man in America that has the color of veracity. For, if they came, these dark Ancients of ours, as our own shamans are fairly agreed, retreating, from some unidentified cradle of the Mongoloid peoples, before or between the great ice epochs, the memory of that passage might well have survived in the creation myths of the Zuñi and Tewa pueblos.

Man, as the Zuñis understand him, came to knowledge of himself in the lowest of the four womb worlds, in Sipapu, the Mist-encompassed Place, and in a state unfinished; tailed, in fact, and web-fingered, "mudhead," as you can still see him learning to be man in the dance of the Koyemishi. Thence he climbed by the roots of the great pine—by the Douglas spruce, say the Tewas—to the world of water-moss, cold, sunless; faint tribal memory, perhaps, of the arctic tundras crossed on the way to the Middle Place. So, world by world, sticky with undried slime, fearful with receding flood and earthquate trembling, man worked upward, having as helpers the Great Twin Brethren, right and left hands of the Sun Father.

In some such fashion the Zuñis, who speak a language having no relation to any known tongue, prefigure their passage from the racial homeland to the Place of Emergence, localized for every tribe in some volcanic crevice or bottomless crater lake. But of an Asiatic origin, there is little direct evidence, beyond facial contours and the fine, gold-colored skin which you see when the young men are stripped for the Race of the Swift-coming Rain; unless you will accept the discovery of a recent Chinese visitor that at Taos the word for hair, and for a certain way of wearing the hair, are the same in Chinese and Tanoan. Also, when Amerind blood is passed through alien strains of the second or third dilution, especially when it goes through the Spanish-speaking stock of this region, very young children will look gravely at you out of doll-like round heads with the slant, enigmatic eyes of the Japanese.

For the rest, we have to accept the conclusion of the ethnologists that the dawn period of the Amerind people was long lived through before our Southwestern tribes appeared on the plateau of southern Utah and Colorado, anywhere from three to five thousand years ago. These we know, by their remains, as the Pit-house People.

Somewhere in their journeying the unripe clans had learned to dig round holes in the ground, roofed over with reeds and grass. Later, as they came to the crumbling soils of the southland, the pits were shored up from within by tree trunks that, projecting a foot or two above the level of the ground, became the support of flat roofs, entered through hatchways from the top, by ladders of notched pines. Scattered over the vast *abras* of the Southwest, as far south as the Mimbres, faint markings of the pit-houses may still be traced by the greener plats of vegetation where the tamped floors and ruined walls gather and hold the evanescent rains. At Luna, near one of these ancient village sites, there is an oval dancing-ring whose bowl would seat an audience of several hundred, and at the burial-places the archæologist's spade turns up the little three-cornered fireplaces of baked clay, having supports for cooking-pots, and the food-bowls, set for the comforting of souls still lingering about the unfinished Paths of Our Lives.

For in the days of our Ancients, the notion that the dead go away immediately to some far, unreachable heaven, had not yet been invented. Heaven was as near, then, as the moon is to little children, and the round, bright shield of the Sun Father hung so low over their huts, that I have always suspected that that name the Tewas have for the rain-smoothed *playas,* Dancing-places of the Sun, came down to them from the Pit-house period.   Still, among the tribes nearest, by their mode of life, to the people of the pits, lingers a myth of the Pleiades as little lost children, who, because their mothers gave them no meat for the play cooking-pots around which they danced in the long Southern twilights, grew light and lighter, drifting skyward till only the vault stayed them.   That is why, as Papago mothers will explain to you, Papago babies are kept as fat as pin-cushions; and ever after, the Pit-house mothers, as the constellation of the starry dance rose over the hyacinthine ranges, came hurrying up the hatchways to stay the feet of some little brown ghost with the comforting flame and the smell of savory dishes.

Not much else is known of the Pit-house people, except that they lived chiefly on seeds and small game, their bows being light, so that more than likely, as Papago boys are still taught to do, they ran down the deer and caught it with their naked hands.   Beyond that, stands out, against all we traditionally believe about primitive peoples, that nowhere in the vast, undefended *abras* which they chose for their village sites, or in the flat-roofed houses and the open-sided ramadas which the Southland taught them to build between the pits, is there the hint of a human enemy. As naked, as unalarmed as flocks of migrating birds, as unplunderable, they moved or settled, following their food and that delicately registering feeling for themselves as a part of the conscious life of the universe, which informs all the Amerind's ways.

It was while they were in the Pit-house period that our Ancients passed from the use of pinched, coiled ware, to smooth pottery, painted black on white, and from the hole-in-the-floor hearth to the baked-clay fireplace with its rude chimney staggering up the wall. Somewhere toward the end of that period, they ceased from being gatherers of wild-sown seeds, and became, as among the still wandering and predatory tribes we find the corn-planters referred to, "People of the Seed."

Long before the Ancients of the Shiwina reached the Middle Place which became their permanent seat, at a time when the present Southwest was unfit for sedentary living,—rains more violent, rivers rolling tremendously, some mountains still belching fire,— there had passed the migrations that produced the cultures of the great central plateaus of Mexico and middle America.  There, in the region of the agave and the tree cactus, those still more Ancients had encountered a full-eared grass that in the hands of unnumbered generations became the six-colored corn.

But before the corn-culture, moving northward by

successive contacts, had overtaken the Pit-house villages, it had become a triad "tied by the lightning," corn, and the great white bean, and the calabaza, mother of all the squash and pumpkin kind; brown bean and pinto, dent corn, pop-corn, round and pointed grain, melons, and two or three varieties of the thin-shelled, pale squashes that unaccountably, in September, grow in halves and quarters from the twigs of dry trees beside every pueblo door.

With the corn, came rites and ceremonies, festivals of seed-time and harvest; also new sorts of pots for cooking it, new methods of storage.  So that the adoption of the corn complex may well have been in the intensive turn by which what we know as the Pit-house culture became the culture of the Small-house period.

Man is an animal of only moderate susceptibility to new tricks. Who knows how many centuries he wandered, looking for the Middle Place of the World, before the hot sun instructed him to abandon his pit-houses, heritage of the Mist-encompassed Place, for walls of woven boughs standing upright on the earth?  Against the hot wind heavy with biting dust, he daubed the wattles with mud, and in that fashion houses are still built in Papagueria. The need of protecting his corn led him to thicken the mud walls, hardened by the sun, until no burrowing thief could find the six-colored ears, and no changes of temperature affect their food values. Farther north, where heavier snows and longer cold rendered the *jacal* impracticable, pit-houses were walled round with cobbles, plastered with clay. Having continued the line of clay-firmed stone a little above the level of the ground, the pit-house builder laid his beams flat across it, and evolved the bonded and cemented wall. For all these processes, corn was a great quickener. Tribes multiplied on the potreros of the San Juan and the Rio Grande, and in the valleys of the Mimbres, the Gila, and the Salado.

Walking there, one of these wide-open summer days, when there comes a sudden silence, and in the midst of the silence a stir, look where you walk. If your feet stumble in a round depression, to the north of which you discover squarish, low mounds of reddish rock, if, beyond the margin of shallow basins, you observe windrows of loose stones pitched out from between the hills of corn long before the leveled space was taken by three-hundred-year-old pines, know that you are in the country of the Small-house People. Always, incredibly, there lingers about these places, where once was man, some trace that the human sense responds to, never so sensitively as where it has lain mellowing through a thousand years of sun and silence.

Look first for the house mound, which was roughly rectangular, of from one to three rooms, facing south, with wing shelters extended from the end walls, sometimes wholly inclosing the *placita,* where most of the domestic life went out; the doorless, flat-topped rooms being used chiefly for refuge and for storage.

South of the small-house, but connected with it by a subterranean passage, lay the kiva, the ancient pit-house, preserved for all sacred and ceremonial use. In the oldest Southwestern tongue, *ki* meant simply "house," and our dark-skinned Ancients clung, as tenaciously as we do ourselves, to the form of whatever connected them with the Allness, and the occasions by which they kept themselves in touch with it. As if they should lose the precious essence if the shape of the cup were changed.   In any of the Rio Grande pueblos you may still discover this round, sunken, ceremonial chamber, the kiva, identified by the skyward-pointing ladder of topped spruce, that spruce by which they climbed up from Sipapu in the Days of the Emergence.   At Taos, there are seven of them, sunk, probably, to the original level of pit-houses. Farther south, as at Santo Domingo and Cochití, they stand almost on the top of the ground.   At Picuris the kivas are so completely subterranean that it is only by the ladder protruding from the hatchway that they may be located. Everywhere, by the symbolic Sipapu, Doorway of the Under-world, by the niche for the sacred meal-bowl and the stepped altar, they are connected in an unbroken chain with the ruined ceremonial pits of the Small-house People.

Persists, also, the urge that drove our Ancients ever south, in the placing of the kiva in relation to the house of the clan that owned it. This year, at San Ildefonso, the pueblo abandoned its plaza, lovely with domed cottonwoods, to correct two hundred years of ill luck, set in motion by its violation of the immemorial precept of the Tewas that "he who would prosper must move ever to the south." In the oldest ruins, there is a marked tendency to bury in the favored direction, and all their Great Ones, going from them as culture heroes go from peoples slow to take the measure of their quality, go southward.

By the water gaps that lead from the San Juan country to the Rio Grande, the tribes came through. The great game-animals came that way, also, of whose movements in determining the flow of human cultures we do not make enough. The elk, of which there is scarcely a trace in the Pit-house period, in the Small-house era made the pastures black with moving herds. Mule-deer and whitetail, within our present memory, kept their ancient trails by Wolf Creek Pass, from the summer pasture of the Rockies, down the

San Juan plateau. The tribes followed the herds, the herds followed the pastures, and the pastures were under the protection of Awanyu, the plumed serpent, Guardian of the Water Sources. According to the Tewas, the Small-house People, except for a few fragmentary clans that were absorbed into later cultures, vanished from the earth because they had lost the favor of Awanyu, who in disdain flung himself high across the heavens and made the Milky Way. Thus the Tewas account for the gradual narrowing of the zone of frequent rains under the great wind river of the Rio Grande.

And if the guardian of the Six Great Springs of the World was not more favorable to the tribes in the Small-house era, how account at all for the thousands of ruins that on the Pajaritan plateau—remnant of the blanket of volcanic tuff that once covered the country between Peña Blanca and the shattered bulk of Abiquiu—make a distinct culture, distinguished for an iridescent pottery glaze, long lost to the remaining tribes? In this country, where now a few lost mavericks feed, one is continually stumbling into the circular pits of their sacred, subterranean chambers, or tracing their ancient fields by windrows of the surface rock. Over in the Rio Puerco district, where the rim rock gathers into domed heads and castled tops, and the light, refracted from red and purple earths, strikes sleepily on the sense with the effect of perpetual afternoon, a hundred villages clustered under the Mesita de la Tapia, where now the sheep-herder seeks, and does not always find, one solitary spring. Lost cattlemen, in the San Juan country, look for the kiva pits and the sage-brush-covered house mounds, as index of a possible water-supply in some ancient artificial reservoir, cupping the muddy residue of infrequent rains.

But it is along the ancient highways such as the Chama, leading from the Mesa Verde and San Juan levels to the Rio Grande, that the Small-house People left their most interesting remains. Here, at the junction of the Chama and the Gallinas, what was once sea-bottom is thrust up, sea-gray, with a green scum of one-leaved pines, wind-sculptured, and worn down to a pale, fertile dust in which the sage, the coral pentsemen and the blue lupin usurp the long-abandoned fields. The ruins are clustered on the terraced tops of the mesas between the rivers, and look south to the blue peak of Jemez and its great World Shrine, southern boundary of the Tewa world.

Here, because the material easiest to the builder's hand was flat, broken rock, it is still possible to trace the movement of the tribesman's mind, as he built up his house, from a grass-thatched hole in the ground to a three-storied stone tower. Curious and revealing motions! The pit-house, to judge from the best-preserved examples, with a thousand years' experience behind it, was as beautifully perfected as a bee's cell;

but the first upright stone wall was a child's heap, having nothing but its heap to keep it standing. Slowly the wall thinned, as the feel of the stone taught the builder balance and precision, until, long before it was firmed by clay or surfaced by the stone adz, it was practically wind-proof. Building clumsily around the axis of his body, as all wild things build, but not with their beautiful perfection, man finally squared his house to his cedar beams, so that on these same small-house sites, in unbroken progression, arose, out of the roundish stone-heaped den, the sharp-cornered watch-tower of an organized society.

Along the Chama, round and squarish towers rise in sight of one another, from point to vantage-point, here thrust up on a detached boulder, or set on some dizzy ledge from which the waving flag of smoke could be descried, calling to council or advising of the movement of the wild herds. If they were used for defense, it would have been only toward the end of the Small-house period. Nowhere on the Pajaritan plateau, where the ruins indicate a settlement almost as populous as the present valley of the Rio Grande, is there any trace of fortification or defensive preparation. Whatever fear walked in the trails of the Small-house People or slept in their huts, it was not the fear of human kind.

Neither was it the fear of God.
In the Days of the New, men did not so much fear

the Secret Powers as yearn toward them with an untutored, vague desire; felt them friendly, and believed
—why not, since we have managed the lightning and
other forces too subtle, almost, for naming?—in man's
capacity to move and manage the Powers to his own
advantage.   One has only to live with Tewa or
Tanoan a while, to see how god-concepts grow out of
the primitive man's greater ease of regression into the
Infinite Subjective Mind of which he was so newly a
part.   Before he built his dwelling, the Small-house
clansman dug himself a safe, secret pit from which his
thoughts could revert to the Unseen and mingle with
it.   Or, walking apart, in dark cañons, or on such high
and lonely places as the Powers have immemorially
visited, man brooded inwardly and built out patterns with the stones, altar-heaps and inclosures, as
children do with pebbles and broken china, wherein he
laid some lovely, valued thing, in thanks or propitiation.   All about the Small-house country you find such
shrines,—miniature Stonehenges, Jacob's pillars, white
shell beads, and sacred prayer plumes.   Coming up
from their kivas, for the ceremony of the Swift-
coming Rain, the young men blew down of eagle's
feathers skyward, or tied it in their hair, to make
themselves light for the races.   Over all their pottery,
black on gray, or black on red, prevailed, throughout
the Small-house period, patterns of the plumed serpent, the earth altar, and the two-turned whorl of
Being.

Whether or not the Small-house period began with corn, its economic and social and religious life revolved around it; for any people that lives by corn becomes bond-servant of all its ways. Corn is a town-builder, a maker of policies, mother of inventions. Out of its necessities were drawn architecture, philosophical systems, and the material of drama.

Here, where I write, on the lower slopes of Sangre de Cristo, as the hills go toward the *plan del Rio,* when the bridle-rein is slacked, your horse brings you, by traces discovered only by the feel of the earth under his foot, to unfenced fields that, except for the wavering furrow of the plow across them, are still of the Small-house period. Here the surface run-off of the August showers is still led down to the great corn plant by dikes and ditches, from the open ends of natural catchment basins; childishly simple to the eye and cunning with the experience of three thousand years.

There is something inexpressibly stirring thus to happen, where all around is silence and the sun, on plants that have come down this long way with man, as though they gave off something of man's personality, absorbed through centuries of aspiration with him, up from the grass. The soul of the corn passes into the soul of the observer; the insistent beat of consciousness soothes to a murmur, faint as the wind in the corn, of godhead in man, to which the Small-house People, giving ear, were moved like the corn in the wind. It is only in such passages that one realizes that the charm of Amerind life, for the modern American, is the absence of those strains and resistances that stiffen us against the wind forever blowing from some quarter of the universe across our souls.

Once the Small-house clans began to coalesce, the determining factor in the fashion of town-building was the clan system, by which descent is reckoned from the mother's side. Not only was woman the food-divider, but the householder. Whether it was so from the first, that the women were the builders, it is not now possible to say; or whether women ever worked in stone, there is no evidence. But so far back as the plastic adobe clay became the medium of construction, excavators are perpetually turning up fine, feminine finger-marks, and the modulation of small, shallow palms, as you can see to-day, in any pueblo before the fiesta, the house-mothers patting new plaster on the walls, and painting them with *yeso* until, between blue shadow and refracted sun, they take on the pure luster of pearl.

Probably then, as now, the husbands of one house cluster went together to cut the beams, days distant, carrying them home on their shoulders and lifting them into place, but the house, however fashioned, was the house-mother's. Seldom her daughters left her, but brought husbands home, and built on another room and another, until the clustered house heap took on that pyramidal form you may observe at Zuñi or Taos, or was strung, roof to roof, in windrows, as at Santo Domingo, or joined in a continuous square, as at San Felipe or San Juan.   So much more, in the days of our Ancients, was the house the woman's domain, that the persistence of the kiva, the size and numbers of them in relation to the house heaps, was partly owed to the inborn necessity of husbands to have some place they could call their own.   If men left women out of politics and the church, when they invented these, it was very largely because the women shortsightedly failed to provide any place in the home where such instinctive male activities could go on; for women in the stone-age had as poor an opinion as we have of the things men do when they get together alone.

A village, in the time of our Ancients, was a group of unit houses, more or less scattered, having usually, but not necessarily, one speech, and a common esoteric or defensive function.   The unit was the mother hive, which might include several married pairs and their children, together with their kiva, called by the name of its chief man.

At the Hopi pueblos, when the Katchinas of the Flute ceremony are out, there is a glint between the dances, like the white glint of a trail between the crowding mountains, of authentic history, which shows how villages were built up out of the fragments of other villages.   Masked in the symbols of the towering rain-clouds and the rolling thunder, walking as if weary, personators of the ancestors of the Flute clan reach the foot of the cliffs where the Snake and the Bear people have already established themselves, halting at the sacred meal road which the priests of the Bear and the Snake, hurrying down, have drawn across their way.

"Whence come ye?" shout the Bear and Snake chiefs from the mesa.

"From the South."

"What seeking?"

"To dwell in your villages and be one with you."

"What bring ye?"

"Medicine of the Blue Flute and the Gray Flute. When the Flutes call, the Invisible Ones roll up the dark clouds and pour down the rain."

Thus persuaded, the priests of the Bear and Snake clans erase the sacred meal bar, and the Flute clan, led by the Flute priests, the Flute maidens, Alosaka with his goat's horns, Kaleotaka with his bow, plant their prayer sticks around the sacred spring, and back along their line of march to the village, that their rain prayers may be surely borne to the gods there, and the blessed rain return. In some such fashion, clans of the Small-house period, with their gods, were absorbed into the Rio Grande pueblos and the scattered remnants of the great-houses of the Gila and Salado reassorted themselves with the walled pueblos of the north. By such coalitions, in the latter end of the Small-house period, populations multiplied and villages grew into towns. Clan house touched clan house, until the rows of conjoined dwellings, having their kivas to the south, took on the forms that characterize the present villages of Hopi and Acoma. But if you would know the veritable appearance of the Small-house People, ethnologists are of the opinion that it may be found among the Tarahumaracs in the Sierra Madre.

Of the influences that determined the local type of town-building, there were two that were fairly constant. One was the gradual withdrawal of the rains over all the mesa country, and the other was the appearance, in successive waves of migration, of that notable stirrer-up of man's activities, the Enemy.

The migrations that came to rest in the Great-house and Pueblo cultures were peace-loving and sedentary by nature. By the time they had bins and treasuries of corn, great jars of pounded meal sunk in their floors, stone cists full of beans, and melons kept sweet under heaps of sand, they became plunderable. In due course, there appeared for the plundering nomadic and predatory tribes, Ute, Apache, Navajo.

It was the nature of the country to which our Ancients had come in migrations not far separated in point of time, speaking at least four languages, but having a common origin legend and a common recognition of this Southwest as their Middle Place, that there was no easy way out of it.  From the high Rockies, the country falls by mesas, flat as the back of your hand, to valleys diverging south, between monumental ranges spread like the finger of the hand, some distance south of what is now the boundary of Old Mexico, into pure desertness.  Westward, the awful dragon of the Colorado cañon cut them from the coast. East the land runs out into waterless, mirage-haunted plains.  Behind them was the memory of sunless Sipapu, and south of the Cerro de Montezuma there was no way but to creep hardily along the foot of the Cordilleras toward central Mexico, already preëmpted by more advanced and hostile tribes.

Within these natural boundaries, the Pueblo tribes settled or shifted, following their food; and from successive tarryings they swarmed.  But by the end of the Small-house period the trails of the various linguistic groups had become inextricably confused, issuing at intervals clear and well defined, and lost again like the track of desert creatures in the sand.

Where it issues at its most engaging, is in the cliffs and caves of the San Juan drainage, and the Little Colorado.  Not, however, as a phase of cultural evolution, but as a mere matter of convenience.  There was no cliff-dwelling age, but an easy adaptation to local advantages.  Why dig a hole, when there is a

hole in a wall already dug for you?   But because
there is no important cliff dwelling without traces of
corn-culture, I am disposed to think it was the supe-
riority of the inaccessible, solid-smooth rooms as
storage-vaults, that led to their long-continued use as
homes.   Every now and then the archæologist un-
covers a wall cache of shelled corn, forgotten as long
ago as the time an English king tended cakes in a
cowherd's hut.

In the north, there seems to have been a Small-
house period of cave-dwelling, and a Tower-house
period, after an interval in which cotton was added to
the squash and the beans and the corn.   Out of a cliff
house in Utah, seed was taken of a distinct species, true
Ancient of our tropical variety, and named *aborigi-
neum;* but how far it was from its native home, there
is no discovering.

Besides convenience, there must have been an immense appeal in the caves for their highness, the unstinted reach of vision, the sense of cuddling safety
against the mother rock.   How far from these aeries,
when the snow lay lightly as cloud on the junipers,
they could trace the movement of the herds of elk and
antelope!   How comfortably they must have snuggled
together around the three-cornered fireplaces when the
torrent of the rain came falling like a silver curtain
between them and the world, or the wolfish wind
howled and scraped against the retaining wall!

CLIFF DWELLINGS . . . WITH A SENSE OF CUDDLING SAFETY
AGAINST THE MOTHER ROCK

79

It is more than likely that the same people moved in and out of their cave homes, as need or wishing drove them.  At the Rito de los Frijoles, which is to say Bean Creek, the Keres, who came into that shut valley with a well-developed craft of stone-working, preferred the cavate lodges, which at a later period they abandoned for the round, terraced pueblo, built up out of whole earth, while other of their clans were still in the cave-backed huts, and still content with them.  As the Small-house People clung to the sacred pits, so the town-builders reverted to cave and crevice for their ceremonial chambers.

That was after the towns grew too large for the caves to hold, or after the enemy, who may have driven them there, had been vanquished or absorbed. Squeezed into the great caves of the Mesa Verde country, there are towns that were able to afford streets, little plazas set about with public ovens, space between the cave and the house walls for the turkeys, rooms for milling and for meditation.

Such magic is thrown about this period, by the wild splendor of the many-colored cliffs from which the squared tops and ruined towers of the cliff villages peer down, that it is difficult to write it into any scheme of tribal evolution.  Eagles mewing about the perilous footholds, great trees rooting where once the slender ladders clung!  You walk in one of the winding cañons of southern Utah or Colorado, threaded by a bright stream, half smothered in choke-cherry and cotton-wood, and suddenly, high and inaccessible in the cañon wall, the sun picks out the little windows in the walls amid the smoke-blue shadows, and you brush your eyes once or twice to make sure you do not see half-naked men, deer- and antelope-laden, climbing up the banded cliffs, and sleek-haired women, bright with such colors as they knew how to wring out of herbs and berries, popping in and out of the T-shaped openings like parrakeets.

Clear October afternoons, when the fleets of aspen, gold at the bottoms of the cañons, set sail for the ruined balconies, and the gobble of the wild turkey sounds between the driving gusts, how can you be sure it does not come from the penned space behind the broken walls, how distinguish between the beat of your horse's hoofs and the *plump-plump* of the mealing-stone, or the roll of the medicine drums from the kivas?

Even more charged with the enchantment of mystery, seem the cliff dwellings when you come upon them from above. Walking the level mesas between scant pines and silver-dusted sage, you observe scarcely any human trace recognizable to the unpractised eye. Here a low, squarish mound of surface stones shows where the Watchers of the Corn set up their towers, there a painted potshard kicked up from some stone-rimmed area of wind-sifted ash, mute evidence of a tender human concern, marks, for the knowing, the place of incineration.

Insensibly your feet stumble into the shallows of some ancient trail, and then suddenly the ground opens before you into a deep, many-colored rift, murmurous with the ripple of a sunken stream and the wind-ruffled aspens. Midway of the cliff, or bent about the blind, rain-blackened head of the cañon, the ruined towers beckon, out of cavernous blueness. There must have been always this quality of enticement about the nested villages, even for the builders of them, so that you can well understand how, long after the clans were pulled, by tribal necessities, up over the cliff-top, to the building of walled towns, they returned to their sacred ceremonial cave as obstinately as the English return to the Gothic for their religious architecture.

Under all color of romance, the cliff towns remained simple and not over-populous agricultural villages, so that if one wanted a marker for the age that built them, I would take it not from the caves but from a feature of their architecture that arose toward the end of the Small-house period, out of the inner necessity of a tribal mind that was, at its profoundest, Oriental. All over the well-timbered mesas of the McElmo, the Pagosa-Piedra and the upper Chama, arose a series of singular structures whose architectural evolution may still be traced, defining the period that produced them as the time of towered towns. They began before our Ancients were fairly out of the cobble-stone pits, and they do not disappear until the towns themselves have absorbed them, stretching up into seven-storied heights from whose tops the voice of the cacique may be heard, waking the village to its morning life.

Consider how they rise in the McElmo district and the Pagosa-Piedra.  East, north, and northwest, great peaks hem in that country, dropping from their shoulders long timbered slopes, spruce and pine, and aspen flaming with the frost, fringed with sinuous vales, silver with sage and slender grass.  Shallow, new valleys they are, cut by huge slanting dikes, walled in by vermilion-and-white and ocher-tinted mesas, over the tops of which creep and cling rosettes of piñon and juniper.  Scattered across the tongues of mesa, between the rivers and the pebbly beds where rivers never ran, are the low house mounds marked by dense growth of sage and chaparral.  Between them, spring the roofless towers.  From Hovenweep and Surouaro and Holly Cañon they spring.

Round towers and square towers, towers squared on the sides and rounded on the corners; towers, like Stronghold House, thrust up on pinnacles of native rock; round towers at the outer corners of great-houses, as at Hovenweep; twin towers, set up over a cliff house; towers on the Mancos above cavate lodges;

towers in the cliff villages, at Far View and Spruce-tree houses. The towers, I insist, grew out of an inner necessity of the tribes, out of that strange necessity of man to be responsible for his fellow-man, of which the dawn impulse lies in the mind of the herd and the flock.

Still, in that region, the leader of the browsing goats climbs up the boulder, to keep his watch where once  the cacique of the Small-house People sheltered his outlook with a heaped round of broken stone. But it was not for the enemy that the cacique watched oftenest: he watched the game; antelope flashing their white rumps or fleeing in great bands like the shadow of clouds, over the grass mesa; whitetail trooping in the shallow draws; but chiefly he watched the corn. He watched the crows settling over the young shoots, and between the glint of their wings he sent the glint of arrows and the twang of the bowstring deeper than their quarreling caws. Many a mid-morning, from his tower, the voice of the watcher scattered the young men for turning aside the hoofs of the wild herds, or the mule-deer moving stealthily between the unfenced rows, ruining with selective bites the finest milky ears. No doubt he watched the sun and the stars, with whose orientation the times of his feasts were determined, and the lines of his ceremonial chambers set.

But of all the necessities served by the tower-houses, the keenest was the need of communication, though it is not until you have lived a while in one of the print-less towns of the Rio Grande, where writing is not used and the bell is uninvented, that you realize why the tower prevailed, in primitive communities, until it was absorbed into the towered great-house and the many-storied pueblo. From the tops of the towers went up smoke-signals to the farthest confederated villages, but chiefly, morning and evening, high priest or town crier cried prayers and the day's directions for a community that was always more communistic than anything of which we moderns have experience.

At Taos, when the wind is falling south from Pueblo Mountain, we can hear three miles away the lieutenant-governor announcing that Juan and Pablo and Hieronimo will mend the intake of the ditch to-morrow, that the young men of the South House will go up to Blue Lake to assoil themselves for the coming ceremonies, and that Feliciano Garcia must hobble the horse that spent the night in the widow Abeta's corn. I recall once going there to take council concerning a matter of land legislation, waiting in the governor's room while a voice from the North House, high over us like a bell, rang out the call to council, taken up sonorously from the South House till the reverbera-tions overlapped and died along the hollow of the creek like the sound of receding waters. So, in the twilights of the upper mesa, along the Mancos and the

Chaco, it must have sounded and resounded from tower to tower for all their centuries.

But of the centuries it took for the towers to grow into great-houses, centers of civic interest as well as of defense, the count is wholly lost.  All that we know definitely, is that, somewhere along the trail, our Ancients crossed that hesitating line on the hither side of which we begin to speak of cultures as civilized. It is the line at which peoples cease merely to accommodate themselves to their environment, and attempt its mastery.

From being half hunting, half corn-growing, loosely coördinated clans, they drew into villages, the villages crystallized into towns, having a centralized organization, with differentiated activities and buildings suited to the same.  But wherever the towns approached the differentiated society which gives the tone of cities, wherever the thin line of cleavage showed between specialized and rural populations, the cities died.

# CITIES THAT DIED

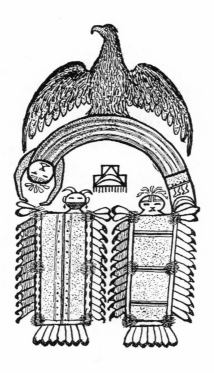

# CITIES THAT DIED

THE line at which our Ancients crossed over from snuggling themselves into the environment, as the wild bee into the hiving rocks, and began to control it, is the line of the *acequia madre*. This was after Awanyu, the great plumed Guardian of the Water Springs, had flung himself disdainfully across the middle heaven, when the Rains walked not on the tall potreros, and the towns had been forced down to the river flood plains for their corn-planting.

When a crop can flourish handsomely on the run-off of natural watersheds, a family may subsist satisfactorily by itself for everything except its social occasions. But when a river is to be diverted in its course to irrigate the fields, then, by the same tie that they bind the river to the service of the corn, men bind themselves by the tie of the indivisible utility. Rain falls on radical and conservative alike, but the mother ditch makes communists of them all. That is, it makes for coöperative effort with psychological implications, to which the term "communism" is a clumsy, crab-like approach.

At the end of the Towered-town period—and that includes the best of the cliff villages—the homes of our Ancients, in the land of their journey's ending, were mere clots and clusters of more or less related farmer groups; as slightly coördinated with respect to their civic functions as any pioneer crossroads; a state of things that we do as much as possible to disguise by calling their remains "cliff cities, "cliff palaces," "Montezuma's Castle," and the like meaningless, falsely romantic names. Of the stuff of which true cities were made, the Puebleños brought little out of the towered towns; a headman, a sun priest, already partly supported by tithing, in order that he might give himself unreservedly to inviting the coöperation of the Holders of the Paths of Our Lives, and many religious fraternities devoted to making some especial natural function work to the advantage of the clans, fraternity of the Rain, of the Hunt, of the Smutless Corn. Then, and still, the pueblo groups were made up of economically and defensively federated clan clusters, often antagonistic and bitterly jealous; and, by their habit of consolidating their house clusters, creating "wards" quite as "solid," politically, as any our modern cities can produce.

Architecturally, they had arrived at the two-terraced house row, and the towered cluster, having as its nucleus the two- or three-storied tower of outlook and communication, the residence of the sun priest, the place where the tithing and the seed-corn were kept, and perhaps a central supply of munitions in the shape of arrows and throwing-stones. Also, if culture is to be ranked by the relative quotas of time and energy given to the making of music, the making of epics, drama, and spiritual exercises, and that given to the business of making a living, our Ancients of the towered towns were even then a highly cultivated folk. They had, though they still entered their houses through holes in the roof, already done what the Greeks did, what Christian Europe strove for and failed to accomplish,—made art and religion so integral a part of the day's performance that the most assiduous of Indian bureaus has never been able to pull them into the duality of business and culture which is the mark of our own time.

The trails by which the Puebleños came down from the mesas and potreros to the river plains of the Gila, the Mimbres, the Zuñi, and the Rio Grande are inextricably crossed. One, at least, emerged definitely, seven or eight hundred years ago, in Arizona, in what is known as the Great-house culture, on the plain of the Rio Salado, which is to say, Salt River. The great-house was a logical extension of the towered town, gathering to itself council chambers, repositories of arms and sacred paraphernalia, observatories for noting the positions of the lord Sun, and the dwellings of the chief priests and citizens. Here the hall-mark of cities, differentiation of function and distinction of caste, had begun to show itself. The peak of the Great-house era, which we measure by the ruins of Casa Grande, half a mile south of the Gila, would have been about, or even before, 1300, for Casa Grande was already a ruin with only a legendary history when Father Eusebio Kino said mass there in 1694. It is also certain that the lumpy, nondescript ruin is only one, and that not the most considerable, of the great-houses that rose on the plain of the Gila and the Salado, citadel and civic center, with outlying temples, public oven and reservoirs, citizen-house clusters, and suburbs, where the rivers fall rapidly toward their junction, from Superstition Mountain, across whose brow runs still the white streak of the foam of the Flood.

Much of the country hereabout must be in the same condition as when our Ancients chose it, rivers issuing from volcanic gorges of the Mogollon Rim, on dense, thorny orchards of mesquite, acacia, palo-verde, and thick-armed sahuaro that might have seen the Great-house People go.

The road which leads through this region, from Casa Grande to Phœnix, cuts the line of innumerable great-house canals. Where it crosses the Salado, opposite the reef of reddish trap called Hole-in-the-Rock, the intake of ditches on both sides of the river may still be traced. These acequias madres, along which the virgin poplars ran, ruffling their white-lined petticoats to the wind, extended for a total distance of two hundred miles across the river plain, bringing under cultivation a quarter of a million acres. At Mesa it is reported that the present Mormon colony saved itself a matter of twenty thousand dollars by utilizing the gradients of an ancient waterway, pecked out of the tufa with hammers of stone, heaped up with wooden shovels, and carried away in skins. Even where their banks have been utterly leveled by the wind, the lines of these meandering canals may still be traced by the *huacas,* water-tamers, placed along them by the builders. For, said our Ancients, along stream-beds and borders, there are rounded and oddly shaped rocks, and where these are, the water flows faster, with a contented sound: therefore let us place, along our mains, familiar shapes of stone, so that the river may be the more easily induced to flow there and feel at home.

Besides these rounded river boulders and concretionary nodules, the little tender flowers remember the place of the ancient acequia. Wet seasons, when all the rest of the *plan del Salado* is bright with bloom, you can trace by flowerless lines the water-borders, tamped hard and baked by brush fires built in the hollows of the canals.

Gathered around the six great-house heaps, spread corn and the fragrant bean fields, cotton bursting white between the golden melons and the little green-white squashes, and the silvery, sinuous acequias.

Far out, beyond even the voice of the cacique, floating morning and evening from the housetops, rose the platforms of the Watchers of the Fields, warding the young corn from the rabbits, and scaring the mule-deer from the melons.  About Los Muertos, one of the lesser groups of communal houses, over whose obscure

mounds the green fields of Tempe close, twelve to thirteen thousand farmer citizens worked their allotments of irrigated lands, living from seed-time to harvest in the lightly built daub-and-wattle *temporales* and under the open-sided ramadas where swung the dripping water-jar and the grinding-stone lay on the metate.  From harvest to seed-time, they gathered at the great-houses for dancing and drama, for trade, and the serious business of aligning themselves successfully with the Holders and Finishers of the Paths of Our Lives.

Distributed along both sides of the main canal, which was about thirty feet across, the great-houses rose from platform-like foundations, terraced to a height of four or five stories, of which the last one was all that was left of the tower, from the flat roof of which a smoke-signal could call the farthest farmer to the citadel. In its lower, doorless chambers would be stored the seed-corn, and the reserve against a possible cropless year, and the tithing of the cacique. In the central cell of all, the sun priest prayerfully awaited the moments when the beam of the Sun Father, turning in his course, would shine through the pierced walls, as the custodian will show you at Casa Grande. Probably no private house was without some marker of its own—as at Zuñi to-day—some spot on the wall or the door-sill where the sun shone at solstice or equinox, and at those times only, from which seed-time and feast-days were calculated. Then, when the sun priest received the appropriate ray, from housetop to housetop would ring the ancient cry, "Spring is here! Spring is here!" and all down the acequia madre the farmers tending the water-gates would take it up and pass the cry like wapiti stags ringing their silvery peals: "Spring is here!"

When the hunt was on, or the salt-train about due from the south, the women went up to the tower story to look for faint smokes in the appointed quarter of the horizon which advised them when to set the fires going in the huge communal baking-pits. These were in open plazas between the great-houses, and when they were packed close with haunches of venison, with savory herbs between, flanked with ears of green corn, with rows of round-bodied bean-pots, or cakes of pounded meal flavored with wild seeds and sweetened with sahuaro, wrapped in clean husks for the baking, the steam of them would have surely hastened the feet threading the silver network of the acequias.

It is likely that the families of all who had to do with the administration of Great-house affairs lived rather continuously at the community houses, and that the smaller dwellings clustered about them were the winter homes of such of the farmers as felt themselves drawn to the winter life of cities.   At San Juan and Santa Clara one hears young Puebleños talk at their summer *temporales* of week-ending at the pueblo, or of going in for a saint's day as the clans of Los Muertos used no doubt to go in for the Green-corn Dance or the seasonal Rain-making.

Whether certain of the buildings uncovered at Los Muertos were halls of the Masons and the Elks, I mean of the fraternities of the Antelope and the Snake and the Rain, or were temples of the Sun Father, or even of some less personalized Holder of the Ways, is one of the unsolved problems of the Great-house era.   Cushing, who uncovered them, thought them temples, any building wholly set aside from secular use is surely a temple, and, dividing the horizon according to the system prevailing at Zuñi, he found his way from them to the ancient shrines and sacred places of the purple mountain wall.   For these and other reasons, such as the finding of the remains of the Maiden Sacrifice to avert earthquakes, after the manner of old Zuñi, and the grouping of the house clusters by sevens, he has called the culture of the plain of the Gila and the Salado, *Shiwinian,* for by such a name the Ancients of Zuñi called themselves. This I leave with the ethnologists; for though Cushing was, no doubt, a changeling whom the Red Gods fathered, too many of his conclusions came the way of my own for me to quote them with complacency.

Most likely of all, it seems to me, three strains, at least, mingled in the Great-house culture, not speaking the same tongues or having the same origin legend, but of a common racial stock. These were: *Outliers,* wild hunting tribes not unfriendly, *Rurales,* farmer peoples, feudally related to the Great-house clans, from whom the present Pimas and Papagos are descended, and among whom still survives a memory of the third group of culturally advanced groups, the builders of the Great-houses, the *Hohokum.*

Tremendous activities went on in these cities that died, while the Hohokum held them. Between the times when the people served the corn and the cotton, there were shrines to be visited, ditches to be dug and mended, loads of arrow-stone and water-worn boulders, suitable for winter working, to be poled in from the river-beds, along the *acequias madres* on rafts of bundled reeds and cane from the river-borders. Between the winter solstice and the vernal equinox, traders came in; fierce, shy, Outliers, with the summer's plunder of dried meat and medicine herbs, turquoise and chalcedony for ceremonial arrows, bundles of yucca fiber, and yucca root for washing blankets and for purification, venders of parrot and macaw feathers, and sellers of strange shells from the gulf and the Pacific Ocean. After the corn-planting and before the first hoeing, there was the annual expedition to the head of the California gulf, for salt, attended by protective ritual, fragments of which still linger among the tribes who have inherited the lands but fallen far short of the culture of the Hohokum.

Between tribal occasions, the women coiled and smoothed and painted their cooking-pots and tended the great communal ovens. In June they flocked to the mesquite thickets that came close up to the irrigated lands, where, between scarlet-tipped thyrses of the ocotilla, the sahuaros, lifting thick arms like priests who pray for rain, ripened their coronals of crimson fruit. Here, while the men made ceremonial wine, and prayed for rain, the women boiled syrup for the winter's sweetening. Young lovers walking apart to find the night-blooming cereus uncurling in the dusk from its dry, rat-tailed stems, lingered to hear the night-singing mocking-bird, pouring its music like round-dropped, molten substance of the moon.

After the corn was harvested, the women braided it, by the husks, in long festoons, hung drying under the *jacales,* on whose roofs presently the ripening cotton pods burst into white drifts for miles and miles.  And always between these and their house-tending, child-bearing activities, the women of the Hohokum were a-building and a-building.  They mixed ashes of brush and grass with the dry earth and puddled it, piling it course by course, as much as would dry well in the shape in which it was laid, into the great pyramidal houses.  They were a long time building the great-houses.  At Casa Grande the custodian will show you, under the oldest foundations, traces of pit fireplaces still older; the gradual disuse of adobe reinforced by posts, withen-bound; and the evolution, through experience of its lasting qualities, of the puddled wall.

These were the cities that died in the south, leaving the ditches full and the walls of the great-houses standing.  The Pima, who occupy as much of their lands as the white man does not happen to want at the moment, claim the Hohokum as ancestors.  But all their legends go to show that the relation of the Pima to the Great-house builders was that of an indigenous agricultural people to dominating clans of a more developed culture.  When the key clans decayed or withdrew, the native population salvaged what it could of what it had learned.  To this day, the Pima have a trace of the manners of *noblesse*.

But if you ask of what the Hohokum died, it would be difficult to say, unless it were of the pride of cities.

For the central fact of their building was that invisible spirit of the hive, which in Europe was so early symbolized in the person of the priest-king and the royal line, which the invisible republicanism of the Hohokum failed to symbolize and so stabilize. Of this, until the psychologists furnish me with a more competent vocabulary, there is more to be sensed than said. It is suggested by tradition that a feeling for themselves as a superior sort of folk, was the undoing of the Hohokum. Clans waxed boastful. Great-house fought against great-house. Dimly appears the figure of a hero chief or chief clan, Civano, suggesting the Civola or Cibola, the seven cities that Fray Marcos de Niza and the negro Estevánico, with rings on his fingers and rattles on his knees, came wandering to find. Fragments of Great-house lore, such as captive women teach to the children they have borne to their conquerors, suggest that the Apaches, who began to trouble the Southwest about that time, might have broken the strength of the great-houses by repeated raids. At Los Muertos there was, without doubt, a devastating earthquake. For any and all these reasons, certain of their clans, concluding that here, after all, was not their Middle Place, fled northward across the hot sands between the painted cliffs, and founded or were absorbed into what we now know as Zuñi, Middle Ant-heap of the World.

There is also a legendary thread upon which to hang

a supposition that others of the quarreling clans
moved south and west, to a pocket of the Sierra Madre,
from which the only outlet south is a narrow volcanic
rift, called the Boquillo, leading along the Cordilleras
to the central Mexican plateau.   It is a long and winding valley, overlooked by the Cerro de Montezuma,
having a river that,
between domed cot-
tonwoods, runs to
broad, shallow *la-*
*gunas,* haunt of water-
birds; called, because
of them, Place of Her-
ons, the fabled Vale
of Aztlan. In the white
argillaceous cliffs of the valley's southern and western borders, there are caves where a corn-growing
people have left walled rooms and granaries.   High
up on the crest of the Sierra Madre and across to
the *barrancas* of Sonora, live the Tarahumacs, nearest of kin to the Small-house People of the Pajaritan
plateau.   Along the Rio of Aztlan, rise, in blunt heaps
strewn with fragments of a rich, bright pottery, the
ruins of Casas Grandes, judged the very flower of
a town-making culture that had passed its peak before
the Spanish explorers found it.

The ruins here are of the same type as the solitary
Casa Grande on the plain of the Gila in Arizona,

towering communal buildings with their compounds and subjoined dwellings, surrounded by fields and farm-houses. But at Casas Grandes there is a perfection of finish about the artifects they buried with their dead in the floors, and a touch of eroticism, such as appear first in cities stationed toward the hot south.

There are no living accounts of Casas Grandes, but north, in the valley of the Rio Grande, and south, in Anahuac, there are tales that seem to meet here and make history. It was from Yunque-Yunque, which is San Juan, at the junction of the Rio Grande and the Chama, that the culture hero Poseyemo withdrew from the pueblos with the most forthright of their young men, never to be heard of again until Oñate came in 1598, with tribesmen of the Montezumas in his train. But of these same tribes of Anahuac, who are named in the order in which they appeared on the central plateau, Xochomilcos, Chalacas, Tepenecans, Tezcucans, Tlatluicans, Tlascalans and Aztecs, it is related that they came out of seven caves, and "these caves are in a country which we all know to be toward the north." Elsewhere it is said that "There are two provinces in this country, one called Aztlan, which is to say a place of herons," and if it were "this land and the Lagunas thereof," from which the last of the Nahuatl tribes set out, in the twelfth century, for the valley of Anahuac, where Cortés found them, then it seems much more likely that they came down the Rio

Grande, rather than across the desert mountains from Casa Grande, in Arizona.

What I think is that the Great-house clans of the Gila and Salado came down the cliff- and cave-way from the San Juan basin, rose on their own roots to unprecedented levels, and, after the disintegration of their culture, struck north to the Chaco Cañon, near the Place of Emergence.

The San Juan takes its rise in the Pagosa-Piedra by innumerable quick rivulets, but at Shiprock it receives from the south the intermittent waters of the Arroyo Chaco, whose tail is a spread plume of dry cañons, trailed down the western slope of the Continental Divide. Hereabouts is a high white country, sloping east by the Chama, sloping south with the Rio Puerco, sloping south-by-west with the Zuñi and the tributaries of the Coloradito, sloping north-by-west down Chaco Cañon.

Going north on an errand for the Spanish Crown, in the year when the Atlantic colonies were determining to have no more to do with crowns, forever, Don Bernardo Miera y Pacheco discovered the Chaco country, and from the clustering of the towns as if they might have been under one chief, and from the fresh condition of the ruins, concluded that he had stumbled at last upon fabled Cibola, or perhaps that Quivira by the tradition of whose splendor Don Francisco de Coronado was seduced. Don Bernardo thought the

Chaco towns could not have been abandoned long, which conclusion was supported by the tribes whom he found in possession of that country, from the Mesa Fachada, north, who insisted that they had been there as more or less friendly Outliers since the building of the Chaco pueblos, which go by the names that the Navajo gave them. It is supposed, indeed, that all that region was called either after a Navajo word meaning "white," in reference to its glistening sands, or from a Spanish word, *chacra,* meaning "house in the field," from the scattered solitary Navajo hogans.

Going up, by way of Jemez, from the Rio Grande, near the top of the Continental Divide you come to a region of great rolling hills, stepped mesas walled with sandstone whose dust is a gray death, wind-streaked in the hollows, leaving bare great knobs of granite and dark basalt, with long tongues of darker forest dropping from the peaks and running out in scattered blobs of piñon and juniper. North, from this country, draws the winding, shallow rift of the Chaco, between whitish sandstone walls in which fierce rain and tireless winds have worn deep bays and beetling capes. The floor of Chaco Cañon was once a gently sloping level, down which cedar and yellow pine, choke-cherry and poplar trooped far beyond the present stations of the last sorry specimens of their kind; the rill of the cañon gently flowing, the mesas that shut it in, loved by the rain. Grass must have grown over the mesa-

FROM PUEBLO BONITO . . . A CUT STAIRWAY UP TO THE RIM ROCK

tops, and antelope fed there in great bands, where now the wind torments the sandstone grits into loose wave-marks, and an infrequent Navajo herder leads his scraggy flock. Down on the floor of the cañon, or mounting occasionally to the sandstone rim, concentrated within the space of a score of modern city blocks, are to be found the traces of a cultural era that, in many of its aspects, rivaled the organization and artifacts of ancient Crete.

Pueblo Bonito, called so because of the beautiful alternation of its courses of large and small stones, lies close up under the cañon walls, and back of it, in a secret, winding crevice, a cut stairway leads up to the rim rock and the trail to Pueblo Alto, accounted the chief's house though perhaps not on any better authority than that it commands a wide, uninterrupted view. A bow-shot from Bonito lies Pueblo Arroyo, which the winter torrents have in part carried away, and just around the cape of jutting rock, rises Chettro-Kettle, House of the Rain. Two miles above Chettro-Kettle is Hungo Pavi, having also a cut stairway in the near-by sandstone cliff, and, on a high point south of the cañon, Peñasco Blanco of the banded wall.

It is not alone for the beauty of its surfaced rocks, for the invention of the staircase, and the roofing of cedar slabs worked smooth as planed boards, with, as yet, no knives but stone, that the Chaco ruins are distinguished, but for the evidence of high social organization in its defense and its adaptations to civic and religious group life. Across from Chettro-Kettle stands the great kiva of Casa Rinconada, seventy-two feet in diameter, set round with niches such as we still build into sacred edifices for the accommodation of saints; and around it traces of a sacred precinct for burying the principal dead. Within the House of the Rain, there is a great subterranean bowl, having an antechamber, and fire-pits between the columns that upheld its roof, so much too large for the mere keeping of the sacred fire as we know it was among our Ancients kept, that one wonders if also the fire demanded sacrifices.

There was an art of inlaying at Chaco, turquoise and pink stone and lignite on wood and bone, there were painted flutes of four notes, trumpets of murex-shell by which the rain priests called the rain, and the beginnings of that subtle art invented once by the Chinese and nowhere else in the world, the art of cloisonné.

Everywhere is the evidence of Chaco as a center of intertribal trade, trade in salt, trade in sea-shells and turquoise from the south, trade in buffalo meat and hides. If the buffalo came so far west and south at that time as they did in 1776 when Miera y Pacheco visited the Chaco, at least they came no farther, so that Zuñi and Hopi clans, drawing into towns across the Painted Desert a hundred miles to the west,—what was a hundred miles to men who ran the mule-deer down and caught him with their naked hands!—must have traveled often to Bonito and Chettro-Kettle, to exchange turquoises and salt for buffalo robes and hides. A hundred miles to the north, the most important of the cliff towns of Mesa Verde must have still been occupied, and from their aeries brought eagle plumes to exchange for the many-colored feathers of the south. Across the highlands of the Chama and down toward the Rio Grande, the pueblos in which the myth of the roving hero Poseyemo was finally located, were a-building.

Over on Las Animas, the broken mounds about what is now Aztec, Colorado, gave form to a rich agricultural culture, which was probably the first or the chief location of the Hohokum when they shook the dust of the Gila Valley off their moccasins. And yet they died. Within the reach of authentic tradition, died the towns of Las Animas, and Chaco died.

From the condition of the ruins, the life of Chaco went out all at once, but not from destructive warfare, though there is evidence in town structure of a need to protect themselves against the growing strength of nomadic tribes. The prevailing ground plan of the pueblos is like the letter E, having a straight, high back, and a defensive wall drawn like a half-moon from wing to wing of the terraced front, except at Pueblo Bonito, where the back of the E is bent and the inclosing wall, fortified by a row of one-story houses, becomes the cord of the bow. The walls are pierced for arrows, and the banded stone made them proof against fire. Only the gods and themselves could have destroyed the Chaco towns, lying in the shape of the constellation of Orion, in a line between Pueblo Pintado and Peñasco Blanco, crossed by another from Kin Klizhin to Pueblo Alto, while Kin Biniola, House of the Winds, lies, like the huntsman's weapon, in a clear space of whitened sand.

The gods, for their part, withheld the rains. The two or three hundred years of the Las Animas and Chaco towns must have seen the alteration in the climate which brought all the Southwestern settlements down from the high places to the flood plains of the infrequent rivers. Legend tells that the drought at Aztec lasted twelve years. The whole country was full of fragments of broken towns, clans and half-clans, gipsying in more favored districts, trading and panhandling, selling charms and instructing their hosts in foreign handicrafts.

Came to Pueblo Bonito, one Blue Feather, from a town on a high rock in the south, selling peyote, that little, low button of cactus to which, to compensate for its lowliness, Those Above gave the power of inducing bright, elusive dreams that, to recapture, you eat another button . . . and another. . . . And when this Blue Feather, whom the Navajo confuse with their

Gambling God whose fetish is a blue stone, had muddled the heads of the Chacoans, he gambled with them for their loveliest town, and won it out of their hand. Out of this there comes a tale of tribal ruin, so enticing that I touch it lightly, meaning to come back to it sometime, with a peyote button in one hand and a sheaf of clean white papers in the other.

For, along with the town, Blue Feather had won the sacred Tabooed Maiden, Bride of the Sun, whom he saw walking by moonlight between her women, lovely herself as a young, dusky moon. Her, sacrilegiously, Blue Feather took to wife, to the scandal of the pueblos and the mortal offense of one of the two superior clans, the Bear and Alligator, from which she was chosen; though what an Alligator clan was doing in the white desert of Chaco, is more than I can tell.

But there they were, traditionally of fairer skin, with brown hair instead of black, connecting themselves with the Hohokum of the great-houses, if by nothing more than their pride of themselves as a superior people.

Among our Ancients, the custom of keeping a Bride of the Sun prevailed generally,—is there not at Zuñi a story of one whom the god visited in the shape of falling rain?—but by her violation at Pueblo Bonito, the towns of the Chaco became accursed. Affrighted, the clans parted and scattered, leaving the walls standing and the sooty pot in the fireplace. But after resettling among the Zuñi or the Hopi peoples, or, as in one case that we know of, among the Rio Grande pueblos, they returned and took away their house beams. Think well of these fire- and stone-trimmed beams, for it is only by these that the last passages of the trail of our Ancients may be unraveled.

From three to five hundred years go to the making of cedars suitable for vigas, at the same time making a calendar of the wet years and the dry. At the time the house beams of Chettro-Kettle were growing, the same record of rains copious, and rains withheld, was being written into the trunks of the giant sequoias of California, together with the record of five thousand other years. Season for season, the rhythm of annual rings would run very much the same for redwood and for cedar. Recently it has occurred to men whose business is about such things, that, since they have already traced in the California forest the drought through which the ravens fed Elijah, when Ahab was king in Jerusalem, it might be possible by locating concurrent intervals of wet and dry on the Chaco vigas, to estimate the approximate time of their cutting. Do not, therefore, when you go by the ruined towns of the Southwest, on your summer's outing, make your fire of the cedar house beams.

If the Chaco fugitives went south, along the Rio Grande, they found cities already dead before them, for those were the days when men owned their homes, instead of being owned by them. If, for any reason, such as rains withheld, or epidemic illness, or their wise men seeing a portent leading them to conclude that this was not the Middle Place of the World, where they felt bound to live, they packed up their sacred *tiponis* and went seeking it. After generations they came back as birds to old nesting-places, for who can tell how the Middle Place circles and shifts? But when they believed most devoutly that they had found it, they died, the cities of our Ancients.

Old Pecos died, that was the most flourishing, the most complex and sophisticated and powerful of the pueblos that Coronado found. Over in the shut valley of Estancia, east of Oku, sacred Turtle Mountain of the Tewa, called Sandia by the Spanish-speaking, died Chilili, Tajiqui, Tenabo, Manzano, Abo, and Tabirá. Paul Walter says they died of fear. In that, I suspect, he comes closest to a fact that hovered, formless as a cloud, behind the pleasant communities of our Ancients.

These pueblos of the Salinas lie mostly on the eastern slopes of the lovely hill cluster of the Manzanos, having the Mesa Jumanos on the south, and looking east to the salt and alkali *lagunas* and the immeasurable, mirage-haunted plains of central New Mexico. Few and steep are the passes by which the riverless bolson of the Estancia is reached. Beyond dreaming, the beauty of the tree-covered slope above it, and the flowery meadows, overshadowed by white blossom clouds, in whose bosom lies the rain.

There were springs then, in the Manzanos, and clear creeks dividing the clan clusters of the summer and winter people. At Manzano, itself, the *ojo gigante* laves the lower branches of the pine-tree under which it springs, and bears water-lilies on its wimpling pool.

Of the origin of the Salinas pueblos, even less is known than of the towns of Chaco, and, though they continued on into the later half of the sixteenth century, not much more of their disappearing. For their beauty and prosperity, and possibly for the docility of their populations, they were chosen to be the scene of the earliest Franciscan missionary effort. Walls of great churches and convents outlast the blunt heaps of the community houses. At Chilili there was a chapel to the nativity of the Virgin and there the false legend of buried treasure first arose. At Manzano still grow pink and white, the apple orchards planted before the general insurrection of 1680. At Tajiqui died, in 1659, Fray Geronimo de la Lana, who built the mission at Quarai, whose bones lie now in the cathedral at Santa Fé. Quarai was a red sandstone heap on a sloping hill, with the walls of the church, for that period majestic, below it. Abo lies in a valley of its own, and its stones are redder than Quarai's, against the piñon green; and the wild verbena outlines its sunken kivas. Something of the feminine grace of the dark women who laid up and plastered its walls lingers still about their ruins. Above Abo, on the mesa, are the painted pictographs such as our Ancients were accustomed to leave about the homes which they had definitely abandoned, leaving the site free to other comers. Also, as was their custom when the next comers might be enemy tribes, they "killed" the springs.

Tabirá stands on a blue limestone hill in the Medanos, the vast bench of sand, now grass-bound and covered, that was once the beach of an inland lake, below the dark wooded level of the Mesa Jumanos. If there were springs at Tabirá, they were too effectually killed for any later finding; only the rain catchments are still traceable on the brow of the bench lands. Pale on the pale grass over which the shadows of clouds race and the wind runs like the waterings in the coat of some great tawny beast, the last of the Tompiros towns took on, long after it had dropped out of history, a golden color of romance. Over it hovered, and at last settled indestructibly, the myth of the Gran Quivira, only now, instead of chiefs eating out of golden plates, there were Spanish *frailes* fleeing from marauding Apaches and burying uncounted treasures of gold, sacred vessels of hammered silver, great candlesticks and chalices of pure gold, ingots mined from secret veins by Indian slaves. And of this, the only truth is that the *frailes* fled, together with the inhabitants of the towns. Also at Tabirá, there are limestone caverns and crevices, giving forth a hollow sound when the ground above them is struck sharply.    And what else, in New Mexico, should subterranean chambers hold but treasure?    But the tales are, in fact, as hollow as the sound.

At the time of which we know most of the Salinas pueblos, and that, little more than that the church of

Tabirá, for instance, was founded by Fray Francisco de Acavado about 1628, the Apaches surrounded the whole of the pueblo country except a narrow arc on the northwest which was held by the Utes.   For these, the corn-fed cities made good plundering.   Within a decade at most, and at a time ten or fifteen years previous to the insurrection of 1680, the Tewa pueblos of the Salinas had reassorted themselves with their kin along the Rio Grande, and the Tompiros had moved south to Isleta del Sur, where still lingers a trace of them.

But in the towns that they left standing, this is singular: that there are no signs of forced sundering.

Out of their walled towns and with a culture immensely in advance of the enemy, they went, if not willingly, at least with deliberation. Fear out of proportion to the occasion worked in them, and what could it work upon but the minds of men too long immersed in communality to be able to turn the sharp edges of decision against an enemy who fought out of a common impulse, each man for his own hand?

# CACTUS COUNTRY

# CACTUS COUNTRY

NOT all the country that the cactus takes, belongs to it. That gipsy of the tribe, the prickly-pear, goes as far east and north on the great plains as the Spanish adventurer ever went, perhaps farther. It goes as a rarity into Old World gardens, runs wild and thrives wherever there are sun and sand to bring its particular virtues into play. For the virtue of all cacti is that they represent the ultimate adaptations of vegetative life on its way up from its primordial home in the sea shallows, to the farthest, driest land. The prickly-pears—*Opuntia* is their family name, and the connection is a large one—run to arid wastes as gipsies do to the wilds, not because there the environment is the only one which will tolerate them, but because it is the one in which all the cactus tribe find themselves fulfilled, triumphant.

Here, in the country below the Mogollon Rim, the business of plants in making this a livable world, goes on all open to the light, not covered and confused by the multiplicity of its manifestations, as in the lush, well-rained-on lands. Here, in this veritable corner of southwestern Arizona, it has traveled the perfect round, from the filmed protoplasmic cell, by all the paths of plant complexity, to the high simplicity of the great king cactus, the sahuaro.

Going west by the Old Trails Road, you do not begin to find sahuaro until you are well down toward the black hills of Tucson, and it is not at its best this side of the toad-like heap of volcanic trap which turns the river out of its course, called Tummomoc. Here it rises to a height of twenty-five or thirty feet, erect, columnar, dull green, and deeply fluted, the outer ridges of the flutings set with rows of lateral spines that inclose it as in a delicate grayish web. Between the ridges the sahuaro has a texture like well-surfaced leather, giving back the light like spears, that, seen from a rapidly moving car, make a continuous vertical flicker in the landscape. Marching together against the rose-and-vermilion evening, they have a stately look, like the pillars of ruined temples.

For the first hundred years or so the sahuaro preserves the outline of its virgin intention to be straight, but in the case of wounding, or perhaps in seasons of excess, it puts forth without calculation immense columnar branches like the arms of candelabra, curving to bring their growing tips parallel to the axis of the main stem, which they reproduce as if from their own roots.

The range of the sahuaro is restricted. Beginning with isolated specimens about the San Pedro River, it spreads south and west, but the true sahuaro forests are not reached until the gate of Papagueria is past, or the flats of Salt River. A small plantation of them has crossed the Colorado and established itself in California. South they pass into Sonora as far as Altár, and approach almost to the gulf shore, where they are replaced by the still more majestic *sowesa*.

The leafless, compact outline of the sahuaro, its erect habit and indurated surfaces give it a secret look. Surmounting the crest of one of these denuded desert ranges, or marching up nearly vertical slopes without haste or stooping, or pushing its way imperturbably toward the sun from the midst of cat-claw and mesquite and palo-verde, it has the effect of being forever outside the community of desert life. Yet such is the succulence of its seedlings, that few of them would survive the first two or three seasons without the shelter of the spiny undergrowth. Once the recurved spines have spread and stiffened across the smooth, infolded intervals, the sahuaro is reasonably safe, even from the hard-mouthed cattle of the desert ranges. In very dry years, small rodents will gnaw into the flutings as far up as they can creep between the spines. High up out of reach of all marauders, the woodpecker drills his holes in the pulpy outer mass; but against these the sahuaro protects itself by surrounding its wounds with pockets of woody fiber woven to the shape of the woodpecker's burrow.

Indians of that country will often remove these

pocket linings before the fiber has hardened, and make use of them for household containers, or you may find them kicking about the sand, hard as oak-knots, long after the sahuaro that wove them has sloughed off its outer layer in decay. For the wood-pecker never penetrates to the sahuaro core, inclosed as it is in a tube of woody, semi-detached ribs which remain standing long after the spongy masses that fill and surround it have completely desiccated, slowly fraying out outward from the top as the ribs part, until at last the Papago carries them away to roof his house or his family tomb.

In the vast *abras* of southern Arizona, there is no woody growth capable of furnishing the woodpecker with the cool, dark house in which he brings up his broods. In a single unbranched sahuaro near Casa Grande, this year, I counted seventeen woodpeckers' holes, ranged up and down like the little openings of the cliff-dwellers' caves. Frequently the vacated apartments of the sahuaro skyscraper will be occupied by the pygmy owl, who may have made a meal of the eggs or young birds before he established his own family there. Everywhere, from the sahuaro towers, little blue-headed hawks may be seen perching, or, from the vantage of their height, launching swift predatory flights. But when in the crotch of some three-hundred-year-old specimen the fierce red-tail has made his nest, you will find all that neighborhood vacant of bird life.

It is not easy to take the life of a sahuaro, even when, just to see the tiny wavering flame run up the ridges, you set a match to the rows of oily spines. Even uprooted, as it may be in torrential seasonal rains, the prostrate column has unmeasured powers of living on its stored waters, and making an upward turn of its growing tip. One such I found at the back of Indian Oasis, toward Topohua, which had turned and budded after what must have been several seasons of overthrow.

If the column is by any accident broken, lateral branches start from the wound and curve upward toward the sun. Successive dry years constrict its columnar girth, as successive wet ones swell it, tracing in the undulations of the vertical outline, a record of three or four centuries of rains. Around Tucson there must be sahuaros that could tell what sort of weather it was the year Father Kino came to the founding of San Xavier, and at Salt River I made my siesta under one that could have given a better guess than any of our archæologists at what became of the ancient civilizations of Casa Grande and Los Muertos.

For I suppose the sahuaro harvest, and the ceremonial making of sahuaro wine to be the oldest food festival of the cactus country. In the excavations of the buried cities of the Great-house culture, buried before the queen was born whose jewels opened the portals of the West, they found little brown jars hermetically sealed with clay, after the fashion in which Papago housewives preserve sahuaro syrup at Cobabi and Quitovaquita.

From the month of the Cold Touching Mildly to the Inner Bone Month of the winter, the flutings of sahuaro stems are folded deep. With the first of the rains they begin to expand, until, if the season is propitious, the smooth leathery surfaces are tight as drums. In May, on the blunt crowns, on the quarter most exposed to the sun, buds appear like clusters of green figs, close-packed as if in a platter. About this time red-tailed hawks, in their shelterless nests in the tallest crotches, will be hatching their young, and the quail in pairs going house-hunting in and out of the *garamboyas*. Within a week or two the green fig-shaped buds open, one by one, in filmy white-rayed circles, deep-yellow hearted, the haunt of innumerable flies. By the latter part of June or July the delicate corollas are replaced by fig-shaped fruits that as they curl open when fully ripe, revealing the full-seeded, crimson pulp, have the effect of a second vivid flowering.

Just before the fruits burst, however, the Pima and Papago women turn out by villages to harvest them with long hooks made of a sahuaro rib and a cross-piece of acacia twig. Often, to save labor, they will peel the fruit as they collect it; returning at night with their great jars and baskets overflowing with the luscious juicy pulp. For this, and for all that I have written of the sahuaro festival in Papagueria, it is counted a crime to destroy a sahuaro.

There is a singular charm of the sahuaro forest, a charm of elegance, as the wind, moving like royalty across the well-spaced intervales, receives the courtesies of ironwood and ocotilla and palo-verde. It begins with the upright next-of-blood, with a stately rocking of the tall pillars on their roots, and a soft *ss-ss-ss* of the wind along their spiny ridges. Suddenly the bright blossom-tips of the ocotilla take flight like flocks of scarlet birds, as the long wands bow and recover in the movement of the wind, and after an appreciable interval the thin-leaved ironwood rustles and wrestles with it, loth to let it go, until it drops with almost a sullen note to the stiff whisper of the palo-verde, while the creosote fairly casts its forehead to the ground.

The ocotilla is not a true cactus, but belongs rather by nature of its adaptations to the fellowship of the mesquite and that leafless thorny shrub often found in its neighborhood, called *corona de Jesús*. It does not store moisture as the cactus does, but remains in the long seasons between the rains in a state of complete aridivation, putting forth miraculously after the first showers, at the ends of its branches, crowded panicles of bloom like the bloody tips of spears. The gray, thorny wands of the ocotilla, growing from ten to fifteen feet, brought together in a lovely vase form by the central stem, a few inches from the ground, are leafless for all but a brief season, when perhaps the first sign of spring is the flush of green creeping up their swaying lengths, in the shape of thin, blunt emerald leaves. After the leaves fall away, the petiole which supports them becomes a spine, for the sake of which the stems of ocotilla are used for chicken-fences and corrals, thick-set in the ground, from which, as the spring comes around, they take heart of life, growing delicately green and scarlet-tipped again.

Ocotilla and sahuaro are to be found growing together on the gravelly slopes of the *abras,* and with them the bisnaga or barrel-cactus, which the stranger frequently mistakes for a young sahuaro. It has the same fluted, branchless, columnar habit, but the bisnaga is a darker green, its spines frequently reddish, its circumference larger, and its height seldom equal to the height of a man. It may also be distinguished from other cacti by having the axis of its growth, like the pointer of a dial, angling directly toward the sun. It is only when the observer finds several bisnagas growing together that the uniform slant begins to appear something more than an accident.

Now it is discovered that there is a crumpling of the surfaces toward the downthrow, and a half-turn of the flutings around the axis of growth, as if the plants had all been pulled by an irresistible force, out of their intention to grow symmetrically plump and upright. It seems probable that this disturbance of the barrel-shaped bulk is due to the more rapid evaporation of the side next to the sun; for the bisnaga is nothing, really, but a huge capsule of vegetable pulp, distended by the water which it collects and carries with the utmost parsimony from rain to rain. When the rains cease, it has been known to subsist on its own stores for a dozen years. Anywhere along the flood basins you are likely to see plump specimens of bisnaga uprooted from the rain-softened soil by their own weight, going on comfortably with their life processes while lying on one side. Also you will find here and there globose individuals, having gray fibrous scars in place of the fruit-bearing crown, which has been sliced off by some thirsty traveler. One stroke of the machete, and a little maceration of the white pulp with a stick or the bare hands, will provide in a few minutes a pint or more of cool, slightly insipid drink. Or if the machete is lacking, the spines may be burned off and the barrel broken with a stone.

There are scores of variations of the bisnaga type, "niggerhead," "fish-hook," and "cushion" cacti, running to fat button shapes or short thickened cylinders, widely distributed through the Southwest. Rendered inconspicuous in the landscape by webs of grayish spines, they prick themselves on the attention by burning, brilliant bloom. But after the great sahuaro, it is only the opuntias that successfully modify the desert scene. Of these there are two general types, the flat-branched prickly-pears, and the round-jointed chollas. If I called the prickly-pear the gipsy of its tribe, it was not without recollecting that the gipsies have their queen in *Opuntia santa rita,* with its coin-shaped disks of grape red and electric blue, touched in the spring with a delicate silver sheen. *Santa rita* is, however, too shy a grower to compete, as a feature of the landscape, with the chollas, which have a tree-like form and a social habit.

Among the chollas, the unaccustomed eye will distinguish the "old-man," having a silvery-haired appearance from the sheaths of its dense covering of spines, from the deer-horn type, slender-jointed, sparsely spined, and with a tendency of the stems to take the general tone of its red or yellowish bloom. Both the old-man and the horned cholla have the habit of propagation by dropped joints, and the same facilities for distribution by hooking their easily detachable sections to passing animals. But it is only the silver-haired varieties. *Opuntia fulgida* and *Opuntia Bigelovii,* sowing themselves across the mesas in thick droves like sheep, that give character to the country below the Rim.

Chollas will grow, in favored localities, as high as a horse, but a peculiar sheep-like outline is achieved by the habit of the fruiting stems. The fruits, bright lemon yellow after inconspicuous bloom, are produced on the topmost boughs, but after setting, remain in place several years, during which a slow movement of the shaggy whitish branches takes place, to bring the fruiting joints closest to the ground on which they are finally cast. A plantation of cholla, which will sometimes cover acres, any plant of which might have sprung from the dropped joints of a single individual, is called a chollitál, place of the cholla, one of those expressive native terms which I mean to spell hereafter as it is pronounced, choyitál.

Between Tucson and Phœnix, south of the paved road, there is a vast cactus garden that I can never pass without crossing my fingers against its spell. Often in the midst of other employments I am seized with such a fierce backward motion of my mind toward it as must have beset Thoreau for his Walden when he had left it for the town. So that if I should disappear some day unaccountably from my accustomed places, leaving no trace, you might find me there in some such state as you read of in monkish tales, when one walked in the woods for an hour and found that centuries had passed. Look for me beyond the last spur of Santa Catalina, where there is a one-armed sahuaro having a hawk's nest in the crotch. Beyond that there is a plantation of thistle poppies on the tops of whose dusty green stems have perched whole flocks of white, wind-ruffled doves, always about to take flight and yet never freed. Then small droves of *Opuntia Bigelovii,* like lambs feeding with their tails between their legs; here and there a bisnaga, dial pointed above its moving shadow; silvery flocks of cholla, now and then a sahuaro pushing aside the acacia under which its youth survived, or a stiff, purple-flowered ironwood, and droves and droves of cholla leading down to the dry arroyo, from which at intervals arise green cages full of golden palo-verde flowers.

Inside the choyital, where ancient black trap overlaps the sand, there will be islands of needlegrass, preferred by the reddish-stemmed *Opuntia* which is called, from the manner of its branching, "staghorn," and dense, globose clumps of *Opuntia arbuscula.* But far down the sandy middle strip, stooping low, you can see the sand thick sown with detached joints, awaiting, with a breathless effect of suspense, the rain that brings the chance to root and grow.

There is an extraordinary feeling of intimacy about the choyital, where practically all the life goes on below the level of the observer's eye. The opuntias are seldom man-high, and the scant grass lends no cover to the intense activity of insect and small rodent life. Only the infrequent sahuaro lifts a bird-flight out of reach, and the wide-searching light pours unstinted around its meager shade.

In this country the chollas are the favorite nesting-places of birds. Early in April, before the sun renders the thin screen of spines inadequate, the thrush and the mocking-bird and the mourning-dove rear their broods on shallow platforms of twigs in the antlered tops of *Opuntia tetracantha,* and the cactus-wren weaves her thick balls of needle-grass in the spiniest depths of the "old-man" cholla. But this excess of safety has its dire results, for at the entrance of the long tunnel leading to the nest, the pygmy owl sits watching like a cat, and now and then one comes upon pitiful fragments of nestlings impaled on the cactus spines in their first clumsy, tumbling flight.

It is the cast joints of cholla which the kangaroo-rat drags about its runways, in mazes in which a coyote would hesitate to set its paw. The road-runner is also credited with using them to fence in a snake it has marked for its prey. Understand that I am familiar enough with the road-runner to believe anything I am told about it, but my observation would lead me to conclude that this fencing in of the prey would take place only after the snake's back is broken with a driving stroke of the long bill, and would have as its object the protection of the quarry from other marauders. Once I saw this sleek cock of the choyital kill a small striped snake by alternately skimming about it in circles until the victim coiled, and then striking at the moveless rings, once, and away again, until, with the snake's back broken in two places, a blow on the head stilled the wriggling length. Usually, however, you will see this *corredor del camino* catching lizards or picking up black pinacate-beetles such as you find in great numbers at certain seasons, standing on their heads in the sand.

Around the outskirts of the cactus gardens, the conical hills of the farmer-ants arise out of circular cleared spaces not more than a yard or two in diameter, though farther north I have seen them as much as twenty or thirty feet. After the first rains, around these clearings, spring up downy carpets of inch-high "Indian wheat," like hoar-frost, whose full-seeded heads are harvested by the ants the moment they are matured. Ripening underground, the husks expand, each one in its tiny ball of fluff, which is carried up and deposited by the farmers in a white, webby ring around the hill, where it lies until the wind carries it away. Warm days toward the end of April, when the heads are bursting fast in the hidden storehouses, you can see the white ring widen visibly, while the particles of fluff seem to boil out of the ant-heap of their own force.

Days like this there is a sense of the concentration of life in the choyital that is only partly accounted for by the movement of bird and insect life, intensified as it is by the withdrawal of the circling ranges behind successive veils of light and heat. By mid-morning the small furred folk are asleep in their stopped earths, the singing-birds retreat to their nests, the hawks rest in the shadows of the sahuaros, wings adroop, but the choyital does not sleep. Life gathers full at the brim of the cup, where any drop might overfill it, and there stays. When the drop falls, the arrested cycle of life triumphant begins again.

Here in the choyital we reach the full diapason of the adaptive rhythms of the spirit of vegetating life. If the word spirit has too much color for you, say the complex of energy: whatever it is we begin to know as a protoplasmic speck in ancient water-borders, shallow enough to be penetrated by the light of the sun and constant enough to keep the dawn-plant perpetually bathed in the sustaining flood. Perhaps the earliest adaptive motion of the undifferentiated vegetative mass, was the specialization of its surfaces to produce organs of anchorage to hold it well within the favoring conditions. Then, as the unstable seas forced upon it the necessity of maintaining itself alive under conditions of intermittent ebb, it learned the rhythms of the tides, holding its breath from ebb to flow. It possessed the marshes, it crept up the rivers, it ventured on dry land. What had been a colloidal mass of vegetable protoplasm, was root and stem and frond.

It grew by nodes and internodes, to rhythms established by the seasonal rains. But all its precious reproductive processes were still accomplished in the element from which it rose. Up grew the spore-producing stem, waxing great, with waving fronds; and down upon the water-film of swamp and river-border, it cast the prothallium in a wafer of green, on whose

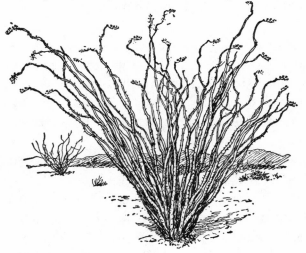

SCARLET-TIPPED WANDS OF OCOTILLA

under surfaces were developed the two essential elements of reproduction. Thus the Vegetative Spirit preserved itself through the medium of two generations, the stem- and spore-producing generation which trusted itself to earth and air, and the reproductive generation, in which what we now know as pollen, could reach the pistil only in the presence of a thin film of water. Along the wet edges of fern-beds may still be seen the mechanisms by which the ancient vegetable world accomplished its double necessity of surviving on land and reproducing in water, in fleets of minute irregular leaf-surfaces afloat on the water-borders.

But before any conquest of the progressively drying earth could be made, some method must be found by which the second reproductive generation could be supplied with moisture by the mechanism already invented by the stem-generation, drawing it up as sap. Thus it gradually came about that the prothallium, instead of being dropped upon the desiccating earth, was retained in place at the tip of the growing stem, and the marriage of the reproductive elements was trusted to the wind.

Look well, then, on that green film which you find floating on the wet fern-borders, for it became the rose! All the lovely intricacies of flowers and the lusciousness of fruit are but so many phases of the adaptations by which the parent generation maintains the reproductive generation on its own stem. Last and loveliest is the filmy-petaled, heavy-pollened cactus-flower.

It is only by keeping these things in mind that you will get anything more than a poet's or a painter's notion of plant life in the arid regions. For there is no such thing as a desert science of botany, no special desert way of flowering and bearing fruit. There are only highly specialized adaptations of the stem-

and leaf-bearing generation, by which the reproductive generation is supplied, under conditions of extreme aridity, with the necessary water-supply. The journey's end of such successive adaptations is found in the sahuaro.

It is probable that the country below the Rim has not changed much since the little *Eohippus* ran about there on his toes. Since there are no fossils of arid-region plants, it seems more than likely that previous to Pleistocene times, since which our southwestern desert has undergone no essential modification, there were no such types. They have, in fact, evolved there in the places where we find them, out of ceaseless operation of the vegetable complexes in contact with desert conditions. Of the moisture-loving plant forms, only such types survive there as are able to compress their flowering and fruiting processes into the curtailed seasons of quick rains. But out of some forgotten ancestry, there have sprung tribes of plants that survived not by hurrying their processes, but by holding them through rainless periods, in arrested states, similar to those in which the great bears pass the winter's snows. Of this type are the creosote, the mesquite, the cat-claw, the smoke-bush, and paloverde. By varnishing its leaves, or dispensing with them altogether, and filling its bark with the green substance of leaves; by reducing its branches to stubs and thorns, each in its own fashion establishes an equilibrium between its necessities and the water-supply. For so much water there is so much growth; and then no growth at all for indefinite periods, prolonged sometimes over several seasons. By this suspension of the functions of growth, the whole life-cycle has been indefinitely extended in shrubs like the mesquite and the creosote. I have reason to believe that the mesquite in the neighborhood of Death Valley has lived at least four centuries, and as far as our knowledge goes, the creosote is immortal. Times when I have had to destroy one of these ancients, to prop my tent or cook my food, I have wished that I knew some such propitiatory rite for the appeasement of its spirit as the Navajos taught me to use before and after the killing of a bear.

To appreciate a creosote plantation, one must be able to think of the individual shrub as having its tail waving about in the sun and wind, and its intelligence underground. Then the wide spacing of the growing crowns is explained by the necessary horizontal spread of the root system in search of the thin envelope of moisture around the loose particles of the gravelly soil. In the rainy season the roots drink by means of minute hairs that are cast off when the last drop has been absorbed, after which the soul of the creosote sits and waits.

Plants of this type will run successfully through the average rainfall from century to century, but for growths of a shorter life-cycle and a more exigent bloom, it has been important, possibly more important in the early Pleistocene than now, to meet conditions of great irregularity in the water-supply with water-storage. For this the yuccas and agaves developed in their pithy stems and the thickened bases of their bayonet-pointed leaves, storage-capacity that enables them to send up, with magical rapidity, great spikes of waxen bloom to grace the rainless years. The obvious difference between yucca and agave is that the yucca produces its blossom crown from a lateral bud, and may go on doing so for indefinite periods, but the agave blooms from the central stem, and, blooming, dies. The great *Agave Americana,* called the century-plant, is a visitor across our southern border, and out of its stored energies,—which by no means run the hundred years with which it is popularly credited,—it throws up, in the course of days, a flowering stalk three or four times the height of a man, bearing seven thousand flowers, in whose fragrance the whole life of the agave is exhaled.

It is the yellow-flowered *Agave Palmeri,* taken just before the expanding growth begins, while the leaf bases are still packed with the sugary substance of the flowering bud, that is the mescal of the Southwestern tribes. Anywhere about the three-thousand- or four-thousand-foot levels of the mountains of southern Arizona you may come upon the pits where the mescal is roasted, or even surprise a group of Indians feasting on the nutritious but not very attractive mass. When I calculate the seasons through which, drop by drop, the agave has collected the material for its stately bloom, eating mescal is to me a good deal like eating a baby.

The long central stem of the yuccas enables them to make much more of a figure in the landscape, particularly the one known as "Joshua-tree," whose weird stalking forms can be found farthest afield in pure desertness, or the sotol (*Dasylirion Wheeleri*), whose dense plumes of long rapier-like, saw-edged leaves and tall pyramids of delicate racemes, are visible like companies of bandoliers far across the mesas. This sort holds its dried flower stalk aloft long after the fruit has been eaten and scattered by the birds; even on into the next season's bloom. There is a humbler variety which goes everywhere, like the prickly-pear, and, under the name of amole, furnishes those who know enough not to despise its narrow, yellowish, pointed leaf varieties, with an excellent fiber, and, from its roots, a substitute for soap. But the final, most successful experiment of the Vegetative Spirit on its way up from the sea-borders to the driest of dry lands, is the great sahuaro, *Carnegea gigantea*.

In the economy of the sahuaro, branch and twig have been reduced to spines, the green of its leaves absorbed into its skin. The need of woody fiber has been perfectly met by the stiff but stringy hollow cylinder of semi-detached ribs that hold the stem erect, and its storage-capacity rendered elastic by the fluted surfaces, swelling and contracting to the rhythm of evaporation and the intake of the thirsty roots. After successive wet seasons, new flutings are let into the surfaces, like gores in a skirt; or, after shortage, taken up with the neatness of long experience. By such mechanisms the cactus-plant surpasses the stone-crops, the "hen-and-chickens," the "live-for-evers" of other arid regions, so that until some plant is found able to make water out of its gaseous constituents in the air, we may conclude that here in the great sahuaro, the Vegetative Spirit comes to rest. Here it has met and surmounted all the conditions that for our cycle, menace, on this planet, the vegetative type. Passing, I salute it in the name of the exhaustless Powers of Life.

# PAPAGUERIA

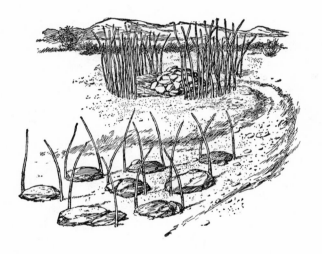

# PAPAGUERIA

THE gateway to Papagueria is past Tummomoc, through Robles Pass. But when Tucson was a Sobaipuri village, Tjuk-son,—"At the Foot of the Black Hill,"—the Papagos came yearly to the river, by way of the Gap in the Tucson Mountains opposite the present mission of San Xavier del Bac. Father Eusebio Kino, who built it about the time the New England colonies, having discovered themselves to be American, were preparing to fight the English on that account, knew where to find his neophytes; knew, too, what he could hold and what not, by the paternal compulsions of his Jesuit faith. Not that he did not go a-missionarying among the Pimas along the Gila River; but, said they with fine native irony, "Are we, perhaps, Papagos?" and in the end San Xavier, white as a shell on the sandy flat, *del Bac,* "by the water," remained the most northerly of that sonorous chain of Jesuit missions: Tubac, Tucumcari, Sonoita, Calabasas, Ariveca, and Santa Ana.

Against native indifference, against Apache raids, against Republican rage over the Mexican revolution, only San Xavier has maintained itself, first by turning Franciscan, and then perhaps by the turning of the rancheria of Tjuk-son into the modern city of Tucson. But the Papagos believe that it owes something of its preservation to its situation beside the five black hills on the top of which they made their own shrines and around which, for at least four uninterrupted centuries, they have buried their dead in open cairns of country rock laced across with ribs of sahuaro, or, more anciently still, with the rafters from the dead man's own house. To this day the little cairns may be found there at the foot of the lava heaps, room to room for company, with each man's olla and food bottle inside. Opposite them, and a score or so of still worked Papago homesteads, the road turns through thick ranks of sahuaro into one of those vast waterless vales called *abras*.

Off to the left, blue wreaths of mountains rise from Old Mexico; straightaway to the south, Bobaquivari, sacred mountain of the *Papa-Ootam,* People of the Bean. Hard red-and-white pinto beans. I give you my word that in this country the great bean-plant with its heart-shaped leaves of deep green, its white blossom-spikes and delicately inquiring tip, is a lovely, a magical plant. But I am not sure that the name is not older than agriculture, for, by strange consent, most of the food-producing plants of Papagueria run to podded fruits: the mesquite, both the straight and the screw-bean, the palo-verde, "big bean tree," and the so-called desert willow, not a willow at all but a catalpa simulating the willow's slender leaf with its long narrow pods. None of these, however, will be met until the first *abra* is crossed. On its farther rim, at about the level of the first village, called Washing Water, the sahuaro begins again. Here the road slips past the tail of Coyote Mountain, past the village of Panták,—"Place Where the Coyote Stayed,"—fanwise into dim tracks down the slope of Papagueria.

Geographically, the whole of Papagueria is a part of that singular vast tract of arid land known as the Sonora Desert, the fall of which for two hundred miles is toward the California Gulf. Northerly, there is a corner that dips toward the incompleted boundary the Gila River undertakes to make by mingling its jade-green waters with the greasy red of the Colorado, failing six seasons out of seven, frustrate in the sand. Except for that narrow divide which the Papagos call Sikulhimatk,—"Place Where the Water Goes Around,"—there is a steady fall of the land seaward of from two thousand to three thousand feet, rendered negligible to the eye by intervening ranges which cut the slope in a general northwest-southeasterly direction. Old mountains these, emerging fin-like from smooth swells of their own detritus, sifted by the wind and its own weight toward the level, treeless *abras,* until in the dead center it is pulverized to a clean, heavy dust.

Had the signatories of the treaty of Guadalupe-

Hidalgo been more concerned with the logical claims of peoples and lands, and less with the pretensions of map-makers, our international boundary, on its last lap westward, would have taken in the whole of the Papago home land, as far south as the Rio Altár, and east in Sonora to Quitovác. Being cut thus in half, from Quitovaquita to the spur of Tinajas Altas, there are no rivers in Papagueria other than the shallow, shifty troughs of seasonal torrents whose waters are absorbed in the wide bolsons, or flood basins, without a sign.

Between the most denuded of the knife-cut ranges, the bolsons are smoothed out as by a hand, in lineless *playas* where the quick rains, pattering down with a sound as of the wooden paddles of the women shaping the unbaked clay of their cooking-pots, makes a thin transient lake like a coating of quicksilver, miles and miles. Over some of these *playas* the mesquite is so evenly spaced, and the low-branched shapes are so uniform that the illusion of traveling through peach orchards has continually to be brushed aside. In and out the road-runner tilts and balances; now and then a rabbit lopes. Not a spear of needle-grass breaks the rain-straightened surfaces. Even the kangaroo-rat avoids the mesquite *playa;* perhaps because the standing rain, when it comes, is too deep for his slight architecture, for on the less-rained-on flats where the creosote weaves its lacy shade, his low mounds appear, with runways that may be traced forty or fifty feet to the nearest available mesquite or *hohoba,* on whose pods and nuts he feeds. Waterways, if there are any, and the sprawling mouths of arroyos may be located by the ironwood and palo-verde, venturing as far as they can on the uncertain water-supply, to make good their claim to be numbered among the trees.

Everywhere, the palo-verde disdains to maintain itself precariously as a shrub. Mesquite will grow anyhow, and cat-claw is able to subsist on a water-dole on which the annual herbs are scarcely able to lift their blossom crowns above the muffling sand. But if you do not see the palo-verde from afar, etching its delicate green strokes above the surrounding growth, then you do not see it at all. The sahuaro will, if it must, march straight across the *playas,* but its choice is for the coarser soil about the rim of flood basins, so that groves of it come circling to meet you as the road swings from ridge to bolson and so to ridge again.

But if the contours of Papagueria give no hint of the coastward fall, there are evidences enough in the changing growth. White brittle-brush, which silvers the mountains of the east, gives place to needle-grass and tufts of gallita. The screw-bean and the serviceable greasewood clothe the llanos; the sahuaro, avoiding the loose sand-belt, is replaced below the Gila Mountains by the more imposing *sowesa;* the ocotilla on the long wands of which appear in early spring bright blossom spikes like scarlet parrakeets, grows tall and taller. The ironwood, which inland is often arborescent, in the vicinity of the gulf becomes an imposing tree. The fine, sticky clay of the *playas* gives place to great wind-rippled dunes; reeds appear, and where nothing else will grow, low on the sand, glimmers the lovely *rosa San Juan,* which is not a rose at all, but an œnothera.

Out here, at the utmost limit of habitableness, runs the old Jornada del Diablo, the trail from Sonora to Yuma, easily traceable now by continuous low burial-mounds. Here, for a three-days journey, the only drinking-place is the group of glassy, volcanic pot-holes known as the Tinajas Altas. But it is only gold-crazy white men whom these things concern. The Papagos, even the clans of that region, who go by the name of Sand-Papagos, make their villages by the lasting waters and plant their crops in the *playas* that, by the best guess they can make, will receive the heaviest of the infrequent rains.

Thus, finding Papagos even in their own land is a matter of knowing the time of wild harvest and the drift of seasonal rains. There are certain village sites, and rancherias such as Topohua, Cobabi ,and Santa Rosa, nearest to their principal shrines, where some houses are always occupied. But always, except, perhaps, in the *Uta-vaokat,* the Inner Bone

FROM PLANTING TIME TO HARVEST PAPAGOS WILL BE FOUND AT THEIR "TEMPORALES"

149

Month of the winter, when the clans foregather for
ceremonial purposes, some members of their communities will be abroad.  It is important to understand
the modes of primitive society in our Southwest, to
realize that the terms in which it is described are
explicit.  *Rancheria* is a Mexican-Spanish term for
any unorganized collection of frail huts, as distinguished from a pueblo, or town, with a headman and
some form of recognized procedure.  *Ranchos de temporales* are the shelters built near the corn lands to
take advantage of the short, swift rain-storms, the
*temporales* of the summer season to which all their
crops are owed.  Thus from planting-time to harvest
the Papagos will be found almost continuously at the
*temporales,* busy about the melons and the beans; or
in the Dry-Hot Moon, which precedes the summer
rain, they will resort to the llanos for the sahuaro
harvest; or in the Month of the Cold Touching Mildly,
be found scattered like ants in the *playas,* storing
seeds of mesquite, scrub-oak, and hohoba.

At Cobabi this year every house was shut, pad-
locked against the souvenir-hunting propensities of
the American tourist; nothing whatever to be learned
of the habits and whereabouts of its inhabitants, except the confirmation of the general report that it was
a village favored of medicine-men and witch doctors.
Side by side we found *two* medicine-lodges, domed
and thatched with grass in the traditional manner,

surrounded with barbed wire to keep the cattle from eating the thatch.

Following the rule that the ceremonial building of any people represents an older, perhaps the oldest, type of dwelling known to them, it may be inferred that the Papagos once lived in round, grass-thatched huts, as the California tribes do to this day. But since the time in which Gothic art gave its confirming touch to our own sacred edifices, they have made their houses of wattles, daubed inside and out with clay, roofed with sahuaro ribs, which are given a slight pitch by being supported in the middle on crotched poles of mesquite. Over this is laid a thick thatch of brush and another of clay, rendering the windowless interior cool and dark, as desert dwellings should be. In most of such houses primitive chimneys of mud and stone stagger up the inside wall, but the family cooking is usually done outside the *jacal,* in an open shelter of mesquite trunks and boughs, placed squarely in front of the door and a little apart from it, under which hangs the dripping olla and all the least intimate functions of domestic life take place.

With this informal community life, the scattered harvests, the widely spaced huts, low, and self-colored like the soil, the stranger in Papagueria might spend days on its white, indeterminate ways without coming across a single recognized settlement. More than likely, the first definite note of human activity is the skeleton shelter, the careful caches of cooking-pots, and the little round hearths of the sahuaro camps.

Late in June or early in July, when the pear-shaped fruits of the sahuaro begin to burst with juicy crimson pulp, the Papagos repair, village by village, to their hereditary orchards for the annual wine- and syrup-making. By this time young rabbits are fat, broods of young quail begin to twitter from the *garamboya*, young hawks, hatched in the crotch of some tall green candelabrum, are learning to pitch and toss. "Soft Child," to whom the Elder Brother gave fangs fine as hairs to protect him against the teasings of the young gods who loved to hear his rattle, has not yet developed the venom of the later *Mársat Tojapik*. In short, it is said that Papagos who come back from the sahuaro harvest are often so plump with content and good feeding as not to be immediately recognizable by their friends.

The sahuaro gathering is the new year of the Papago, and all its occasions are ceremonial and prophetic. It begins with the ritualistic fermenting of the expressed juice of the first gathering. With the dark of that day comes the call to the singing-place, where the holy men sit, under long strings of eagles' plumes, and the dance begins. The Papagos are the only Indians of my acquaintance who hold one another's hands as they dance, and their ceremonial circle is against the sun. Within the grass-thatched medicine-lodge, the great jars, with heavy spume rising through the heart-red juice, stand round the fire that keeps them an even temperature. Outside, under the direction of the Keeper of the Smoke, old men alternately sleep and sit at the ritualistic four quarters of the world, persuading the gods with song and admonishing the people to "Look for the shining house in the west where the black clouds are." For, with the commendable Papago habit of making one hand wash the other, the sahuaro wine-drinking festival is also a rain-invoking rite. The drunker the company, the more rain.

As the sahuaro harvest comes just before the month of summer rains, by which the field crops are either lost or made, you can see how admirably this works out.

Between the gods and men, each season has its own mediator. For the sahuaro festival there is the night-singing mocking-bird, which can be heard at all hours shattering the moonlight in round, mellow notes and scattering them like rain. In the towering white cumuli reaching from Papagueria to heaven, lives his prototype, the mystical god-bird whom thus the Keeper of the Smoke invokes:

"Through your strength come all the clouds, all the lightning, all the thunder: from the mountain, clouds spring, meeting clouds. . . . However wide the earth is, clouds touching all its sides, . . . the clouds and the winds get up and stop in the west; the rain spreads over this poor earth. When shall we see this again!"

Ceremonially, as from the four world quarters, the old men reinforce the prayer, and as the condition of the wine permits—about thirty-six hours are required for complete fermentation—the drinking begins. Fortunately for the Papagos, the sahuaro wine acidulates at the end of three or four days, and its ecstasies are of a mildness almost Greek.

The rest of the harvest-time is spent in boiling down the juice to a thick syrup, sealing it hermetically in native jars, with fresh clay, and in making a kind of meal cake of the pounded seeds. After the sahuaro, fruits of the smaller cacti, under the general name of pitahaya, are eaten, as almost everything in the desert can be, once you know the secret of preparing it. Bare as they look, in the mountains of the Papa-Ootam there is still mescal. Catkins of the mesquite may be eaten with no more trouble than stripping them like currants between the teeth, and of the ripened pods is made a yellow nutritious bread. Root or fruit or young shoot, the Papago housewife is excelled only by the Chinese in the skill with which she renders its full food value.

There could be no greater mistake than to confound the quality of cooking with standards of culinary cleanliness. The Papagos are as well nourished as they are well grown and well natured. Six feet and over is not unusual among their shy, glossy-haired, always-smiling men.  Even the dogs are good-natured in Papagueria, though I do not count that altogether in their favor.  I do not go so far as to say that I do not like dogs; but I can never forget that the dog is a lazy wolf who preferred to follow the better hunter, man, rather than rustle his own kill, and by the usual process of parasitism became more or less a gentleman.

There must have been good pickings for the original lobo who followed the first Papago, for in the days when there were whitetail and antelope feeding on the rich browse of the detrital slopes, the *burro-burro* of their young men was he who could run down a deer and take him with his naked hands.  Even now this is said to happen occasionally, and the children are still brought up to catch rabbits in the same fashion.

To-day the business of the Papagos is chiefly about cattle, which they have had since the middle of the seventeenth century.  With all its rich wild pasture, there is not enough water in Papagueria to make agriculture anything but a secondary means of subsistence.  Even to keep their cattle alive the people must build *charcos,* banks of clay and wattles, to retain the drainage of favored slopes, and in exceptionally dry seasons, such as the past three years, even the deep-driven and not very efficiently managed government wells have not furnished sufficient drink to keep the cattle from dying in their tracks.

There is something appalling and yet immeasurably raising our appreciation of the human spirit, in the way this people maintains itself in the presence of the hourly promised and ever-withheld bounty of the sea. Always from a fixed point on the horizon the gulf signals with great thunder-heads of cloud, glittering white, gray with withholden rain or taking fire with the sunset, blown inland. Even on the stillest days there is continuous streaming of cloud banners, dry storms enfilading with thunder and streaked lightnings between the ranges. Day by day the play and promise of the sea's gesture goes on, and though it rains seldom in any particular place, any hour the blessing might descend, slanting silverly across the *playa,* or infolding some sharp sierra in its dim blue veils. Then the short arroyos roar, the moon-colored *playas* are rendered impassable by thick, inelastic mud, the wild growth greens and plumps visibly.

There is no class of vegetation so deeply experienced in the business of translating the qualities of the soil into food and seed-producing stores, as the spined and scantily leaved plants of the Sonoran zone. As if all their secret processes were primed to catch the advantage of the rainy hour, the desert growth produces in the observer a sense of expectancy more poignant than the sense of desertness. This curious feeling of aliveness of the plant world, waiting like a wild creature of the cat kind, every tree and shrub clawed like a cat, crouched for the spring, with the dramatic announcement of the sea's intention going on overhead, plays its part in the  quality of the human product of Papagueria.

The Papa-Ootam have never acquired that solemn sense of themselves as the apex of the scheme of things, characteristic of peoples who have more or less mastered their environment. Like children, carrying on their small concerns among half-attentive elders, they adapt themselves to the naked process of nature and the inappeasable proximity of the sea. Since it is impossible that either of these should be completely understood, why worry? They move with their cattle and their household goods around Papagueria in the track of the rains, returning in due course to the same slopes and the same houses, many times. The freedom they have had to move back and forth across the Mexican border has, no doubt, kept them from feeling unbearably the pressure of white life, to obvious phases of which, such as clothes and farming-implements, they conform easily.

So much of their earlier myth and ritual has been let go, that we know little of it except that it closely resembled that of the Pimas, but is loose in outline and lacking in detail, as though they had allowed the Pimas to make it up for them. Nominally Christians, and arranging their cosmogony around the activities of Earth Magician, the creative force in, and Elder Brother, the saving force apart from nature, there is still free and unritualized worship of the sun among them.

When they go down to the sea for salt, the neophytes make their ceremonial race around the *salina,* and their prayer for all the good gifts of the sea: rain, good health, and handsome wives. This they ask, standing all hand in hand, knee-deep in the sacred sea, facing the morning. But they do not bathe themselves therein, considering it far too holy to be so defiled. I do not know where, in that rainless land, the Papa-Ootam find water for bathing, in any case. It must be that the sun assoils them, since they do not, at any rate, announce their presence by their smell, as is said of their cousins the Akimult-Ootam, the River People.

The principal shrines of the Arizona Papagos are near Santa Rosa, which is also one of their most important farm centers, at Cobabi, and in the great cave of Bobaquivari. At Santa Rosa, between the rancheria and the large mountain which gives the place its name, we found the Shrine of the Children's Sacrifice freshly visited. In this place, in the days of our Ancients, a flow of water opened from the Great Deep, and threatened not only the valley but the whole land of the Papagos.

There *was* such a flood once. Does not every South-western tribe hold a record of it, and is there not proof, as good as the rainbow that certified the flood of Noah, in the white brow of the Sierra de la Es-puma, Mountain of the Foam, that marks the highest level of receding waters? It is more than likely that the breaking forth of this stream, and the way the Papagos dealt with it, is a matter of historic reality, for the place, when we found it, had evidently been the site of one of those artesian springs the force of whose deep-sprung waters has raised a cone of sedi-ment, in this case about twenty feet wide and six or eight feet above the surface of the llano.

It was noon when we reached it, one of those wide-open days in the moon of yellow flowers, when the young leafage of the mesquite makes a lacy shadow, and every palo-verde is a cage of green that holds a swarm of golden flies. This was a week or ten days after Easter, and we saw at once that no longer ago than that, the Shrine of the *Alihihiani,* "where the children are buried," had been freshly set in order. In the center of the depression from which the spring had emerged, an altar had been built of slabs of greenish shale, and around it, open on all the four world quarters, an inclosure of peeled wands of ocotilla, thick-set and leaning outward a little of their own weight.

Opposite each of the four openings, next to the altar, stood two wands of about the height of a five-year-old child, for the threat of a second world deluge had been met by the Papagos in a natural, primitive fashion by the sacrifice of four children,—two boys and two girls,—to the Powers of the Deep. It was all too consistently human not to have actually happened, and even the tradition of how the children had been symbolically painted, and what songs were sung by the medicine-men while the elders rasped their singing sticks and made mimic thunder with their basket drums, has more than a trace of veracity. Outside the rim of the miniature water crater, which inclosed both altar and stockade, are neatly piled the blackened wands laid aside whenever the inclosure is renewed. It is impossible to guess how many renewals went to build them, for though there seems to be a four-yearly cycle in Papago ceremonials, any tribal emergence might have been the occasion of new attention to the *Alihihiani,* and the heap of discarded ocotillas, man-high, dropped to dust against the ground.

The trader from Santa Rosa who brought us there, said that the last renewal had been accomplished by a few old men, each carrying his appointed number of wands, and had been followed by a night of singing and exhortation at the rancheria in remembrance of the spirit of the Children's Sacrifice. About a hundred feet to the east, where the runnel from the spring disappeared in the sand, little heaps of greenish flat stone and white wands marked the spots where the children were buried. Only—this was strange to us— the tradition tells only of four children, and the burial-places were eight. Was, then, the sacrifice, like the furnishings of the shrine, also renewed?

There was something inexpressibly touching in this simple monument, so swept and ordered; prayer and propitiation to the sea. Around us the desert spread immeasurably. Overhead, too high, the gulf piled its pillars of cloud; beyond Comobabi white thunderheads gathered; over Kukomalik gray veils, rent by sterile lightnings. Only the night before, the Indian Agent at Oasis had told us how, the past season, the cattle had died of thirst, upon their feet, around the ineffectual wells. This year a thousand Papagos who had been independent cattle-owners, would be working the copper-mines at Ajo. And still the Papagos are, of all the Indians I know, the most cheerful.

At Cobabi, where we found the women squatted around tubs of soaking marytina pods, splitting them for basket-plaiting, we dared not go up to the shrine, though the path to it on the nearest hilltop was wide and clean. It was too steep, for one thing, and I doubt if we should have been permitted. But leaving the rest of my party to worm, if they could, the secret of the purplish red dye from the basket-makers, I slipped aside into the new shrine of the Crucified, which you will observe, if you know the signs of your own religion—which more than likely you don't!—in all the larger Papago villages. It was windowless like the huts, but whitewashed within, the mud floor carpeted with rags of mail-order rugs, wild skins, and mats of bear's-grass.

There, on the familiar stepped altar of the Southwest, the earth-and-cloud altar, in ten-cent store presentments, was the whole collocation of our own Blessed Personages. In and about Mary and Jesus and the saints, stone beads, dried bright berries, and scraps of Christmas tinsel were laid in patterns that, as they shone out for me suddenly in the dusk, shifted the whole machinery of consciousness. Where was I, then, but back in that dim, absorbed hour when low mounds of patted dust, and patterns traced upon them with white stones and broken crockery and stemless flowers, bring the child home to long-forgotten consolations of the race!

It was here that I first understood what I said earlier about why the Papago had found an easier release from the ways of his Ancients than other of the Southwest peoples. Walking daily with the Powers that bless or withhold blessing as seems good to Them, he does not take his own thought patterns too seriously. It is only peoples whose gods, having revealed themselves, have gone away to some distant and barely attainable heaven, who cling injuriously to old customs.

As such evidences go, the Papagos are a young people, having been on their present site from four to six hundred years. Their migration legends are of the slightest, and all referable to the country described, since the sixteenth century, as Papagueria or, including the *abras* north to the Gila River, Pimeria Alta.

Ethnologically they are grouped with the culturally superior Pimas, but not in a way which makes it easy to declare that the Papa-Ootam are merely undeveloped, or degenerate, members of the River People. It is true that the Papago arts have declined before the white invasion. They once had looms, and flutes to play upon and counting-sticks on which the tale of tribal happenings was kept by a system of grooves and notches. But if their baskets are not so well made as formerly, the Papago women still know what the patterns mean, while the Pimas admit that their own patterns are largely copied from potshards of the Hohokum, "Those that have Perished," out of the Great-house of the Casa-Grande culture.

And when the Papagos come down yearly to San Xavier del Bac to celebrate the saint's day with singing and dancing, there is a rhythm in their step not referable to any tribal dances that I know; and you will perhaps allow that I know something of Indian rhythms. There is a cadence in their song, almost caught and lost again, which is not Spanish, not the influence of Gregorian intervals such as the Franciscan missions left upon the music of California tribes, but something more elusive, like the fragrance shaken out of folded garments. It is not Piman, and yet if the Papagos are but a backward branch of the Piman tribes, what then?

The Pimas are believed to be the reorganized fragments of the once-great culture of the ruined cities of the Salt River Valley. If this is so, then the Papa-Ootam must also have been somehow related to that culture; peasants, perhaps, mountaineers, too remote to be touched by the series of catastrophes that broke the power of Hohokum, five hundred to a thousand years ago. Does it seem too unlikely that this indefinable overtone of Papago music, this persisting unfamiliar pulse of their dance, should be reflected color of that vanished Great-house culture?

The Papagos have no such tradition. They believe themselves made on the spot, out of the selfsame earth that sustains them. Nevertheless the road that now leads out of Papagueria to Casa Grande and the Salt River flats, where the mounds and waterways of the Great-house People are fast disappearing under

orange-groves and alfalfa, was once a road leading
*in*.   If one had time for it, I am sure it would be possible to find at the end of it, as one finds in the Ten-
nessee mountains, songs that were once the entertainment of baronial halls, fragments, faded but firm, of
the vanished culture of the Hohokum.

# DOWN ON THE RIO GRANDE

# DOWN ON THE RIO GRANDE

WHERE the great granitic knot of the Colorado Rockies begins to fray out in loose ends of ranges, arise many rivers: flowing south by east, the Arkansas, the Red, and the Canadian; flowing south by west, Las Animas, Rio Piedra, and Rio Mancos. Between these two groups, the Rio Bravo y Grande del Norte. It creeps out from under thin crusts and bosses of snow, and stony flats of detritus, frothing in a trough of broken boulders: it runs, already a true river, slanting east across the Colorado plateau, until it is turned south by the Culebra not far from the boundary of New Mexico.

Here, in the midst of that plain, which was dark with herds of deer and spotted with white markers of buffalo skulls, Zebulon Pike, looking for the head waters of the Red River, and supposing he had found them, raised the American flag upon the Rio Grande. Pike had come up the Arkansas, seeing the peak that now bears his name, blue like a cloud on the western horizon, and then white above and blue below like sea-water under a pointed sail. Having climbed it, Pike made too direct a trail to the Rio Grande for any one familiar with that country to believe that, as his diary naïvely professes and as he swore to the Spanish authorities, he mistook it for the head waters of the Red River.

The Red River, in fact, rose several days' journey south and east of the point on the west bank of the Rio Grande where Pike built his blockhouse. And what need had he of a blockhouse, since, if he were where he supposed himself to be, every day's journey found him nearer home—unless he carried secret instructions to get himself admitted one way or another to the Spanish domain? That, at least, was the result of his adventure.

Down the Rio Grande he went, under military escort, and finally along the Jornada del Muerto, to Chihuahua, where he met one of Nolan's men and, in a "Gazette," the first he had seen for two years, learned of the romantic attempt of Aaron Burr to wrest for himself an empire from the West.

Pike's camp was on the west bank, some distance above Ute Peak, around whose foot the Costilla hurls its tributary waters. Thence, south to the valley of Taos, the Rio skirts high mountains on the west, receiving from the slope of the Culebra, snow-water and torrents of swift rain. Down past abandoned mines and timber cuttings, the creeks come singing. In every trough between the tilted slopes, and crowning every terrain, great spruce-trees crowd the silver firs. Above them, scalloped crests burn purple with the heather, or rust-red with frost like dull heated ores.   Rock crevices, too sharp to grow a tree, nourish dwarf oaks and flowering shrubs. Along the water-borders, scarlet patches of pentstemen and painted-cup make seasonal flashes of the mountain's inner heat.   Red of the salmon-berries, a clear, approaching red, floats above the pale green of their palmate leaves.   What you cannot find in the way of mountain bloom along the upper Rio Grande, is hardly worth finding.

In the narrow flood plains the quaking aspens, secret treasure of Western mountains, make thick plantations; slim, pale-greenish boles, branching level like clipped yews, thirty or forty feet from the ground. And never a day so still that it is not alive with the click and patter of their heart-shaped leaves, going on interminably as the river goes, in the currents of mountain air that stream from the vast fronts of granitic planes, tilted every way to the sun.   But when the bright shield of the sun-god is hung straight from the zenith, the trees are worshipfully still for an interval in which you can hear the leap of the trout in the dark pools under the Douglas spruce.

After it issues from the Culebra into the valley of Taos, there is no sound but of the river's own making in the Arroyo Hondo, where it runs, or perhaps, as it passes Valdez and the village of Hondo, the high squeal of the *pitero* and the steady fall of the *disciplina* as *Los Hermanos Penitentes* trail out from the moradas to make their lenten obligation. Old settlements these, of the Spanish occupation; low, earth-colored, like fowls dusting themselves in the sun, bees droning in the cups of the tall, bright "staves of San Juan."

Up over the *barranca* to the east, Pueblo Mountain looms blue as summer midnight, as the Culebra uncoils around the valley of Taos, through the Sangre de Cristo range, toward the clustered peaks of Santa Fé. Behind Pueblo Mountain are glimpses of the dim, snow-dusted, fawn-colored scallop of Mt. Wheeler, the highest peak hereabout. South, beyond the Rio, rises the flat-topped phantom shape of Pedernal. West, the horizon lifts in the Continental Divide.

Taos pueblo lies under Pueblo Mountain; Pueblo Creek coming down between the summer and winter houses from the sacred Blue Lake and the domed cottonwoods of Glorietta. The creek that issues nearer the Rio is called Star-water, clear like the light of stars. Rio Chiquito comes from the mountains called Blood of Christ, under U. S. Hill, so called because the winding road goes over it in the shape of those letters, between the well-spaced yellow pines. Taos town, whose true name is Fernandez de Taos, lies well down the valley, and draws to itself the trade of half a dozen hamlets and *placitas,* Llano, Talpa, Ranchos de Taos, Cordoba, Cordillera, which is a musical way of saying Stringtown—all the ancient settlements of the Spanish heyday.  Fernandez de Taos was for years the end of overland commerce along what afterward became known as the old Santa Fé Trail.

Beyond U. S. Hill is Peñasco Valley, and the slowly starving pueblo of Picuris, with its crumbling scalp-house and its land diminished by as much as our honor is attainted, who made treaty with them that it should never be.

Out of Peñasco the road goes on toward Questa la Osha, toward Trampas and Truchas, until it comes out again through the last knot in the Culebra, called the mountains of Santa Fé, from whose eastern slope descend the head waters of that Red River which Zebulon Pike supposed himself to have found.

There is another road out of Taos, dropping to the river level down the dark and narrow basaltic cañon which shows across the mesa as a dim grape-colored streak.  Between Hondo and the point at which this highway goes over the cañon rim, there is but one place at which the river trough is accessible.  Here a mineral spring breaks out at the trough's edge, called, since the Spanish caballeros first broke their way down to it, Horse-go-down.  But before that it was known as Young-Forever, and the way to it was marked by sacred symbols pricked into the dark rock. The waters of this spring are loosening to cramps and humors of the body, to a degree that sanctions the mile-long pull up and down to enjoy it. No other guide-post being furnished, the stranger finds his way to Young-Forever by tracking the habitual frequenters to be seen at any hour, but especially of a Sunday, converging toward a common point along all the shallow highways. Just opposite the trail to the spring is another zigzag down the west bank, white and perilous, by which the wandering goatherds bring their flocks to drink in rainless seasons. Elsewhere in the upper cañon, footing neither for man nor beast, until at the southwest corner of Taos Valley the east wall of the cañon gives back to admit the state road.

All this way in the upper river there is never a fall of importance, never a cascading rapids, never a mirror-polished lake nor a gliding shallow. It runs, the Rio runs on its own self-centered errand. At the bottom of its stony trough it slinks and grovels. From the top of the mesa the upper courses show frothy white with driven air of the rain-torrents, turning to chrysoprase, as from the heights of Fiesole you see the Arno. Where Taos River gathers its tributaries, virgin-clear as they came from the mountains, but now charged with the valley clay, the descending flood turns a bright, bilious yellow. So, as you come up along the cañon, you read the weather in the distant mountains by the color of the Rio Grande—brown where Peñasco water makes its *entrada,* red for

the greasy Chama.  Between the flood seasons the
river reflects the umber and vermilion of its basalt
walls, and in the shadows its own secret, unaccount-
able green; never dramatic, never beautiful except as
it borrows from the season or the sky; yet somehow
memorable, knowing its own way and the reason
therefor.

The state road follows the east bank, except for
occasional *rincones* and narrow intervales, just clearing the walls that in midsummer are too hot to touch,
and on the other side keeping level with the hurrying
turgid flood.  Beyond Peñasco water, its volume is
notably increased.  From Peñasco Hills millions of
railroad ties are floated down on the spring and summer freshets.  After one of those thunderous down-
pours called *temporales,* they come leaping like dol-
phins, and at low water, line the sandy shoals for another hundred miles.  Otherwise there is no life on the
Rio Grande except the occasional whir of water-fowl
making their migratory rests in its rock- and willow-
fringed borders.

There is life enough on the road, however.  Every
tiny *rincon* and cienaguilla has its mud-walled ranch
house, its orchard crowding the road against the
cañon wall, its campo santo opening on the highway
as on a street.  Once at least your mud-guard scrapes
the windowless wall of a morada.  Once, going to Taos
late of an April afternoon, we came upon the peni-

tentes issuing toward their *Calvario,* shining upon its little hill, out of blue-black mountain shadow, with an unearthly gleam. Once we passed a door open upon a line of lighted candles across the floor whose owner entertained in honor of the local saint. In early summer you turn out for the line of covered wagons going up with peaches and melons from Cienaguilla to the mountain towns, or the road gang from the *penitenciario* turns out for you. When I began first to visit the Rio Grande, these convict road gangs were mostly Spanish-speaking natives, effecting a reconciliation with a culture they could not understand, by pecking the road out, mile by mile, from the cañon wall. In those days you stopped and bought silver trifles from them, bracelets and rings hammered out of Mexican coins and etched with patterns that advertised the craftsman's derivation from the mixed strains that came into the country with Oñate. But now you will meet chiefly Hi-jacks and such like members of your own tribe, always ready to flout but not able completely to circumvent their own civilization.

In all this district, which is called Rio Arriba, there is not anywhere in the cañon a memorable tree. Nothing taller than the dwarf juniper and piñon and an occasional cottonwood. Rabbit-brush and willow crowd the water-borders, virgin's-bower, Virginia creeper, and stubby thickets of wild plum. Yet with this slender scale there is never a season, in the cañon of the Rio Grande, without its appropriate, its inevitable color scheme.  In the snowy months there will be cumulus clouds topping the cañon walls, white as cotton bolls, burnt-orange tips of the willows repeating the note of the cliffs, and bright flecks of bluebirds' wings, interlacing earth and sky.  When the snowdrifts in the shadows begin to take lilac tones, the drift of wild plums is feather white, the rabbit-brush white fluff over green, and the water shadows as green as the junipers.  In September the wild plums are vermilion, with a bloom like the purple haze of the mountains, and after the plums the Virginia creeper tones with the frost-bitten red of the cliffs.  Then the squashes piled in the fields, and the bright gold of the rabbit-brush bring out the yellow of the clays, and the adobe huts which otherwise tend to disappear into the earth from which they have been drawn, are blots of flaming scarlet and vermilion.  In Española Valley where *chile* is raised for export, not only the house walls, but great racks of threaded pods make splashes of heartening color, clear and detached, color that gives you a full sense of its being eaten and absorbed. About this time the cottonwoods along the acequia madre begin to bear, in place of leaves, little heart-shaped fruits of light. . ... Along Tesuque River they come up burning like the bush in the midst of which was God.  Toward the end of October the deep, self-contained blues, the delicate fawn, and the grape-black shadows of the winter landscape emerge.

The river, issuing from the narrow gorge above Velarde, swings off to the west, while the road climbs and crosses the San Juan mesa. Here the Pliocene sands on which the later volcanic formation was laid down, shape as low, fantastically eroded hills along the base of the Santa Fé Mountains. Off to the west the Pajaritan plateau lifts directly from the river plain, and above it the blue silhouette of the Jemez range. It seems likely that the whole course of the Rio Grande from Taos, south to El Paso del Norte, was shaped by an ancient synclinal fold, lying along east of the Continental Divide, interrupted from point to point by more recent volcanic intrusions. Above any of these volcanic barriers, is the evidence of how the river scuffed deep into the flood plain, laid back its ears, and bit straight through the thousand-foot lava-flow into its original bed. From San Juan it is easy to surmise that the valley of Española was once a lake which received not only that river which was first called Bravo, but Rio Chama, Santa Clara, Santa Cruz, Pojoaque, and lesser seasonal streams.

This is that San Juan which was called San Juan of the Gentlemen by Oñate and his men, on whose account the clans of Yunque-Yunque, across the river at the mouth of the Chama, were received into San Juan to make room for the caballeros. Still you can

see, to the south of the old plaza, the plaza about which
the households of Yunque-Yunque were accommodated, and beyond that the Plaza of the Strangers,
with the store and the church and the statue of Mary
Virgin under which at the set
time of the year the six Corn
Maidens dance. Of Yunque-
Yunque, between the Rio Grande
and the mouth of the Chama,
which became the first capital of
Spain in New Mexico, there is
nothing left—only low, shapeless

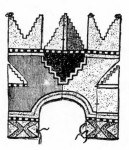

mounds of the house rows where the first European
drama was played by the first settlers, and the
aborigines sat on their roofs and wondered.

San Juan is a waterless town, set on the puma-
colored mesa's thrust-out paw, with the acequia madre
curving about its lower edge. Below the acequia
stretch the green patterned fields of corn.

Five minutes' walk from San Juan brings you to
the Rio Grande and the *entrada* of the Rio Chama.
The Chama has its source in that region of bright
desolation called Tierra Amarilla, and circles the
ancient cones that come to a head in the vast shattered
bulk of Abiquiu. Out of Abiquiu poured the huge
blunt heaps of pumice, the streams of dark trap, and
the storms of volcanic ash that make the western
barrier of the Rio Grande.

North of Abiquiu the ash-storms must have fallen into the sea and been lifted again, perhaps with the lift of Jemez Mountains, superimposed on the volcanic plateau. Where the Chama cuts through a thousand feet of the apron north of Abiquiu, it is all sea-gray and ghostly, but the Gallinas, cutting a burnt region, imposes on the milky flood a bright Indian red which gives the river its name. Much of this country, if it were marked truly on the maps, would be marked black, unexplored, perhaps unknowable. I have been three times over the Abiquiu road, bringing away from it not much but the sense of desolation on a scale of deific grandeur. Pedernal, which from a hundred miles away floats blue and flat-topped, an enchanted mountain, is hidden behind great eyeless heaps, blind guardians of the untrodden ways.

The town of Abiquiu itself is perched half-way up the mountain like one of these lightly indicated villages that float in the upper corners of Japanese kakemonos. Above Abiquiu, along the Chama, old trails, older than history, climb the sea-gray escarpments to the shrines and ruined homes of the Small-house Country. From lookouts perched on solitary boulders, the Small-house People watched the passes for the movement of deer and elk, for stranger tribes trekking the way they had come themselves, from the Colorado plateau to the *plan del Rio*.

Nothing that has happened since, in Española Val-

ley, equals in human interest the records left of endless migrations over this ancient thoroughfare.   At
least two, possibly three, distinct periods of migration
can be traced, as well as the movements of solitary
groups, such as the Pojoaqueños who came, by their
own account, from the stone pueblos of the Chaco.
As Pit-house Dwellers, our Ancients must have
drifted along the Rio Grande for generations, before
as Small-house People, they took possession of the
Pajaritan plateau, where it is still possible to trace
their advance from small-house and cavate lodges to
the great community dwellings of Shufine and Puyé.
This would have been in the period when the Rio
Grande used almost the whole of the Española Valley for its flood plain, and the rains roved happily over
the high western plateau.

When the Small-house People had gone to look
for their vanished rains, then came the Puebleños,
down the Chama, already advanced in town-building,
still seeking the mesas for their town sites, but spreading their fields across the river plains, as you find them
at San Juan to this day.   Five or six miles down the
Chama from Abiquiu lie the ruins of Po-shu-ouinge,
with its impressive quadrangle, where, by tradition,
occurred the quarrel that resulted in the splitting of
the Rio Grande pueblos into two ceremonial groups,
one of which made itself ritualistically responsible for
the summer weather, and the other managed the rites

by which the Powers of Winter were appeased. Along Rio Caliente, which reaches the Chama from the south, are the ruins of Poseunge, where was born, of a virgin, Poseyemo the culture hero. All along the Chama mesas, it is still possible to find the curious "outline houses," clean ground-floor patterns of communal dwellings laid out in small boulders, room by room. Very many explanations of these, the ethnologists have drawn out of their own heads, but Ascencio of San Juan told me they were simply staked homestead claims, possible sites for new pueblos should any sudden reason arise for changing towns, as our Ancients were accustomed to change, overnight, as the spirit moved them.

At the time that Yunque-Yunque was chosen for the capital of New Mexico, all the existing pueblos of Española Valley were already established along the Rio Grande. It is more than likely that the accessibility of the original site of the capital, to raids of the Apaches de Navajo, down the ancient tribal thoroughfare of the Chama, led to its removal, first to the lower end of the valley, and finally to Santa Fé. But nothing could be more peaceable now than the level flood plain of the Chama, green with fields against which it shows a brighter red as it swings into the smoky, buckskin-colored Rio Grande.

The farmers who came in with Oñate accepted the native corn- and bean-culture as complacently and with as little disposition to give credit for it as the Pilgrim Fathers, on the other edge of the continent; planted their crops in long, narrow fields running down to the river's edge, and built their homes on the mesa's edge around the four-square, clean-swept patio, with the addition of the dug well under its carved, blue-painted well-head.

All the way through the valley of Española the Rio hugs the west wall; on the east in the piedmont of the Sangre de Cristo, along the upper reaches of the rivers of Santa Cruz and Pojoaque, are the towns where the years still sit in the plaza: Santa Rosa, Santa Cruz, Chimayó.

> Whoever saw the years go any where?
> They sit in the plaza mumbling.

Anywhere, from this southern end of Española, can be seen rising from the east bank of the river, a mile or two from the pueblo of San Ildefonso, the dark hulk of Black Mesa, where still the altars of our Ancients are visited. Black Mesa is of later, intrusive, volcanic origin, contemporaneous with the flow of basalt and lava which divides the district of Rio Arriba from Rio Abaja. To reach the lower river the traveler must turn out to the east, by the oldest highway, the *camino real* of Spanish New Mexico. But the Rio, which knows its own course as a homing pigeon knows its cote, has bitten a thousand-foot gorge for itself across the flow.

The highway runs out of Rio Arriba, past Pojoaque and Caymungé. It follows Tesuque River to Tesuque. It turns in at Santa Fé, and turns south again past the turquoise mines, south and south to the district of Rio Abaja. Meanwhile, to meet it there, the Rio snakes its yellow length through White Rock Cañon, at the foot of the Pajaritan plateau.

The plateau is the remnant of that blanket of volcanic tuff which the cones of Abiquiu once spread over all that region. Behind Santa Clara and San Ildefonso it rises by rounded grayish slopes, spotted with rosettes of juniper and piñon, divided by sharp, dry arroyos, to erosive islands, flat-topped, round as cinder cones, or long lizard shapes like Puyé, having a steep talus at the foot and above the talus a vertical escarpment. From Puyé, which is ten miles back of Santa Clara, the eye follows the mountain called Blood of Christ, back into the windings of the Colorado Culebra. Across the dim gap by which the road goes out toward Santa Fé, floats the turtle shape of Sandia, sacred Tewa mountain. North of Puyé, separated from it by the gorge of Santa Clara Creek, rises the yellow rock of Shufine. West and south of Puyé and Shufine stretches the land of the Small-house People—small-house and cliff house and community house, and intervening valleys where in Sep-

NEVER A DAY SO STILL THAT IT IS NOT ALIVE WITH THE CLICK
AND GLITTER OF THE ASPEN'S HEART-SHAPED LEAVES

185

tember the rabbit-brush outlines, in the gold of remembrance, fields and acequias in a land where the deer ranges no more, and even the rabbit fares badly.

Puyé was a cliff city, girdled all about the foot of its escarpment with cavate lodges; on Puyé and Shufine rose great community houses, the focus of populations vast compared with the present settlement of Española Valley. The ruins go everywhere, past Pininicangwi, past Otowi with its tent-shaped rocks, past Tsankawi and Tshrigi, past Navahu, place of the well-planted fields, past terraced mesas and intermittent creeks and dazzling red and white and yellow bastions of unearthly beauty, past trails worn hip-deep in the country rock by moccasined feet, past shrines and dancing-places.

The relation of the Pajaritan peoples to the existing tribes of the Rio Grande Valley is confused and uncertain. Santa Clara claims Puyé, Cochití traces its movements to the cliff dwellings of the Rito de los Frijoles, which is to say Bean Creek. The Rito is the only one of the watercourses cutting the lofty west bank of the Rio Grande, which runs, a year-long stream, dropping over the basalt barrier of White Rock Cañon, unapproachable silvery veils.

To reach the Rito, the road crosses the river, climbs the plateau winding between the dwarf oak and well-spaced pines to the verge of the north wall of the narrow box of the cañon, which was the earliest remembered home of the Cochiteños. For two or three miles along the foot of the north wall the soft rock is pierced by the cavate lodges where still one finds the wall niches for the sacred meal-bowl, the tiny fire-boxes with the ineffectual, twisty flues, the ridges in the floor that held the sleeping-mats in place, and, high over them all, the clan signs, Sun clan, Snake clan, and Lightning clan, cut in the cañon wall.

One goes to the Rito not only to discover by what stages man progressed from holes in the rock to many-storied apartment-houses, but shut in there with the purling creek, the feathery pines between whose tips one looks out from the great ceremonial cave, the cool air and the warm sun, the magpie flying over, and the faint gobble of turkey cocks from the potreros, to correct impressions of cave-dwelling man, to discover the shy, home-loving, beauty-worshiping animal man was. Never in the cliff period so harried and hate-ridden as in this civilized age of ours.

The plateau abuts on the Rio Grande by many pointed tongues of land whose tall, flat tops are called potreros, over which the Cochiteños wandered to their present home where the hills give back for a semi-circular space on the west bank below White Rock Cañon, from which their ancient shrines are still visited. From the shrine of the puma hunting-god on Potrero de las Vacas one looks across a puma-colored plain at the foot of the black lava wall called La

Bajada, dividing the district of Rio Arriba from Rio Abaja.

Down La Bajada the highway twists and sidles, and along its foot the Santa Fé River seeks the Rio just above the present pueblo of Cochití, still distinguished for witchcraft and a special way of dancing the *Matachine.*

Beyond the dry plain, livened by the black-beetle shine of racing automobiles, the Galisteo turns its intermittent flow past the pueblo of Santo Domingo, to the rapidly widening middle valley. Santo Domingo is the most conservative of the pueblos, where one must have friends to be permitted to enjoy dances such as Europe has not known since the great days of Homer. It was down the Galisteo the Domingueños came by successive removals, from some unremembered place of origin; but San Felipe, six miles to the south, came over the potreros, on the sheer edge of which the wall of their last tarrying still perilously hangs.

The district of Rio Abaja begins properly at Bernalillo, where Coronado wintered, and burned the two hundred hostages. Between these two points Jemez River makes its *entrada* from the west. Up Rio Jemez are Santa Ana, Jemez, and Sia pueblos, and down the Jemez came the Navajo from Saydegil to raid the prosperous haciendas, or be made slaves to the hacienderos.

Rich was Rio Abaja in the days before the Gringos came, when the Oteros carried their money in baskets, when the blond Chaves, called El Guero, had two million sheep and twenty-seven hundred peons to tend them, and the Governor of Isleta even lent the American Army of Occupation eighteen thousand silver dollars to pay off their troops.    South and south as the Rio runs, the fertile flood plain alternately pinches and narrows.    Below Bernalillo is Sandia, and below Albuquerque, Isleta, pueblos on which the effacing hand of Christian civilization has been too long laid. At Los Lunas a road goes west to Laguna and Acoma, to Zuñi and the Painted Desert.    At Belen a by-road passes between the Manzanos and Los Pinos Mountains to Estancia Valley and the cities that died of fear.    All down the middle reach of Rio Abaja the awful wall of Sandia lifts between the river and the east.    Toward the west, Mt. Taylor, Madalena, and San Mateo stand off, solitary, uncomforted.    Along the borders of the flood plain are gravelly, grassless heaps of river wash and lava waste to prove that the Rio Grande was once a mightier stream.    Half-way between Belen and Socorro the Rio Puerco makes tribute from the west; a graceless river eating its own banks, charged heavily with the red sand it drags down from the western slope of the mountains that give rise to the Chama, and a red mesa where the stained light lies on the eyelids like hot afternoon.

At Socorro, the ocean-to-ocean highway, which entered at Albuquerque, turns west and south toward Deming and Lordsburg and the far West. But the old road, *el camino real* of Rio Abaja, the oldest road our Ancients knew, follows the river south from Socorro to San Marcial. Here it crossed, where the river plunged again down one of its basalt gorges, and the road was forced over the mesa to the Jornada del Muerto. But just there, below San Marcial, practically while our backs were turned, watching the nations of Europe tear out one another's vitals, the Future put down a peg in the history of the Rio Grande.

Here, where you cannot see the glittering modern road, you will not find things changed so much as you have imagined, since Oñate came marching up the Rio with banners and arquebuses, priests, and a poet, and the solid-wheeled carretas—first turning of wheels in these United States. Just so the dim outline of Chupadero rose on the east, just so the Rio rusted with the flood of Rio Puerco; then as now the houses were piled up out of the earth, and their rafters cut from the cottonwoods thick on the flood plain. All this section from San Marcial to within fifty miles of Albuquerque was country of the Piros, friendly to the invaders. San Marcial was a pueblo, Socorro, Sevillita, Alamillo, and Senacú. It was about here that vines were first planted and wine made. There were Piros among the Salinas pueblos on the east. North of these the Tiguas dwelt in several towns around Bernalillo, and beyond the Manzanos, in Chilili and Quari, well built and prosperous. All up the Rio Jemez there were towns, and up along the Galisteo. On the rich alluvial plain of Rio Abaja, field touched field; six-colored corn, ears of it as long as a man's forearm, beans, brown and pinto, squashes, melons, gold-colored and red-hearted— Oh, even in their cave-dwelling days Americans loved water-melons! Around Bernalillo and at Algodones there was cotton-growing. In Rio Arriba, Cicuyé, a walled city boasting five hundred fighting men, was a focus of population along the Pecos. The valley of Española was full of villages. Abiquiu was a pueblo, also Ranchos de Taos and many smaller settlements denying, perhaps forgetting, their aboriginal strain. Picuris was a town of three thousand, Taos, then as now, the chief pueblo of the Tiguas.

Into the heart of this culture the conquistadores snuggled themselves and might have been assimilated, for they brought blood of the native strains of Old Mexico. But along with the Tlascalans that marched with Oñate, marched the Cross, and that was a time when the Cross meant bitterer things than it had ever symbolized since it was the terror of Roman slaves.

Not that the earliest Americans objected, any more than Americans to-day, to adopting a new method of squaring themselves with the Powers. What they resented was finding all their other methods thereby held in contempt.

Actually, in Santo Domingo, about the time they began burning witches in Massachusetts, there was an *auto-da-fé*. With a complete consciousness of doing the admirable thing, Spanish empire and Catholic observance were pressed upon New Mexico. There was also forced labor in the Spanish mines.

Finally, in 1675, at the end of a long sequence of missionary intolerances, four medicine-men were hanged as wizards, and one, Popé of San Juan, along with forty others, imprisoned and severely punished. "Come now," said Popé, brooding in the kivas of San Juan, "let us drive out the intruders, for my medicine is good, and my familiars promise me success."

It is believed that the chiefs and caciques of the pueblos were reluctant. Because he doubted the fealty of his own son-in-law, Popé killed him in his own house. But the clansmen rose. They rose on the tenth of August, 1680, because at Tesuque the rumor of the revolt had leaked out, and lest it be forestalled, they fell upon the enemy at once. In Taos Valley all died but two men, who fled south, leaving their wives and children dead under the charred house beams. With the exception of the settlement of La Cañada, all died in Española Valley. In Rio Abaja, Lieutenant-Governor Garcia gathered the refugees at Isleta, and having heard that all the settlers in Rio Arriba had been massacred, including Governor Otermin, moved on to the friendly Piros at Socorro. There arrived to them Chaves and Herrera of Taos, reporting that as they skulked past the capital they had seen the Indians beleaguering it, and heard the dull roar of Spanish artillery. Also arrived messengers from the revolting tribes to the Piros, who confirmed an already aroused suspicion of their loyalty by concealing the messengers for two days.

Not all the fine and moving things in American history were done in English. If you think so, read the *auto* of Garcia, which recounts how, lacking clothes and food and ammunition, the fleeing settlers of Rio Abaja sat down by the Rio Grande, in sight of their enemies, to consider whether they might not in some fashion succor their friends of Rio Arriba. They looked for succor from El Paso, but before its fortunate arrival, Otermin, having made a sudden sally against the Indians, then drunk with seeming success, had brought his own party forth, threatened at every step, but uninjured, leaving the towns sacked and burnt, the churches desecrated, the dead unburied, to overtake Garcia at Fray Cristobal.

So passed down the Rio Grande a hundred years of Spanish pioneering. But when Don Diego de Vargas Zapata Lujan Ponce de Leon came clanking back twelve years later, armed for reconquest, it appeared that the Indians had not done particularly well for themselves. It was August when the Pueblenos rose, corn standing in the fields, wild plums bending over crimson by the creeks, and the first golden flush of the rabbit-brush along the arroyos. When they had driven out the colonists, they scoured themselves in amole suds, of the contamination of baptism, and, as soon as the harvest was over, began to move the town sites to more secure positions on mesa-tops and mountains. They abandoned their pueblos, to quarrel at Santa Fé as to who should live in the *villa real* and rule. The roving tribes of Apache and Navajo, more or less held in check by fear of Spanish arms, pressed in on the disordered pueblo world. The Cochitenos returned to their potreros. The people of Zuñi barricaded themselves on Thunder Mountain. San Ildefonso retreated to the top of Black Mesa.

Humanly they might have welcomed the return of the settlers. But when De Vargas came marching up the ancient road with arquebuses and armor and "the wagons of our Lord the King" he carried at the head of his expedition a figure of Our Lady, which you may see at the Rosario chapel of Santa Fé, any Lady Day, in a new silk skirt, amidst a winking galaxy of candles.

Of how Don Diego, who was as astute as he was courageous, first invited the Pueblenos to return to their allegiance and the Catholic religion, of how they pretended acceptance and secretly defied him, of how he stormed Thunder Mountain and besieged Black Mesa, there is much that is better told in fiction.

When you study history for the sake of the land, you quickly learn that the story of a military conquest may just as well be told in any way that makes a good story. The Puebleños were not militant, and seem to have cherished no animus against the conquistadores. The resistance that they opposed with heroic and

cunning persistence, was to the destruction of their own way of reconciling themselves to the universe. But the Spaniards had also learned something. After the reconquest they hanged no more medicine-men, professed themselves satisfied with baptism and a reasonable attendance at mass. Neither was there forced labor at the mines. Rather, the settlers united with the Pueblos to make retaliatory raids on Apache and Navajo, furnishing themselves, out of the prisoners, with necessary slaves.

There were three types of Spanish settlers along the Rio Grande: younger scions of noble houses, pure Castilian, as witnessed by the appearance still, among

their descendants, of an occasional milk-white skin
and dazzling Titian-colored hair; there were artisans, for the most part immigrants direct from Spain,
and there were peons, servants, and soldiers and small
farmers, pure Mexican or, at the best, mestizos. These
were by far the most numerous, and, to the Pueblos,
menacing. There is something at once pathetic and
revolting in the desire of the mixed blood for the pure,
as if they might assuage their sense of inferiority by
pressing back into the untainted strain. For two hundred and fifty years the Pueblos maintained, against
the contamination of their blood, a resistance so forthright and sustained that there are yet towns where
no Mexican, so called, dare mingle with their festivals
or smile upon their maidens. But where there was no
such resistance, as among the Piros, the Indian strain
was dissipated, mixed indistinguishably with the
*paisanos* of the Rio Grande valleys. Thus Socorro
was transfused and Senacú and San Marcial and
Sevillita. Thus Abiquiu became a Spanish-speaking
hamlet, and Ranchos de Taos, though there are those
living who remember when it still danced the Corn
Dance and the Race of the Swift-coming Rain. Thus
at Tesuque the old men say, "Remember the fate of
Pojoaque," while Picuris and San Ildefonso live in the
shadow of dissolution.

Judging from what has happened in Old Mexico,
this crossing of the blood-streams might not have mat-

tered, seriously.   No strain so pure and long-founded as the American Indian, can be lost by one dilution. After Spain was cut off and Maximilian slain, the tide of native blood might have risen again, had not Zebulon Pike come riding down along the Rio Grande with his United States troopers, and by his published diary turned the interest of all America in that direction.   When the gringos came, they despised the Spanish-speaking even more than they did the Indian. And the Protestant missionary, with the Indian Bureau behind him, has made a dull, debasing smear over the lovely and æsthetic culture of the pueblos.   Looking back, shall we come at last to see Christianity marching across the world as it marched along the Rio Grande, with dull, effacing foot, always confusing the teachings of its Founder with the particular obsession of the time in which it is expressed?   But the Franciscans, at least, for the beauty they destroyed, left such beauty as they had, and a type of architecture destined to prevail throughout the Southwest.   Beside the terraced houses and the old Franciscan churches, the alien, inappropriate buildings of the Indian Bureau eat into the beauty of the landscape like a pox.

From any of these gravelly detrital slopes above Rio Abaja, streakings of the three occupations affront one another.   But turn now down the way the Rio goes, and find the Future betraying itself in a great thrust of power. Below El Paso, the Rio Grande carries an international boundary on its flood, but not with any sense of responsibility—or perhaps with a sense that outreaches our appreciation. Through the soft, deep alluvium of the coastal plain it loops and wriggles. Flood-plain ranches of years' standing are drowned in a night; whole settlements, that were American or Mexican when they began, find themselves shifted to the other bank. Clearly, international boundaries must not be carried so lightly. Elephant Butte Dam was built to curb the wilful Rio,—three years' flood will scarcely even fill it,—but not without due consideration for both its borders. During the years that loose-thinking Americans were talking about intervention in Mexico, Mexico quietly reached out and acquired a visible stake in us. Between San Marcial and Elephant Butte, the Rio is constrained by the United States, in the State of New Mexico, to serve equally Texas and Chihuahua. Below San Marcial the river runs in red with the silt of mountain and mesa; over the dam's vast apron it runs out in shining arcs as clear as glass.

Many years ago, when I began to know the Rio Grande, it was somewhere about this green thread of river plain, at the bottom of the stopped waters under Fray Cristobal. I recall brown huts and strips of tillage, young leafage and the rosy glow of peach-blossoms against the warm adobe walls. And on the winding river road a teamster walking at the team's

head, singing—and that was the first time I heard it—
the teamster's song beginning,

Cliffs of yonder lofty mountain . . .

I think it must have sprung from hereabout, both
song and melody, taking the rhythm of slow-plodding
oxen.

Ay, Peña Hueca
No me vayas á olvidar!

There is a Hueco range over beyond El Paso;
Spindle Mountain is, in fact, apt enough for any of
these vertically streaked mesa fronts, like ancient
Spanish doorways. But there sticks in my mind a
queer feeling for the place of hearing, as lying now at
the bottom of the checked river waters, so that I think
of it all going on there still—the creaking axle, the tender note of the blossoming peach, and the song rising
through the clear water. . . . Ay, *Peña Hueca,* forget me never more! . . . as I think some passionate
plaintive note of the Spanish occupation must continue
to rise long through our strident modernism.

The Rio goes on below Elephant Butte, threading a
series of fertile intervales: Paloma, Rincon, Mesillia,
and, beyond El Paso, the valley of Juarez. But the
highway is forced up over the black lava wall to follow
the Jornada del Muerto.

This is how the last lap on the El Paso road was

called when the only transportation was the heavily loaded *atajo,* or the ox-drawn, solid-wheeled carreta. The mesa here is said to be the oldest land in the world, and looks it; burnt scoria and ghostly sand of the long *medanos* patterned by the wind, stiff bayonet-pointed yuccas and low, lifeless-looking grass. Once there went great country-colored bands of antelope, swift as the shadows of clouds, but now nothing stirs except the sullen rattler, or the coiling and uncoiling *torneos,* that, while the traveler watches, seem mercifully bent upon covering the bones of dead men and pack-animals, exposed by the shifting *medanos,* only to turn in an unsuspected moment to fling their torrents of pulverized grit in his face.

Of all the *pasears* down the Rio and over the Jornada del Muerto, the most memorable was the annual *conducta.*

At the time of the year when, rising early, you catch the footsteps of the morning on the wings of the magpie for good luck, men whose business was the management of trade caravans, trail masters, *arrieros,* armed escorts, gathered at the rendezvous below Socorro; to whom resorted trappers with mule-loads of skins, *cibolleros* with sacks of jerked buffalo meat, hacienderos going down to exchange bales of homespun blankets for blooded stallions to improve their stock, miners with ingots of smelted silver and bowl-shaped, government-stamped lumps of soft New

Mexico gold, pueblo traders with turquoises and *osha,* that aromatic root which, bruised and sweetened in a hot decoction, gives such delicious comfort to your perturbed insides, beaver-skins and *serapes de Navajo.*

From the first that we hear of them, Navajo blankets were especially esteemed, though they knew no color then but natural black and white wool, dark blue of a forgotten dye, and red which the women picked out of the crimson lining of Spanish officers' cloaks and rewove, the demand for which made such a scarcity of officers that the Government bethought itself and made *bayeta,* as the crimson cloth was called, a regular article of trade.   The *conducta* went armed and cautiously along the Jornada del Muerto.   At the water-holes in the Organos Mountains, which the *atajo* must visit or die, they were quite certain to find Apaches in ambush, to see that they died horribly. Some weeks later, when the *conducta* returned with silk and cutlery, pineapples and carved leather, high Spanish combs *por las señoras,* and brazil-wood for dyes, it was all to be risked over again.   There were also government supply-trains going up with gold coin to pay the official salaries and gold altar furnishings to content the missionaries, drawing bandits out of the mountains that to this day are called *Los Ladrones.*

At the ford of El Paso del Norte the Jornada and the Rio Grande come together again, but there was nothing on the north bank when the footsore refugees of 1680 reached it, nothing much on the other but a mission founded in 1659 to the honor of Our Lady of Guadalupe, and the indefatigable Father Ayeta, who settled them in three groups about where the city of Juarez now stands. Nor was there anything on the north bank but a trail through the mesquite and sand in 1883, when Zebulon Pike came riding down; nothing, in fact, until Texas tore herself free from Mexico, and then only a trading-post until after the Lone Star of Texas became fixed at last on the flag of the United States.

El Paso is now the chief city of our Southern border, but if you go there you will be astonished to discover how few of its citizens can tell you what journeys passed or came to an end there. For El Paso is a city whose journey is but just begun. There is little besides a date or two, and the fragmentary clans of the Piros at Isleta del Sur, to connect it with the Spanish occupation. Cabeza de Vaca is supposed to have forded the Rio here, making his troubled way across the Big Bend country; and down about the *entrada* of the Rio Conchos, the village of Almaden crossed on its unauthorized adventure up the Pecos. For the rest of its four or five hundred miles the river has no history. But you cannot live beside the Rio Grande and not know it for a history-maker.

# PASO POR AQUI

# PASO POR AQUI

W HEN Don Francisco de Coronado lay with the advance-guard of Spanish exploration at Hawikuh of old Zuñi, while the inhabitants entrenched themselves on Corn Mountain, came to him certain *principales* of Cicuyé, which is Pecos, bearing gifts of buffalo-robes, and offering submission. Now, this was singular, for Pecos was farthest from Zuñi of all the Rio Grande pueblos, walled and towered, having a force of five hundred fighting-men and a clear way on the terraces all about the great pyramidal house heaps. Nevertheless the *principales* of Pecos asked terms and gave them, and Coronado, whose own mind was too full of anxiety for gold and his disappointment at not finding it, to inquire what was in the minds of the aboriginals, sent one of his captains back with them.

Going up out of the valley of Shiwina, the embassy, with Captain Hernando de Alvarado, had to right and left of them many tall islands of banded red-and-white sandstone, flat-topped and straight-sided, their escarpments weathered into pinnacles of unearthly shape and proportion, of which Toyoállanne, sacred mountain of the Zuñi, is a notable example. Between them were lovely shallow intervales, somberly wooded with cedar and piñon, and very little water, so that at the end of the second day they made camp under one of these island promontories, pearly white like a bleached shell, around whose castellated top they heard great eagles mewing. Because of its inaccessible towered front, the Spanish-speaking called it El Morro, but now it is recorded as a national monument under a name coming naturally to the first American discoverer of it: Inscription Rock.

We know that Captain Alvarado's party camped there, because it is in the direct ancient trail from Zuñi to Acoma, which he visited. So that there passed by here for the first time something of which you will find not a hint in any Spanish narrative, because it was not even in their suspicion, something that ran shiveringly through the tribes like the wind that runs in the corn before the rain. This we shall come back to. For the present it is enough to know that under one of the *cuevas,* these eyebrow-shaped weatherings of the Rock, there is a *tinaja,* a natural cistern of seepage-water such as still supplies the pueblo of Acoma, taking jade and azure tones from refracted light, but sweet and self-renewing.

Up the straight-sided cliff, exceedingly plain at that time, since there are still some of them visible, went a row of foot- and hand-holds, by means of which the women of the now ruined towns on the top of the Rock went up and down with their patterned

water-jars poised lightly on their heads.  Had Don
Hernando taken the time to circumnavigate the Rock,
he would have found its ground-plan triangular, with
a cleft in the peak leading to a bay—round, steep-
walled, with incredible secret access down the rain-
streaked cliffs—within which one
of his beloved Spanish cathedrals
could have been hidden away
whole and unsuspected.

But anything the Spanish captain heard or discovered about Inscription Rock would have been
pushed out of mind two days later
as he climbed the *peñol* of Acoma
by similar shallow holds in the
sheer sandstone wall, and from the
terraced roofs of its village looked
across at the shadowy splendor of
the Enchanted Mesa.  As for Coronado, his mind was
so full of his second disappointment about the seven
towns of the Moqui, which he visited in the person of
Pedro de Tovar, that he not only missed knowing what
brought the eastern Indians whom Alvarado found at
Pecos so far from their homes, but missed the trail as
well, so that on that journey at least, in all probability,
he saw neither El Morro nor beetling Acoma.

Don Juan de Oñate, Adelantado and Captain-
General of New Mexico, rested there, however, on his

way back to his capital "from the discovery of the
Sea in the South," and, with a mind more at ease,
accepted the hint of earlier visitors and cut his name
and achievements in the smooth sandstone cliff, in
good Spanish script. Don Juan had need of some such
monument of discovery. Having neglected the business of colonization, for which he had been sent into
New Mexico, to dash about its irreconcilable spaces
in search of gold, he had finally, to offset the rebellion
of native tribes and the clamor of starving colonists,
made one last snatch at glory by rediscovering the
Colorado River, which was then called River of the
Brand, and renaming it Rio de Buena Esperanza.

He had set out from Zuñi with thirty men and four
hundred horses, when the roofs were piled with the
harvest of six-colored corn and the fields yellow with
ripening squashes, had followed the river from a point
opposite the fork of Bill Williams River to the inset
of the gulf, and incidentally had seen in that passage
the last flick of the tail of that glittering rumor of
precious metal which had set the whole Spanish exploration in motion. Oddly enough, this last flash of the
sea-serpent's tail was the only one which proved to be
true. One day, when Oñate was eating his dinner off
the silver plate which in the baggage of an explorer of
those days was as indispensable as tin in ours, though
he had little to eat off by this time, except the flesh
of his own horses, an Indian out of what is now the

Navajo country, remarked that there were quantities
of silver where he lived.  But what was silver in
those days to a man whose wash-basin was made of it!

In the month when the willows redden and the
rabbit-brush is faintly blue under silver, Oñate
camped at the Rock again and wrote:

> Paso por aquí el adelantado de don Júan de Oñate . . .
>         a 16 de Abril a (ñ) o 1606.
> Passed by here the adelantado don Juan de Oñate . . .
>         sixteenth of April, 1606.

Now, Oñate began his thus-recorded expedition
from the capital which he had established at the con-
fluence of the Chama and the Rio Grande, opposite
the pueblo of San Juan of the Gentlemen; established
under the protection of San Francisco, whose gift of
holy poverty was so little appreciated by the colonists
that they shortly transferred their spiritual allegiance
to San Gabriel, whose banner flew from its mud walls
when the adelantado set forth from them for the discovery of the sea in the south.  Exactly what happened in the year and a half of his absence, has been
variously obscured, but the likeliest version is that
the colonists, in the absence of the executive, and under ·pressure of tribal hostility and insufficient crops,
moved the capital to the place which it now occupies
beside the little river of Santa Fé, where the long
trail up from Chihuahua turns off to climb the high-

lands between Santa Fé and the *plan del Rio Grande*. This saved the long pull of supplies over the broken hills of Tesuque, and was in direct line of flight (if flee they must, as in the absence of the captain-general they might at any time be obliged to) down the river in the only direction from which help might come.

And if Oñate did not find his capital moved when he reached there, he moved it himself immediately afterward. Or, perhaps, disinclined for the two days' further pull, he sat down at the Indian village which was already there, and sent for his capital to come to him, which I think both likely and unlikely, since anything that the adelantado did himself, especially if it turned out well, he was never shy about admitting. At any rate, the capital was at San Gabriel in 1604, and in 1608 we find it officially described as at Santa Fé, and the governor's salary two thousand ducats. Though there was little besides the Holy Faith after which it was named, to be found at Don Juan's capital, it was a faith sufficient for maintaining the flow of romance over the road past the Rock as it had been from the beginning. As it had been time out of mind.

There is no way of determining how early the wild tribes had made their passing camps beside Inscription's spring and graved their clan signs on its smooth, inviting surfaces. Snake clans, deer clans, clans of the mountain sheep and the lightning, left the count of the game, pointers to springs and suitable camping-places, votive hands, sacred symbols of the sun and the four world altars.   Parrot-peddlers making their way from Old Mexico to the Chaco towns, advertised their wares.   For what else would be the long-tailed birds, beak to beak on artificial perches, but the same red parrots still imported from Mexico and precariously kept in the houses of fraternal orders who find their plumes indispensable symbols of the intercessory powers of the air?

Certain of the inscriptions appear to be of ribald intent.   That one of the heap high chief as primitives draw him, which cuts into without obliterating the inscription of Oñate was it not done with the tongue in the cheek?   Done, more than likely, by the secret emissaries who went to Zuñi from Taos in 1680 to stir up the pueblos against the Spanish colonists and the priests.   So, if I know Indians, and if the pueblo fireside legends of Spanish explorers mean anything. Spanish histories, too, for it was Governor Don Francisco Manuel de Silva Nieto who, on an expedition to Zuñi to install Perea, the new Father Custodian of New Mexican Missions, issued the wise and necessary edict that "no soldier should enter a house of the Pueblo, nor transgress in aggrieving the Indians under penalty of his life," as cut into the Rock by Juan Gonzales in 1629.

It was on that passage, also, that the governor undertook to secure the safety of the priests by setting an example of extreme reverence, himself and his men falling on their knees when one appeared, kissing the hem of his gown. This was a business so little relished by the Indians, that, although in the official inscription made on the return journey, in July, the governor expressly states that he had "put the villages in peace, at their petition, asking the favor to become subjects of His Majesty the King , . . . which they did with free consent, knowing it prudent as well as very Christian," he was obliged to return in August of the same year, "with the wagons of our Lord the King," and carry the faith to Zuñi, having in his own magnificent phrase already "conquered the impossible."

Six years earlier Lujan, a soldier, records in an inscription long undecipherable, that "they passed on the 23d of March of the year 1623, to the avenging of Father Letrado." There was also a matter of Father Martin whose hand had been cut off, as well as his scalp, so that between the writing of Lujan and the almost obliterated names of three colonists who escaped massacre at Santa Clara in the rebellion of 1680 by swimming the Rio Grande, there passed by here not much but fierce Christian fanaticism and fiercer pagan hate. There was more to Governor Nieto's inscription about what a fine fellow he was and how much everybody loved him, and another dateless statement to the effect that Vicente Sinor-

gosta and somebody fought together of a question
which somehow failed to get itself stated, perhaps
on account of the *licor* which seems to have had more
than a little to do with the occasion. Also, it is written how Joseph Domingo and others passed by here
in September "with caution and some apprehension,"
which might have been in the troublous September
after the pueblo revolt of 1680, or more likely the
September of the return of De Vargas in 1692 to the
reconquest. All Spain wore its heart on its sleeve at
that time; not its heart only, but its vices, its intimate
spiritual aspirations.

In 1692 came De Vargas, recording that he had
"conquered for our Holy Faith and for the Royal
Crown all the New Mexico at his own expense."

Doing things at your own expense seems to have
been one of the prerogatives of royal officials in the
days of the founding, since *por aquí* passed on February 18, 1726, Ensign Payba Basconzelos, "the year
that he brought the Council of the Kingdom at his
own expense." But the coming of Don Diego de
Vargas Zapata Lujan Ponce de Leon brings us back
to what was passing so obscurely in the dark hearts
behind the shields and under the helmets of buffalo-
hide that came to Coronado at Hawikuh to make
terms of an uninvited peace.

At Pecos, when he had gone back with them, Captain Alvarado fell in with an Indian from the north-

east who described to him as well as he could—for
how was he who had never heard of gold to know it
from copper?—a country where yellow metal was to
be found in great masses. And what should Indians
from the copper country be doing in the first pueblo
they would naturally reach if they were looking for
creditable news of pale, magic-making men heard of
in the south?

What we have yet to realize about our Ancients
is that they were, in their own fashion, charged with
that strange human hunger to know, which drove the
ships of Columbus over the edge of a new world.

Thin trails and well traveled threaded the country,
making with the instinct of the buffalo herd for the
easiest grades, and of the wood-pigeon's flight for the
shortest distances. What news would travel faster
over them than that rumor which edged their knowledge with fear, of white men wearing skins of
stone, for so steel armor appeared to the stone-age,
armed with the thunder and the lightning? By this
time the Basques had touched at New Foundland,
Jacques Cartier had ascended the St. Lawrence to
Mont Real. All the time Coronado was crossing
sacred meal roads and burning hostages, De Soto was
collecting pearls from Cofitichique and burning Talla-
hassee.

Just about the time Don Francisco turned back the
half of his army, to pursue in lighter fashion his

quest of Quivira—could the French word for copper, *cuivre,* have had anything to do with fixing that fabled region toward the north and east?—the discoverer of the Mississippi with his ragged band had crossed from the east bank to the west, where later a pueblo woman, escaping from the loving attentions of one of Coronado's lieutenants, found them. Whisper and foreboding, fear of the French in the north and the Spanish in the south, *se paseron aqui* with the embassy that went from Pecos to make voluntary terms with the man of magic-might at Hawikuh. But it was to come nearer still to the Spanish journeys' ending, that far-reaching finger of French encroachment.

In 1689, when the colonists—what were left alive of them—were huddled below El Paso del Norte, near what is now Juarez, a detachment of soldiery, sent hurrying on rumor of attempted French settlement on the Texas coast, picked up, among the Indians there, several Frenchmen who admitted to having crossed the sea in the flotilla of Monsieur de la Sala, who could have been no other than Robert Cavelier, the Sieur de la Salle, who five years earlier had, with that high spirit and inadequate equipment which characterized the time, undertaken to found a colony on the coast of Texas. Of these, one was that Jean l'Archevêque who had stood on the river bank when the commandant had come to ask the whereabouts of his nephew, already lying murdered in the tall grass that moved all about them like a sea, with the eagles flying low for a sign of death. But the Sieur de la Salle was a brave gentleman, if somewhat overbearing, and when Jean led him on with insolent replies to where in the grass the conspirators lay hidden, well knowing that insolence was the one offense the Sieur de la Salle would never let go unpunished, he came on steadily. Then the sound of a blow, and, "Lie there, Bashaw!" cried the hateful Duhaut whose servant Jean was, and did such disrespect to the poor body that the French lad's heart turned in him.

So with Grollet, a sailor, who knew of the murder but was no party to it, Jean withdrew himself and found refuge with the Indians for five years. These two were brought to the viceroy and sent to Spain to give an account of themselves, and it was supposed that they died there in the galleys. But it was the custom, when the Western hemisphere was all new for the taking, to give minor offenders the choice between hard labor and enlisting in the army of the Americas; and for a lad of sixteen to have been party to the killing of a Frenchman trespassing on Spanish Crown lands, would, I suspect, have seemed a minor offense indeed.

Back they came, then, Jean and Grollet, to the West, whose taste once it has got into a man's blood can never be got out, undoubtedly with De Vargas to the reconquest. For according to the ancient *informaciones* which Bandelier uncovered a couple of hundred years later at the pueblo of Santa Clara, Jean, now Juan, was present at the siege of Black Mesa,—that island of black trap whose dome curves darkly behind the yellow hills on the west as you go toward Taos,—on which the Puebleños of San Ildefonso intrenched themselves during and after the rebellion of 1680. And if there, then undoubtedly with De Vargas when he carried the faith at his own expense to Zuñi, and made a note of it upon the Rock.

Not by any means his last passage, for as may be gathered from the *informaciones,* Captain Juan el Archebeque, as he was finally called, became also a trader and a *muy rico* whose notes of hand even the provincial government endorsed, at whose wedding with the daughter of the alcalde of San Ildefonso, the Governor of New Mexico, no less, was witness. And if a trader, then he would have had his part in the annual *conducta* to Chihuahua, which remained the capital of colonial trade, passing by here many times in the collection of *serapes de Navajo* and hard turquoises, for the turquoise of Arizona holds its color much longer than that of New Mexico, and other items of provincial trade.

Nevertheless the Trues knew where and when to lay hand upon him; for in 1720, when he was sent with Don Pedro de Villazur toward the Arkansas to reconnoiter the advance of the French on Spanish territory, as the result of a skirmish the body of French Jean lay in the long grass by the river, as dead as ever La Salle was. This was the last touch of French influence in the Southwest, until, perhaps, in the early half of the last century, when French trappers might have strayed as far south as the Rock, which by now you discover to be not so much a landmark to me as a symbolic focus for many evanished streams of human interest.

The last official Spanish inscription on the Rock is that of Governor and Captain-General Don Felix Martinez, passing to the reduction of the pueblos of the Hopi in 1716. About that time the road must have been shortened to its present route, leaving the Rock to the south, for between then and September 17, of 1849, when Lieutenant Simpson, U. S. A., rediscovered it, and placed his neat *carte de visite* thereon, apparently but one English-speaking traveler had left his initials, "O. R.," and the date "March, 1836." But the place was not, on that account, unvisited. The spring, when Simpson found it, was still deep and sweet. Therefore it was bound to have been the resort of wandering bands of white men and brown, Navajo herders with their flocks, great caballadas of wild horses, the men who hunted them, and the roving deer. The buffalo hardly came so far south, but the *cibolleros,* professional buffalo-hunters, men of mixed blood and habits, heir to that mysterious aboriginal capacity for "thinking buffalo," tall men in buckskin clothing lined with *bayeta* and decorated with fox, armed with bow and arrow, and with powder-horn and ancient, wide-mouthed fusils stoppered with a wooden plug and well tasseled, tassels, indeed, wherever they could be applied, with that superior taste in ornament which the human male displays wherever the fashion gives him leave to indulge it.   Men such as these made their rendezvous at the spring of El Morro.

One of the engaging things about New Mexico is that there are still men there who are not afraid to introduce a little color into their dress.   There is one at Zuñi having bits of the bluest turquoise inlaid in the rims of his ears, between his black locks, so that I can never take my eyes off him.   These tall, dark hunters also wore ear-rings, and their bow-guards were studded with silver *conchos.*   *Cebolleros* followed the herds in twos and threes, killing and drying, and annually resorting to the *conducta* or dissipating in the settlements a year's profit in one splendid spree of aguardiente and four-card monte.   Of that same stripe, but a finer breed, were the trappers, whiter, and as much more intelligent than the *cibolleros,* as a beaver is more intelligent than a buffalo.   There were also *gambucinos,* pocket hunters as I have already described them in "The Land of Little Rain." *Se paseron;* they passed themselves by here. But it is impossible to say which of the undated, undescribed names they carved upon the Rock belonged to one or the other.

All this time, between the Spanish journeys' ending in the Southwest, and the unending westward movement of the English-speaking, lay fordless rivers and immeasurable hostile plains. But in 1805, a merchant in Kaskaskai had furnished Baptiste la Lande with goods, and instructions to break through from the Platte River to Santa Fé if he could. Which he did, and, profiting by the example of Jean l'Archeveque, became also a *rico,* forgetting, it is said, to make a report of his profits to his employer, thus furnishing an excuse of legitimate business for Zebulon Pike, when, looking for the head waters of the Red River, he lost himself in the wooded slopes that bent toward the Rio Grande, and was escorted by a detachment of Spanish soldiery down the Jornada del Muerto to Chihuahua.

What Pike wrote of what he saw on that expedition, by giving it a plausible objective, set a roaring torrent of superabundant Anglo-Saxon energy pouring down the old Santa Fé trail. Trade with the Spanish settlements was a good enough business proposition, but it was a better excuse. I never go by the turn of the road on the way to Lamy, by which the

old trail from Raton Pass comes into the highway,
but I see the wraiths of the rocking lines of high-piled
covered wagons swinging between the dark piñons,
and I never come back past the twin breast-shaped
hills but I hear the fusillade of the teamster's whip-
cracks, and the inhabitants crying, *"Los Americanos!
La entrada de la caravana!"* But I know very well
that the whole business was chiefly an excuse for the
itching foot: *"Se paseron por aquí"*!

Kit Carson, on his first *pasear* to California, since
he is known to have visited Zuñi, must have been in
this neighborhood; and later, on that expedition
against the Navajo which made the name of Bosque
Redondo a dread to the Indian and a disgrace to
America,—supposing Americans capable of feeling
disgraced by their own conduct, which I doubt,—his
scouting parties must have played hide and seek
among the tall stone islands hereabout. Kit Carson
I understand; the blue eyes, the broad forehead; the
relentless disciplinarian, the beloved leader, the tem-
peramental breaker of new trails. Many faces of
that type you can see looking out at you from any
gathering of young people in the Southwest, breed of
their blood, fierce but gentle, chivalrous toward
women, and, after their notions of honor and justice,
incorruptibly honorable and just.

But along with them, and between their coming and
the generation capable of creating a national monu-

ment around Inscription Rock, there came hordes and types of men that were no more to my purpose than the froth on the lip of a wave that spilled over from the Old World and ran far on the sandy wastes of the new. Either that, or at this point all my gifts fail me. For, plainly, my business is prophecy. What I would know is the far journey's end of all these threads of human enterprise, and my sole purpose, besides the pleasure of playing with them, in showing you the many-colored skein of the past, limp in my hand, is that you may presently feel with me the pull of the shuttle that flies to the pattern's completion.

Men like the Patties I understand. They left a record of human achievement, broke new trails, mapped them, touched the plains of the Gila, and sent back the first American notice of the cactus country. But between the times of men like these and Buckie O'Neil the rough-rider, there were loosed upon the land men whose record, so far as we know it, was of violence and destruction; men to whom all Indians were "varmints"; all Spanish-speaking, "Greasers," therefore plunderable. They accepted the hospitality of Spanish rancheros, and forged titles to their property. They found the Pimas hospitable, peaceable, with broad fields of corn and the roofs of their *jacales* white with bursting cotton-pods, and beggared them. They guffawed at the courtly ritual of daily life as they found it in the haciendas, spat tobacco juice over everything, swore vilely, drank hard, and killed one another on slight provocation. They massacred the game and gutted the mines; cast down the shrines, seeking buried treasure; built nothing, preserved nothing, roared muddily through the land, and ran out like Western rivers, in the sands of a time that shows every disposition to forget them.

I suppose there must be always survivals of these freebooters at large in society, whom the report of a new country to be plundered draws as carrion draws buzzards. Of their inconsiderable names carved on the Rock, the custodian has erased as many as encroached on the clear, personable script of the Spaniards. Nothing shows now on the pearly-white front of El Morro but the names of famous men, with the ancient rubrics at the tail of their signatures, and the occasional ribald sketches of the aborigines. I commend you to the fat man with the full front feet, in particular.

In three hundred and thirty years the spring had filled with sand, but since the Rock has become a national monument it has been cleared, and the blue- and amber-shadowed water has come back. On the way to it the custodian called my attention to what can be so easily mistaken for a fall of the island rock that only a lover of the Rock such as Evon Voght discovered it to be fine, pale pottery clay brought from

unknown sources, on the heads of patient women,—
stored there how many centuries since? Of the ancient trail at the back of El Morro, up to the crowning
towns, there is now no trace. Nevertheless I went
up, and thought well of myself until a few days later,
when, having declined the short trail up the rock of
Acoma, which is a good deal like climbing the outside
of the Woolworth tower, I struggled up the mile-long
drift of sand. Sinking at every footstep over the
ankles, and breathing heavily, half-way up, was overtaken by two Acoma women walking with bales of hay
on their heads, who courteously stepped out and
around me, where the slope of the shifty dune is about
forty-five degrees.

Probably the two ruins on the split apex of the
triangular sandstone called Inscription Rock, were
the summer and winter clan groups of a single town,
and of the early Chaco period. So this might have
easily been the pueblo on a rock from which he whom
they call Blue Feather came to the undoing of Pueblo
Bonito—this, or that other ruin on the banded red
island that you pass on the way from Ramah.

It is a perilous business, getting yourself from wing
to wing of the split triangle, though there must have
been a trail once, and every available space is marked
with pot-holes where the women worked, dyeing cotton, grinding corn, bleaching buckskin, having always,
a hand's throw to left or right of them, the dark drop

of the cleft whose floor must have been the dancing-place. High up, under the towered front, they would have made their shrines, and at all hours the eagles would be crying. The best thing I know about our Ancients is that they were unlonely. They would have looked out from their rock over the tall islands, to the blue of the Sierra Zuñi, and found it natural and satisfying that the smokes should be so few, and the lovely intervales full of grazing deer that, of moonlight nights, would come in long lines to their own spring to drink.

I have wondered if ever there passed by here the camels that, in the secretaryship of Jeff Davis, were expected to find in our Southwest footage as native to them as the Syrian desert from which they had been imported with much diplomacy and expense. For it was our American way to think of our newly acquired desert merely as a place to be crossed, and its aboriginal population, unfriendly to invasion, as creatures to be hunted. "What," said Mr. Davis, who as Secretary of War was keen upon the hunt, "could be of more use in that business than the Ship of the Desert?" This was the poetic way in which Americans referred to camels before they became personally acquainted with them. Seventy-two camels were shipped to Indianola, Texas, in 1857, by means of a committee, one of whom was that young Lieutenant Beale who had passed by here recently on his way to Washington from California with the news of the discovery of gold.

Half of the animals made the trip under pack from Albuquerque to California several times. So they must have passed over the Jornada del Muerto, and if not actually *por aqui,* then on the road which runs a little to the north of the Rock, about the present line of the railroad. The rest of them were used for pack-animals on the plains of Arizona, and for all purposes of desert travel proved themselves invaluable. Except that the American mule-whacker could not be taught to love them! For one thing, as Jimmy Rose-meyer, who had tried it, explained to me, a camel can never understand when he is being cussed. Mule- and horse-trains stampeded at sight of the animals, and the Apache, who was to have been hunted, turned hunter, developing a taste for camel meat that, together with the protests of the mule-whacker's union, speedily put an end to the Davis experiment.

Several of the beasts were bought by Beale, now First Commissioner of Indian Affairs in California, who told me how his son drove a pair of them tandem in a sulky from the Rancho Tejon to Los Angeles, over a road that is now one slithering line of automobiles. The rest were turned loose in the Arizona desert, where they were heard of from time to time, as late as 1891, frightening pack-trains out of their wits, or topping the mesa sky-line unexpectedly, causing

TOPPING THE SKY LINE UNEXPECTEDLY . . FRIGHTENING MULE TRAINS HALF OUT OF THEIR WITS

many hard drinkers to reform forthwith. They were used at Papago Tanks, and left a mark there, inscribed on the Papago mind; the landlady at Casa Grande Hotel may show you, wrought into the native black-and-white basketry, the strange, remembered forms.

Two drivers came from Syria with the camel band, of whom one, because of his frequent use of the Oriental salutation, *Hadj Ali,* came to be called, in the way of the West, Hi Jolly. The other became a trader, and I have always believed it was he, under the name of Abdullah George, making with his pack the rounds of the herders' camps, from whom, at a shearing in the country of Lost Borders, I bought what proved to be, when I had scoured it, an enameled copper bowl of undoubted Syrian workmanship. I kept it at my wickiup with the hand-wrought bronze bell of the bell-camel at Tejon, which I had from Jimmy Rosemeyer, until the interest of casual visitors in these reminders of a time that had passed, advised me to remove them to a less conspicuous situation.

I suppose that a Syrian loosed in the country between the Rio Grande and the Colorado must have found many a touch of home there: the large, low stars set alight like lamps in the twilight space; the faint almond scent of the wild-peach orchards; the pregnant misshaped moon walking cautiously the keen straight line of the mesa. I do not know what the dweller of the Syrian desert thinks of the Milky Way, but I am sure if George knew of it, he would have found adequate the Zuñi notion of the middle drift of little curled feathers across the heavens, where the lesser gods gather prayer plumes for the greater. More nearly to his mind he would have found the shifting camps of sheep-herders and cattlemen.

In Arizona, north of the Mogollon Rim, there is still good cattle country, but New Mexico was always, in spite of a flurry of recent years in favor of horned stock, a sheepman's country. In broken bands of one to three hundred, with dogs and men, they drift across the landscape, while the *capitan,* with his sturdy saddle-mule and drove of pack-burros, weaves in and out, carrying them supplies, selecting camps, advising of the condition of water-holes* The spring under the Rock would have been a well-known watering-place to *boregos* on the way to the meadows of the Sierra Zuñi, . . . and now I know the exact shade of the pale sandstone hereabout: it is the color of a sheep's coat a month after shearing.

In those days, any inhabitant of the Rock must have been witness to the dramatic skirmishes between sheepmen and cattlemen for the possession of the crowded ranges. For cattle disdain to graze where sheep have lately passed, and will not drink where

* *The Flock:* Mary Austin.

they have just been drinking. For which natural antipathy the cow-boys used to scatter the bands of sheep where they found them, running them until they died, or until the coyote and cougar defeated the struggle of the dogs and men to round them up again. Then the herders armed themselves to cripple the raiders' horses, but the horsemen shot first and farthest, so that many a herder lay face upward among his silly sheep, mourned over only by his dogs. But they passed, those days, as old times and older. Cattle go by on the worn trails under drawling, peaceable drivers, and at dusk you can still see from the Rock, over toward the Sierra Zuñi, the *borego* making his nightly round with a torch, flashing it in the silly sheep faces, until, affrighted, they turn head inward, and so remain until the rising light releases them to the pastures.

Since the custodian put up the fence around it, nothing has come to Inscription Rock but an intermittent tourist stream, requiring federal enactment to prevent it from destroying one of the most interesting of southwestern landmarks, with that strange passion of the touring American, not so much to see notable places as to prove to other people that he has seen them. It is curious to note how much more character there is in the ancient Spanish inscriptions than in such modern print-cut names as have been allowed to remain. Even so, I suspect, the quality that the conquistadores wrote into the land, as they passed by here, will outlast the brisk conventionalized pattern stamped over it since 1848. If I did not believe this, I should not so wish that I could make my home here, in one of the ancient plazas on the Rock. Not, however, having accustomed myself to walk a mile and a half, mostly straight up in the air, for my daily drink, and carrying my marketing home on my head, I suppose that would not be convenient, though I can think of no place more suited to my purpose. But if not to live, then, perhaps, equally to my purpose to be buried here; and from my dust would spring the crêpe-petaled argemone.

Here, at least, I shall haunt, and as the time-streams bend and swirl about the Rock, I shall see again all the times that I have loved, and know certainly all that now I guess at. I shall hear the drums far down in the dancing-place, and talk with feather-venders going up to Chaco and the cliff dwellings of Cañon de Chelly. I shall see the Fire Dance on the top of Toyoállanne, and know what was in the hearts of the men of Pecos when they came down to Hawi-kuh in 1540. You, of a hundred years from now, if when you visit the Rock, you see the cupped silken wings of the argemone burst and float apart when there is no wind; or if, when all around is still, a sudden stir in the short-leaved pines, or fresh eagle feathers blown upon the shrine, that will be I, making known in such fashion as I may the land's undying quality.

# THE LEFT HAND OF GOD

# THE LEFT HAND OF GOD

WHEN the All-Father-Father, having thought inwardly, breathed outward into space, then came into being, earth and sky and the world-encompassing water. Then, with his beam, the Sun Father impregnated the foam-cap of the cosmic ocean, of which were born the divine twins appointed to be man's helpers, Ahayuta, Matsalema, right and left hands of sun-power. Thus, in the Days of the New, all life was shaped as it flowed from the right hand to the left, pulling the dust up through the corn to be man, pulling man down to the dust again.

There might be truer accounts than this of how the world was made, but I find none more pertinent to my subject. It was so, I suspect, before men endowed the Father with their own liking and misliking, calling them good and evil, that all myths of twin brethren were to be interpreted. So long as the two hands were open, men experienced the one without boasting, and suffered the other without complaint. It was not until they fell into the clutch of this most Christian but un-Christlike civilization of ours, that with anguished certainty our Ancients fell close over them the Left Hand of God.

By 1540, when Coronado and his gaudy, gold-greedy young Dons came swaggering out of Culiacan, not so gaudy but none the less greedy and swaggering by the time they came to Hawikuh near Thunder Mountain, the streams of tribal migration had followed the rains down from the high mesas to the river-bottoms, the great-houses crumbled, the banded walls at Chaco lay roofless to the sun, the cliff dwellings, occupied if at all, only by fragmentary clans, that by the time Oñate crossed the river at Paso del Norte, with seven hundred Spanish settlers and soldiers in his train, had passed completely out of remembrance.

Of the Rio Grande pueblos, Taos, a bow-shot from its present site, Acoma, fast as a limpet on its rock, Pecos, now in ruins, are all that we can certainly identify in place. Zuñi had seven towns, Moqui seven; Tiguex, where Coronado wintered and burnt two hundred hostages at the stake, was probably near the present town of Bernalillo. Altogether, with the Piros at Socorro and south, and the Salinas along the riverless trough of the Estancia, the Spanish found, according to Castañeda, eighty self-sustaining, republican, co-operative commonwealths, of which we have left a scant score in New Mexico, and the Hopi villages in Arizona.

Castañeda says, further, that he found the pueblos industrious, and so prosperous, that often, when they came to plant, there was corn of last year's raising, ungathered on the ground. But even at that time the peak of building activity was passed. No more banded walls of dressed stone, no more great ceremonial bowls as at Chettro-Kettle, no sun temples, wall within wall, as at Mesa Verde. Practically all the pueblos, at the time Spanish sovereignty was forced upon them, were of puddled adobe, but larger and handsomer than you see them now.

Of how, in 1680, when the land was well parceled out in lordly grants, the pueblos rose against the Spanish, of how they killed the priests and drove out the settlers and scoured themselves clean of the contamination of baptism, in amole suds, of how, after De Vargas came to the reconquest, the towns rose like flocks of startled birds, how they circled and fluttered before they settled again, must be told in boys' tales, full of sallies and surprises and futile heroisms. What we have to keep in mind throughout is that the point of all rebellion was their predilection for worshiping God after the dictates of their own hearts, so native to the soil that it is everywhere spoken of as American.

The reconquest ended, there ensued a period during which the multiplying raids of Apache and Navajo drew the pueblos and the Spanish settlements into protective coöperation. The nomadic tribes had learned a casual agriculture from the sedentary peoples; horses they had taken from the conquistadores, and sheep from the colonists. By the opening of the eighteenth century the Navajos were better horsed and provisioned than the settlers themselves. Then came the Utes, and the rise in fighting efficiency of the Comanche nation. Following soon on the establishment of the Republic of Mexico, entered the Americans, knowing neither the land nor its inhabitants, caring only for what they could get out of them. Thus they closed, Spanish, Navajo, Apache, Comanche, and gringo, five fingers of the Left Hand, on the terraced towns.

In this fashion, passed into the keeping of the United States the vase, the cup in which had mellowed for a thousand years the medicine for the want of which the civilized world is tearing out its own vitals. For in the cultural frame which we hold so obstinately that it can never refill from its original sources, and so stupidly that the precious content is spilled and fouled by the least creditable elements of our own culture, lies the only existing human society that ever found, and kept for an appreciable period, the secret of spiritual organization.

The government of the pueblos is republican. Only the cacique, whose business it is to go between the people and the Deific Powers, is elected for life, but in everything but his sacred office he is amenable to the common law. Inasmuch as the business of prayer is one requiring time and withdrawal from distracting affairs, a field is cultivated for his benefit, but betweentimes he works in it himself, rears his children, and instructs the acolytes among whom his successor will be selected.   In general, the civil affairs of the community are in the hands of a governor who may not succeed himself, and a council composed of ex-governors and war captains.

The governor has his lieutenant and an *alguacil,* or constable, and the war captain, by the natural reversion of his office, has become the executive of foreign affairs.   All of these serve without pay and without distinction of their offices from other items of communal labor, such as mending the community ditch or cultivating the widow's field.   There are no specialized classes, as of artists and artisans.   Every man, as he feels impelled, makes songs, carves the ladders of his house, or decorates his articles of daily use.   He makes his own tools.   Once he wove and spun, minded the young children, and sang to his women as they bent over the neatly boxed metates in the milling-room.

There were always these three smoothed stone slabs, for the three grades of fineness of the meals demanded by the discriminating housewife, and the three manos or hand-stones resting on them, in a clean little room by itself, or perhaps several of them grouped together where the women of one hive could be found *plump-plumping* to the rhythm of the grinding-song, sung by the young men between pleasant quips and cheerful laughter.   Such is the power of song over labor that not only the corn was ground, but the upper and the nether stone also, so that a saying has come out of that country to the effect that every man in his lifetime eats one metate and four manos.

Besides the milling-room, every pueblo home has a general living-room, along one wall of which runs the low *banca,* and in one corner, or midway of the long wall, protected by a wing, the triangular fireplace where the pot simmers and the cheerful flame runs up the cedar logs. Hung from the smoke-browned vigas by a thong, the "pole of the soft stuff" carries the bright blankets and robes of skin and the silk rebozos of the women. Rolled into a convenient seat, the family bedding lies all day against the wall. Near the door, in its niche, stood, until very recent years, and stands even yet in devout households, the cloud-and-altar patterned meal-bowl, from which the courteous guest blows a pinch of sacred meal in the six ritualistic directions.

In the great pyramidal house heaps, where the rooms are small and the inner ones dark, there is likely to be a special room for cooking, and for storing grain and treasures of ceremonial use. But in the long-house pueblos, the grain will often lie heaped in its own corner, and the cooking-utensils in another, the bed roll against the long wall, and no thing usurping the corner of any other. Nowadays you will find all manner of unlovely modern utilities: sewing-machines, cook-stoves, victrolas. But among our Ancients there was never an article of the meanest use which had not its own æsthetic quality, if no more than that form of beauty which comes of perfect mastery over the material.

Outside, the cone-shaped oven cluster, on the roofs if the house be of the many-storied type, or in the *placitas* between the house rows. Beyond the house heaps, the corrals of the live stock, and the gardens spread away into acres of beans and corn, from which blue smoke of the *temporales* rises between planting-time and harvest.

Walking early, in one of these still, brown towns, you may see the cacique climbing the nearest hill to pray, so the cacique at Tesuque told me, first for the pueblo, then for all the Indians in the world, and for the President of the United States, for all white men in the world, then for all the Mexicans. This being the extent of the world's population, so far as he knows it, the cacique charges the rest of his petition with the welfare of the corn, the water in the acequia, or any other matters that require to be brought into harmony with the Deific Powers, always conceived of as being friendly and amenable to the desires of men.

Here and there, as the sun rises, gilding the tops of the corn with liquid rays, the elders appear on the housetops, making their oblation to the east, and women, blowing sacred meal dust or a light prayer feather, unobtrusively, as they come down the ladders with lovely patterned *tinajas* poised upon their heads, to bring the morning water-supply from the acequia. Presently the village goatherd leads the community flock into the field, and the day's occupations are absorbed noiselessly into the wide, bright day.

At evening when the light breaks, before it dies, into unimaginable splendor, there is a stir of cheerful domestic life, smell of cooking, laughter of women. The goatherd brings in the flocks, children play out toward the fields from which presently the fathers return, with a flower, a bright pebble, a branch of purple-berried juniper, anything to make their pockets worth rifling. What an old human custom that is, and how unregarded! Out of the oldest days of our elders comes a fragment of a myth charged with a sudden poignancy . . . of a woman whose young sons had been fathered by the Sunset Cloud standing toward the west, she keeping it from them . . . and a day when the children come questioning: "Mother, why have we no father to run and call to when the men come in from the hunt? Why have we no one, Mother, to run to and call?" . . .

The evening meal at the pueblo is taken before the fire, with the smoking food-bowl in the middle, the platter of bread beside it, the swinging cradle within reach, the children leaning on their parents' knees and taking their portions by the only rule of table manners the pueblo knows, with slowness and dignity. After supper the sack of native tobacco and the heap of soft corn husks, and the quiet stealing away of one or another of the house group for the hour of meditation and the last salute to the Sun Father; then the voice of the *pregonero,* sounding from the housetop, with directions for to-morrow's labor. If it should be evening at Taos, you will hear the young men, ghostly in their white sheets, on the bridge between the north and south houses, singing their wordless moonlight melody, or at Zuñi they will foregather on the terraces to moan melodiously until the protest of some sleepy elder cries them silence.

In the summer months sleep falls on the pueblo almost with the darkness, but when the great winds between the rains get up and shake themselves dustily, when the snow lies in an unbroken fleece over dune and stubble, then there will be tales by the fire, and mysteries in the kivas, from which the *tombes* may be heard, going all night, steady and quick like the pulse of their ancient life beating. Then the children cower by their mothers, and nobody looks out if he hears an unaccustomed noise, for, in the dark witches creep and black prayers have power. It has been long since any one has been killed for witchcraft, but the primitive belief in the power of thought has this evil in it, that evil thoughts take form and substance, and any strange noise in the dark, a flitting owl or a lurking coyote, starts the prick of uneasiness. It is better, in any case, not to be found with owl or raven feathers in your possession.

Living in such fashion, the pueblos, at the time Spain found them, had no rich, no poor, no paupers, no prisons, no red-light district, no criminal classes, no institutionalized orphans, no mothers of dependent children penalized by their widowhood, no one pining for a mate, who wished to be married. All this is so much a part of their manner of living together in communities, that three centuries of Christian contact have not quite cured them of their superior achievement. By breaking down Indian custom marriage, the missionaries have contrived to increase the number of unsatisfactory settlements, and added to the irregularities, formerly at a minimum for their populations.

The Government having refrained from enforcing the rights of the pueblos to the lands signed to them under Abraham Lincoln, pauperism eats in upon them like a discreditable sore. Trachoma, tuberculosis, and that other scourge in which Europe writes its sign manual across the world, has brought down the vitality of the population. Over all the inestimable treasure of their culture lie our ignorance and self-conceit as a gray dust. Yet still, in that dust, blossom and smell sweet, concepts for the lack of which our age goes staggering into chaos.

If we could blot out of our sight all the materiality with which man, even in our inmost vision of him, is forever in contact, we should see him floating in the bubble of his selfness, aloof, shut in by iridescent films of his own experience with the universe. What he thinks he sees, what he feels he knows: these give color and texture to the irised globe in which he moves, and, like a bubble, blows out and contracts with his own breath. I find this figure of the many-colored foam which the rain priest lifts through his cloud-blower in the Tewa rain-making, better suited to my use than the stiff phrase of the psychologists. When the yucca suds swirl in the ceremonial bowl, rise, under the rain priest's breath, heap on heap, shining half-globes that crowd and coalesce and break into one another, until something of its neighbor's wall has become a portion of every filmed inclosure. This is the figure of our sort of society, in which there are a million souls shut in the foam cloud, for whom the color and shape of the universe is the shell of their neighbor's thinking. Here and there great souls detach themselves and go sailing skyward in a lovely world of their own seeing, poets and prophets. But what happens in the pueblo is the gentle swelling of film into film, until the whole community lies at the center of one great bubble of the Indian's universe, from which the personal factor seldom escapes into complete individuation.

I doubt if any white man ever completely knows an Indian. There is perhaps no such thing as an absolutely knowable Indian, any more than there is a completely individual Japanese. All that I propose to show you is something of the rainbow-shine of the pueblo bubble, fouled by our handling, but unbroken. Even then I shall probably not be able to show it to you without at the same time dimming it with my own breath.

The root whose substance makes all the bubbling shapes, is Life, conceived as a reality, forever flowing and reforming through all phenomena. At the bottom of the Amerind mind, this reality is probably seldom personalized. Anthropologists, who have agreed to speak of this universal element by the word describing it among certain of the plains tribes, *wokonda,* agree that there is less of manness in the names it goes by in the terraced towns—the Trues, Those Above, All-Father Father, Finishers of the Paths of Our Lives—than goes to our own notion of a Supreme Being. Certainly it is never thought of as being weary, jealous, complacent, or avenging. This *wokonda* is, in some degree, in every created thing, stick and stone, bird and beast and blowing wind. It flows endlessly from shape to shape; the great bison is a majestic form of its tarrying, the sun a place where *wokonda* is concentrated, the corn one of the blessed disguises which it takes on in order that men may be fed. There is a pueblo myth of how Life assumed the deer, from which it is released by the huntsman's arrow, to take on fresh shapes for his following.

"O younger brother," said Cushing's Zuñi host to him, concerning the water turtle, "it *cannot* die; it can but change its house."

Thus the dead are spoken of as "Those who have gone away," and it is wholly consistent with the notion of the easy flow of life that they may come back again. Among the Keres, they linger about for four days, during which their personal belongings are not disturbed,—is it not natural to wish to look at their own things in the familiar place?—and if not placated during that period, they may come knocking at the door. But at Hopi very young children are laid in rock crevices with a guide-string pointing the way to the pueblo, so that they may find their way home to wait till their mothers are ready to hold out a hand to them on the way to the under-world. Would it not make death less terrifying to feel, the next moment after, a small familiar hand slipped into yours? For death, like life, is a thing to be learned.

The distinction made, until recent times, between the dead whose bodies were burned and those who were buried between the walls, was a distinction of spiritual progression. The burned needed thus to be released from the bonds of the flesh, as the life of the burial bowl or basket had to be released by breaking, before being deposited in the burial heap. Those whose bodies were built into the dwelling were the saints, far enough along the Path of Life to be able to go forth of their own volition, as finished beings.

Among the Zuñi, many states of being are recognized, of which some are mystical and others states of progression, some of which are passed as "unborn men of the under-world, who are like the smoke, taking form from the outward touchings of things, while the dead are like the wind, taking form from within of their own wills." But the masked impersonators of the ancestors, who come to dance with the fraternities to which they belonged, are not ghosts as we conceive them, identic selves of our friends, with all their individual traits and passions. They are the real life of the ancestors, thought of as something other than the breath body or personal envelop of the psyche, which remains in the under-world while the spiritual substance comes back to cheer and advise the living.

Both incineration and intramural burial have passed out of Pueblo practice, but there is still no cult of the dead among them, such as is expressed among us in monuments and mausoleums. Never having feared death, they make no to-do over it, often foreseeing, with that singular prescience of primitives, the very hour of their dissolution, and willing, except where the church intervenes, to have the outworn garment of the spirit added to the communal rubbish-heap, as was the custom with their fathers.

Every creature is thought of as having his share of *wokonda.* But not a fixed or certain share. By methods arrived at partly by intuition, and in part empirically, the Puebleño can charge and recharge himself with the precious essence. And not himself only, but the earth, the corn, his sick and ailing neighbor. The more *wokonda,* the heavier the crop, the greater the success in the hunt and the triumph over the enemy. Out of this primary belief grows a society quite simply and literally founded on the idea that the chief consideration of its members is to increase the amount of god-power in themselves. To this end, every rite and every important social or personal function is directed. Failing to understand this, neither the Amerind's art nor his literature can be apprehended. The "happy ending" of a Pueblo tale is not the marrying of a particular woman, nor the adding of a certain feather to the war-bonnet, but the attainment of magical power.

This is the objective of every song-cycle and dance-drama, the incident which set it going, or the situation to which the power is to be applied, being so irrelevant that it is lightly mentioned, or even left entirely to be inferred by the audience. Thus, the nine-days Moun-

tain Chant of the Navajo is designed to make the smell
of a young man's own tribe seem a good smell to him.
In the Corn Dance, a drama by which the necessary
water and fruiting power is won for the corn, the
climax comes when the People of the Middle Heaven
dance with us, the clouds grow big with blackness, the
thunder rolls responsive to the drums, and the rain
comes down.

One of the empirical discoveries of our Ancients was
that by the making of rhythmic movements and noises,
the whole plane of tribal activity was keyed up; not
only the actual capacity for fighting and hunting and
procreating, but the powers of invention and discovery.
Intuitively they arrived at knowing that by suggesting their desire in symbolic acts, they stood a better
chance of having it realized. Behind all Amerind art
and religion, lie instinctive movements of this nature,
half-remembered or childishly explained experiences.
One of the curiosities of mind stuff is that it works
quite independently of the explanations. The Tanoan
youth who ties eagle's-down in his hair to make himself light for the Race of the Swift-coming Rain, does
actually run better in consequence. By the painting of
the symbols of fearless power on his forehead, the
warrior becomes powerful. If, then, by the mimic
thunder, by the wearing of rain-masks and cloud-
calling head-dresses, we invite the rain, does not the
rain come? Well, . . . prove that it does n't!

IF BY MIMIC THUNDER AND CLOUD-CALLING HEAD-DRESSES WE CALL THE RAIN, DOES NOT THE RAIN COME?

The world with which the Puebleño thus harmonized himself, is of a color that only poets and children for a brief period keep. The Sun, clad in white buckskin worked with glittering beads, walks the sky bearing a burning shield. The earth is sentient, and if you dance for it, thrills and flushes with the power of ripening the harvest. The great spruce-tree is knowledgeable, its roots reach down to the six great springs of the earth, its tip touches the clouds. The thunder is a bird, the most majestic, whose wings are made of the dark cloud, whose feathers are clashing flakes of obsidian, in whose claws are serpent-darting arrows of the lightning. Springs are sacred, and under the protection of a symbolic concept made out of the analogy of snakes to the zigzag lightning and the sinuous course of rivers, and the use of plumes to symbolize the bird-flight of prayers on their way to Those Above. Thus, a cleverly constructed effigy of a great snake having feathers growing out of his head has become the chief fetish of a desert people.

Such a one is kept at Zuñi in a secret cave in the mountainside, brought to the town by chanting processions for the festival of the Snake fraternity, under a canopy of everliving boughs. Where it comes to rest in the kiva, arises, out of the hatchway, the sacred spruce-tree, whose roots reach to the under-world, through whose tops our hearts ascend on the mountains of the north. At Hopi, when the Snake Dance is on, the Tcamah-heehe strikes the sounding-board before the *kisi,* where the gathered snakes are kept, to summon the Ancient from the four world quarters to the ancient obligation, and the Snake priests as they dance between the files of the Antelope priests pound with their feet upon the earth to notify their ancestors of the under-world, dark Sipapu, that thus the obligation is fulfilled. But the worship of the Awanyu is a dying cult.

From old Pecos come fireside legends, dating from late Spanish times, of a huge serpent appeased yearly by the sacrifice of a plump brown baby. Maria, our *cocinera,* says that once to the rancho of her grandfather, came a young Pecos woman concealing her *niñito* under her shawl, weeping and begging to be hidden until the festival of the Awanyu was past; and if confirmation were wanted, was there not a woodcutter, who, going early to Pecos after fresh snow was fallen, saw the track of a snake clear about the town, huge as if an ox had been dragged!

Better evidence is the prevailing decorative pattern of the plumed serpent, frequently assimilated to the pattern of the lightning, associated with life-giving water. At San Felipe I found it circling the baptismal font and the bowl of holy water.

As old, as widely spread, perhaps older, is the cult of Fire, now shrunk to fragmentary rituals except among the Hopi, who still keep the ceremony of New

Fire. But certain of the Hopi clans derive from cliff-dwellers, among whom, if we believe the evidence of New Fire House, recently uncovered in the Mesa Verde cliffs, the Fire cult had a temple to itself, and was perhaps carried south from there to become the source of that magnificent ritual of the New Fire in far-off Anahuac.

There it finally became the symbol of the mystical reality of the communal bond, flashed from the tops of teocallis, new-made, carried by swift runners to announce the end and the beginning of time-cycles. But in the cliff caves the worship of fire, as the symbol of the magical power of life, is associated, as at Hopi, with the phallic being, Kokopelli, whose figure appears painted on the walls of New Fire House. Fire, to our Ancients, is a being; the fluid, formless, Elder Life. That was why the pueblo of San Ildefonso sent recently to Zuñi for fire priests to reinstate the cult of Life-increase among their dwindling clans. It may very well be that the whole clan system is based upon the primary human group of those who used the same fire, and the ancestral clan mother not necessarily the mother of them all, but the Keeper of the Hearth, the priestess of the community-creating Flame.

At Hopi, when the New Fire is made, every hearth

is dark, the women and the children keep themselves hidden while the men perform the ancient perilous adventure of bringing fire to be a creature of daily use. But at Zuñi, the fire priests go further and profess to control the fire which they have created. Issuing from the kivas, they plunge their naked bodies into the red embers of the fire-pits, and come out scatheless and unwincing. Also they make, as do the Navajo, the fire a medium in which the spirits of those who have gone away materialize. When, on the high top of Toyoállanne, the naked dancers thread the concentric circles of the fire-piles, when the smoke arises and the call to the spirits sounds to the rhythm of the drums, . . . Come, come, come, . . . come, among us, . . . come be with us! . . . Are not their shapes seen descending as the smoke goes up? Sleight of priests, . . . trick of the mind's excited response to the wreathing smoke and the ghostly echoes from the rocks, or shadow thrown on the smoke-screen of some reality deeper than the self? The more you see of this sort of thing, the less you will dogmatize about it.

It is at Hopi that the association of fire with the idea of life-increase and the god of germination, takes most definitely the form which it naturally would take in a society where procreation is still associated with worship. Not that it is the only ritual touched with the sense of the sacred functioning of the principle of male and female, but it is the one most recognizable by our debauched sense of such things. That the objectionableness of phallic rites is chiefly in the mind of the observer, is proved by the fact that they seldom appear objectionable unless we know that they are phallic, and we never know except when they obviously violate our particular taboos.

When they lie, as many of the most enjoyed life-increasing ceremonies do, outside our prepossessions, we are stirred and recreated by them. In the translating of Indian songs I was often told by the interpreters that they could not always translate to me correctly, because all the "white men's words," to describe the matter of the song, "mean bad." There are things symbolized and experienced as part of the religious life of the pueblos which cannot even be interpreted by Christians, since all our thoughts of such things "mean bad." But in fact, the current rumors of unwitnessed and much-whispered-about phallic rites in the pueblos, are of the stripe of the story of the great snake of Pecos. The life-increasing rites that I have seen myself, I should n't know as being of that character, if I had not read about them in the reports of the Bureau of Ethnology.

What is meant for humor is another matter. The key of pueblo fun is set by the Koshare, the Delight-makers. These are the black-and-white spirit clowns with corn husks in their hair, who may be seen circling the communal dances with light steps and ghostly, giving forth hollow, fluttering cries, such as immemorially the disembodied dead are supposed to make. White streaks of *yeso* on black-painted bodies, black-and-white stripes of the night and the morning, the white upper world and the dark nether, such as clowns have worn "ever since we came out of the ground." At Zuñi they tell how, before the primordial mud was dried or the earth made stable, our Ancients wearied, seeking for the Middle Place, and the corn, catching their sodden humor, would not fill out in the ear. Then came the ancestors, back from the spirit world, to comfort with their presence and cheer with quips and laughter, for the corn has a soul also. That is why the spirit dancers are called Delight-makers, as, between the intervals of the dance, they break into inimitable clowning. Also, though they wear the black-and-white spirit livery, husks of dead corn in their hair, and rabbit-skins such as the dead were anciently buried in, and strings of deadly nightshade berries, there is always tucked behind one ear or under their belts, or worn as an armlet, a sprig of the evergreen spruce, symbol of life everlasting.

In their religious function the Koshare are invisible, and as they dance, or, early mornings before the dance begins, as they circle the village in search of those whose hearts are bad, whose words have left the straight road, no eye is lifted to them. Where they come in to break bread with the householder, happiness flashes, for the moment, like a sudden sunburst, for do not the beloved dead come in their persons? While the movement of the dance is on, they dance with incredible spirit lightness, stooping to tie the loosened foot-lace of a dancer, to untangle the blown hair of another from his neighbor's arm-band, or bringing young children on their backs, to learn the steps and take on the joyous solemnity of the dance occasion. Between the intervals of the song-cycle they enliven the dancers with buffoonery of a type often broader than our sort of society admits, but never so slimy.

The social function of the Delight-makers is to keep the community in order, with whips of laughter. These humorous interludes often take the form of dramatic skits based upon the weakness or the misadventures of the villagers; they will even found themselves upon the absurdities of white life, with a penetration and a power of mimicry that leaves the white observer speechless. As, for instance, when they set the stage for their simple dramas, the presence of a white man is indicated by a pile of tin cans.

Every now and then they turn up the roots of the human mind with lumps of our common clay sticking to it. Odd how you can tell by the throaty turn of laughter, even among folk whose speech is unpronounceable to you, when the spirit clowns uncover the tremendous ancient joke the gods played upon men when, male and female, they created them. Once at the end of one of the winter dances, at a Keres pueblo,

at the red fall of the day, we stumbled upon a farce of
the once frightening Apache raids, and a joke, a modern type of which turned up multifariously during the
late war, in connection with what were known even
in the stone age as "atrocities," the only joke which our
age could tell but not print, in that connection, . . .
and it was the same joke! "How long," said I to
Tomacito the teniente, "have you had that joke?"
"Ever since we came out of the ground," said Tomacito, and I believed him.

Also, you understand why we have to teach our
children not to laugh at a natural accident occurring in
connection with stewed beans, when you have run it to
earth in the cave-dwelling period, as an origin legend
for the pinacate beetles who may be found standing
on their heads in the sand on summer evenings in great
numbers. But with the ancient jests, go still more ancient proprieties. You would n't, for instance, if you
were obliged to change your dress in the long-room of
a pueblo, be noticed any more than a cat washing its
face or a pigeon preening itself among other pigeons.
And you never see an Indian, as you occasionally see
our males, thinking himself more of a man because of
his susceptibility to sex attraction. If he did, the
Koshare of his clan would find it out and correct him
with ribald laughter.

It is for this capacity for showing us the mind in the
making, that pueblo experience is priceless. If you can

slip inside the bubble of pueblo thinking, quiet, till it clears of newer matter, you see shaping on its iridescent surfaces, chiefly through the medium of dreams, vague large shapes of the life before we lived this life. But to come as close as that to the back of an Indian's mind, you must first realize that all this modern Freudian slough is no more the reality of dreams than the slime of a stagnant pond is the protoplasmic stuff from which Life made us.

All early cultures are introspective, having no record of the past beyond the memory of their old men, and the writing on the deep self, most easily accessible in states of trance and sleeping. That is why Indians attach so much importance to dreams. And if it were not the case that in dreams a deeper level of experience is uncovered, why should the dreaming take the form of animals charged with mystery and patronage and kinship, as it was in the beginning? As it must have been! Was not man among the animals soft-bodied, hornless, not clawed nor fanged, puny beside the buffalo, laggard to the deer, pupil to the coyote?

When you have seen the Buffalo Dance at Tesuque, under the low, pointed hills behind the pueblo, then you will realize that once, or perhaps still, in some subterranean chamber of the mind, man thought as a buffalo. How else, with horns, a scrap of hide and a handful of eagle feathers and a pebbled gourd, could he make you shiver with the power and mystery of animal being?

At Taos, the Deer Dance is dramatized in a story of a time of scarcity caused by the retreat of the deer into a crevice of the mountains. Great the hunger, and profound the device for luring them back within reach of the hunters. In the dead of winter, when the great-houses are like pinkish clouds, white-tipped with snow, and the dancers are placed according to the ancient ritual, the women, reverent and majestic, come out of the kiva. Moving subtly, with strange, mask-like impassivity, they approach the hiding-place of the Deer people. The sound of the *tombes* is like a hurried pulse, the gurgle of snow-water mingles with the singing; the deer stamp and whinny as they feel the earth-power of the medicine-women.

There is an unearthly mimicry in the painted bodies with deer-heads and antlers, and sticks for fore legs, in the shivers and prances, as they follow the waving prayer feathers of the women. They come, the horned ones; they fear and come! Behind them small shivering boys dance, as antelope, in the falling snow; the drums flutter like a pulse in the throat, as with increasing cries the quarry is drawn down the mountain. The great deer lead, tossing their antlers; the women beckon them on and hold off. . . . The power of singing draws them as the women shuffle ever more softly toward the hidden hunters, . . . they have come . . .

"*Heya, heya, hi—ya,*" sing the dancers. "*Ah a—h,*" shouts the bow-string. They are surrounded, they wheel, they huddle. The drums increase, the cries of the hunters, the groans of the wounded! What mimicry in the death-leap, in the dying shudders, in the limbs, relaxed as the boys and the old men carry away the game. We also have been both hunter and hunted!

The animal dances belong mostly to the cycle of winter ceremonies. For the summer clans, there is the business of making the crops grow, the rain come, and the harvest ripen. They are best known as the *tablita* dances, from the tall cloud-calling head-dresses worn by the women, prayer dances for Life-increasing. Distrust anybody who proposes to tell you all or very much about them. The most I have got myself is a mosaic, bright glints and fragments of multifarious experience; the charm of bodies moving from centers of self-realization, the charm of color and symbolic design so intuitively harmonized with place and purpose that without knowing anything you know all that is necessary for that spiritual participation which it is the business of the dance to evoke. You are caught up into rhythms, the pound of feet, the silver clash of conus shells, and the arm- and knee-rattles, . . . the finger-touch of *yeso,* white where a white woman places a black patch for the enhancing of fire dark eyes, . . . and oh, the long blowing hair!

When and why did we conclude that long hair is unsuited to manhood?

And the masked dancers, the metamorphic forces of nature, painted with the symbols of their beneficent metamorphoses, cloud and thunder and the roving rain, do they now lurk, still unmasked, at the bottom of all our thinking? In the Hopi villages, at the time of the New Fire, they tie prayer plumes to everything of which increase is wished, a prayer going with it. . . .

> Corn I wish much.
> Hard goods I wish much.
> Offspring I wish many.
> All things I wish much. . . .

Is not this a most American proceeding?

The recreational value of these things is inestimable. In primary art sources, in the unself-conscious translation of first-hand contacts with environment into rhythm of color and design, no other national heritage touches it. But the uniqueness of the Pueblo contribution lies in its being, sole among the peoples of the earth, a society in which there is no partition between cultural and economic interests. Here is the only organized group in which group-mindedness runs higher than the individual reach. This is the only society in the world in which culture exists as an expression of the whole, unaffected by schisms of class and caste, incapable of being rated in terms of power or property.

Behind this cultural wholeness, making it possible, is a psychic unity, so foreign to our sort of society that we have not yet a name for it. Sometimes in intervals of the Corn Dance, when the wind comes up and blurs the long, rhythmic line in the dust of its own dancing, or waiting outside the governor's house at Taos, where the sky over Pueblo Mountain holds on blue until long after midnight, while the council deliberates within and the young men are singing to the moon between the North House and the South, the word swims up and circles, flips its bright tail, and vanishes. It is a word woven out of the belief that there is god-stuff in man, and the sense of the flow of life continuously from the Right Hand to the Left Hand. But why seek for a word defining the state of the whole, who have not achieved wholeness? Somewhere at the edge of that experience the word lingers, intuitively felt, and still to be brought to consciousness by some happy observer if the Pueblos live long enough.

For this is what we have done with the heritage of our Ancients. We have laid them open to destruction at the hands of those elements in our own society who compensate their failure of spiritual power over our civilization, by imposing its drab insignia on the rich fabric of Amerindian culture, dimming it as the mud of a back-water tide dims the iridescence of sea-shell. Robbed of his lands, wounded in his respect for himself, all the most colorful expression of his spiritual experience filched from him in the name of education, the great Left Hand of modernism closes over the Pueblño. But if the Holders of the Paths laugh at all, it is at us they are laughing. For we cannot put our weight on the Left Hand of God and not, ourselves, go down with it.

# KATCHINAS OF THE ORCHARD

# KATCHINAS OF THE ORCHARD

AMONG many curious inquiries, I recall the reading of a pamphlet, by a learned gentleman, to prove that the Fruit of the Tree, which the Serpent plucked for Eve, was no apple, but a peach. Of the argument, nothing sticks in my mind except a statement which seemed to be soundly supported, that the peach came to us in almost its present perfection out of that region around the head of the Persian Gulf where the apple does not flourish, and the Garden was situate between four rivers. And how, in that case, would it get out of the Garden at all, unless Eve carried it, a keepsake, and thus began the still disappointed hope of women to have both the Fruit of the Tree and the innocence of Eden?

I trust there is no flaw in the argument of the pamphleteer, since it fits so happily with what I have to tell about the peach-tree's long journey from Andalusia, where it halted two thousand odd years behind the Pillars of Hercules, to the place where it went wild again and made itself at home in the fields of the Hopitu-shinumu, between the first and second mesas. Where else would it naturally come, if actually out of Eden, but to the only place left in the world where the great Snake is still a deity and has dances performed in his honor? If you are disposed to think of such things as an accident, recall that an accident is merely a happening of which nobody knows the complete explanation.

According to a telling of the Hopitu, the peach-tree showed itself, at such a time that it failed to connect with the coming of the Spaniards, a blooming wonder of the spring. This would have been, then, either after the visit of Don Pedro de Tovar, who explored the province of Tusayan under Coronado, or after Espejo, forty years later. So it must have been without design, other than the purpose lurking at the heart of the Katchina of the orchards, and we still wonder in what cook's bale or forgotten pocket of a Spanish caballero the Katchina hid the fruitful seed, since the legend bears no mark except that of having preceded the Franciscan foundation of 1629.

But there were brown gowns with Pedro de Tovar; that same Juan Padilla whose martyrdom heads the list of bleeding Kansas names, with Espejo also, and that nameless one who taught the Cruzados whom Oñate met, to tie crosses in their forelocks when they went to visit the whites, and were found as early as 1776 in possession of peach orchards along the Colorado River. Of the Franciscans, it is known that they had an affinity for gardens, and a habit of going about with pinches of seeds in their pockets. Also, they loved long rosaries clicking pleasantly below their knees, and in the country from which they came it is still possible to find prayer beads made of carved peach pits, not necessarily pierced so that the seed would be killed, but linked by small wires. Thus, by a dropped bead weighted with a sacred Name, the desire of the peach might have passed by a path as straight as, to this day, Hopi children are taught to speak, "straight as the sacred meal road over which the Divine Ones pass into the images of themselves." And what tenderer image of the divine metamorphoses of nature, I ask you, than a peach-tree in full, rosy bloom?

By 1629, the Hopitu, the peaceful ones, who even more than the Zuñi abhorred the use of force to gain an end, were nominally Christian, with a mission and *convento* at Awatobi, which in 1680 they destroyed along with the other revolting pueblos. Not without, however, a residue of "singing men," more than likely the choir trained in the Gregorian intervals of the mass, upon whom, as sorcerers and heretics from the Red Divinities the other mesa towns fell, in the year 1700, with destruction. That was in October, when the gold of the rabbit-brush was passing into invisible fluff, the terraced roofs covered with drying fruit, and the walls glowing with strings of chile crimson like thick streakings of blood. Softly as the evil owl, whose wing feathers are edged with silence, the enemy came creeping, when the children were asleep beside their mothers in the inner rooms, and the principal men busy with the hated rites, in the sunken ceremonial chambers. Suddenly, at dawn, the ladders were drawn up, and the thatch lighted above the trapped workers in things accursed.

Of what avail, then, the arts of the "singing men," when the enemy threw down into the flames the strings of crumpled red peppers, that they might perish the more miserably? Only the children were saved, and of the women, such as knew any good prayers, that is to say, rituals of the Ancients of the Hopitu-shinumu, and one man because "he knew the secret of making the peach grow." This would no doubt have been the mission gardener, who had been taught pruning and possibly the art of budding the superior varieties on wild seedling stock. So the peach was established in the life of the Hopitu in the hollow between the high earth-altar mesas, and season by season slipped thence and chose out places of its own.

The origin of the Hopi clans is as dubious as the way into that country is difficult. Cliff-dwellers from Cañon de Chelly,—incorrigibly stupid rendering of the Navajo; Tseghi "place among the cliffs," fragments from the broken Chaco towns and the Great-house cultures; and, latest comers, fleeing clans from the Rio Grande to whom the very smell of the Spanish-speaking had become an offense; Eagle clans, Bear clans, Snake and Antelope people, Blue Flute and Gray Flute, building mud and stone-shingle towns on the three-fingered mesa, between which the desert bites deep and slowly widening cañons.

Here still, from any one of the six villages, smoke trees of the other five may be seen wavering skyward while below them the gray-stemmed batamote—batavota, water-shield—covers and indicates the source of hidden waters at which a tap-rooted peach-tree may drink.

Only Oraibi, on the third mesa, hides itself at the far end of the chain of soft-sounding names, Walpi, Sichmovi, Shipaulovi, Shimopavi, Shongpovi, Mishongnovi.

From the mesa, one overlooks the basin of the Colorado Chiquito, toward the sacred peak of San Francisco Mountain, and south to the ghost-white Sierra Blanca. West and north toward the Grand Cañon, Tusayan is walled by the altar lift of the Painted Desert, glowing warm yellow and red as a ripe peach through a fruity bloom of desert haze, and by the noble desolation of Moencopie Wash. East, but north-reaching, begins the Cañon de Chelly, whose gray sandstone walls are gathered into great sweeps and folds of wind-sculpture work, among which the cliff-dwellers built their nested towns. It was up these narrow box-cañons and around the springs and wind-scooped water-holes that the peach-tree ran to spread its rosy cloud of bloom. Was it, then, homesick, all these centuries of trim orchard rows, for a dark-skinned desert tribe, mud huts, and the call of the five-notched flute?

Here, every year, the Navajo women come to the wild plantations and cover the bosses of the peach-colored limestone bluffs with drying fruit. When there is a full moon like a pearl in a peachblow sky, and the fruit about to set, they dance here, and mate, . . . as the peach remembers. In 1836, when Kit Carson came to drive the Navajo into the dread Round Wood, he found it necessary, as a measure of reduction, to destroy three hundred peach orchards in the Chinlee country.

As for the Snake, of which, if it really came out of Eden, the Katchina of the peach may have had a better opinion than any of us, at Walpi, around a mushroom-shaped rock, its dance is still celebrated at the time of the year when the peach begins to ripen on the bough, alternating yearly with the ceremony of the Blue Flute and the Gray Flute, that the Rains may walk the great wind roads. Then you see the young priests of the Antelope clan holding one hand with another against the natural impulse to defend their faces from the snakes writhing between their teeth. But when the

old men dance, with that perfect relaxation of the outer
self beyond which no mere animal can reach to do them
harm, a state that, in our culture, only a few mystics
reach, suddenly the story of the Snake and the Tree is
touched with mystery more
insightful than theologians,
have been able to give to it.
For this is the last place left
in the Western continent
where all the life of the people pulses with a sense of the
sacred spirit quality of all
things, so that the women de-
sirous of motherhood make
prayers to the Mother Rook,
and do not speak above a
whisper while their lovely
white-and-yellow pots are being fired, lest the spirit of the
*tinajas* be disturbed in its
communion with the flame,
and break.   Here also at the

festival of the Gods Going Home, the caged eagles are
killed ceremonially on the housetops, and all disease
and evil whatsoever goes out of the towns of the Hopitu-shinumu by the Eagle Road.  Always the Katchinas
come and go, the masked powers and spirits of the
earth, the air, the orchard, and the corn row, changing
and changeless.

If your fortune does not take you so far as to the wild-peach orchards, go out along the *acequia madre* at Santa Fé, or by old waterways, from the haciendas below Santa Cruz and Alcalde, till you find growing of itself a red-stemmed, briery rose, small-leafed and sturdy, such as you may be happy enough to remember opening its pointed, clear yellow buds in New England gardens, along with the white mock-orange, about Decoration Day. It does not, however, come, where you find it, from New England, but, by a more devious route, from Cadiz and the gardens of the Alhambra, where it was known since Roman times as the Persian rose. But whether, like the peach, it too originated in the Eastern cradle of civilization, I am not certain, since it is also reported wild along the Danube and in Austrian valleys, and is perhaps the mother of all yellow roses.

As far back as I can find garden lore among the Spanish-speaking towns of New Mexico, I find its pale, sparsely petaled moons unclosing, but no legend, even, of its coming, so that whether it was brought purposely, or by accident of a seed hidden in the soil around the roots of vine and orchard stock, it must have come the long sea journey to the ports of Mexico and thence by land to the walled gardens of New Spain. The place of its first going wild, I guess to be the river borders near Chimayo, as you go toward the Sanctuario, past the little hill thick planted with "estancias" where the dead have been let down from friendly shoulders, on their way to their final place in consecrated ground.  You will know it as a neighborhood of purer Castilian strains, by the ornate Spanish forms of the crosses, though I forget whether the footpath to the rose thickets turns to the left or the right, or on which of the river banks.  Such is the effect of unpremeditated beauty that it stuns the recollection for a little space around, in order that it may exist in the soul of the beholder, sole and incomparable.

Down along the Rio Grande, in the series of fertile flood plains of which El Paso is the focus, and in the reëstablished Great-house country, the red geranium flourishes in rubbish-heaps, though not as it does in the deep window-seats of almost every *casita* of the Spanish-speaking.  Out of tin cans and broken *tinajas,* glow, toward the end of winter, in the meanest of the adobe huts, bright windowfuls of generously flowering geraniums and fuchsias.  Fuchsias of this red-and-purple ear-drop pattern grow thick about old wells in Spain, and in the gardens of the Alhambra, back and back to the time when Roman maidens strung them under their dark locks for jewels.  Geraniums have rather lately come out of Africa.  Both of them travel by slips and cuttings, so that what holds your attention in almost any New Mexican window is more than likely branch of the branch of the branch that came across seas and up by the old Chihuahua trail and over the Jornada del Muerto, from the home land of the Spanish-speaking, the symbol of some warm, secret aspiration lurking still in the blood of their far-called descendants.

In some such fashion came many herbs of healing, *yerba santa, contra yerba,* and the horehound which may be found widely escaped from mission gardens.

The Franciscans, however, are hardly to be credited with the occasional tall plant of marihuana, the dream-provoking hashish, a leaf of which mixed with the tobacco of a cigarette is responsible for so many border outrages.

Lately, there has slipped across the border, *guayule,* a low weed, at a casual glance resembling a bush of lavender, with a rubber-yielding sap that science has undertaken to increase a hundredfold. Did it come, then, looking for the hands that could teach it to run as automobile tires on the highways of the world? I am not by any means convinced that under all the multitudinous devices of barb and wing and burr, by which the plant world make use of the movement of animals for its distribution, it does not sometimes touch the deep-seated intelligence which teaches it also how to make use of man. For I am deeply intrigued with the faith of the Tewas that the universe, Every-thing-that-Is, is alive to itself, and one in itself, as Opa the Universe Man. There is no good reason why a plant may not be, in its own degree, aware of man, as

"SOMEWHERE IN THEIR WANDERINGS THEY FOUND A
FULL-EARED GRASS"

279

foot is aware of hand. There are, at any rate, men who have a special power of "in-knowing" the virtues and habits of plants, who in our kind of society become botanists or horticulturists or plain gardeners and fruit-growers, as in the society of the Hopitu and the Tewas they became herbalists and shamans. Is it so unlikely, then, that there should be plants having a special affinity for man, coming along with him the road that he has traveled, since, seeking to discover what had become of the breath of the first man that died, he discovered a hole in his dark home, lowest of the Four Wombs of the World, which led him upward toward the light?

Was there not equal evolution of man and the tufted grass called teosinte, "grass of the gods," as one became the author of ordered society and the other six-colored corn?

Opinion inclines to make this wild grass, still found growing in the central highlands of Old Mexico, the mother of the foodful ears on which our material welfare founds itself. For corn, as we know it, is a Lady. It has lost the power to maintain itself without the careful attention of man; cannot go wild again, can only flow in his hands as the type of sheltered woman flows and shapes to his desires. This, our Ancients discovered so long ago that reverence is paid to its essential energy as the Corn Mother, and its many-colored varieties figure in the drama of the corn as the Six Corn Maidens. All of which became fixed in their usage so anciently that the other parent of the maize, mixing with the slender, grass-leaved teosinte, has been lost both to tradition and to science.    So long ago it was, that there has been time for corn to fossilize along with the fossil remains of man, in the shape of short, roundish, pointed grain, close-packed ears, as the oldest cereal in the world.

It must have been in a summer flood basin, between the mountains, that our Ancients found the grass of the gods.    Huge, heavy-branched tree cactus kept it company, and the tall agave, and the sahuaro, uprooted, curving, with the force of its own stored waters, to the sun again.    By the wet borders, its leaves turned reddish, as you see them sometimes remembering in the lush river-bottoms of the middle West; as also the minute scale at the base of the grain, grows into a distinct infolding sheath.    As it came up beside their huts from chance droppings of the seed, the corn instructed men in all its indispensable ways: how with too much water it grew leafy and sparsely eared; how in a dry season it must have the soil light and deep above it; how it clung in clusters against the uprooting summer flood; what times and seasons it had for its own.    When, and by what natural plant affinities or what skill of man it added to itself the bean to climb its mounting stalk, the squash to run between the stalk clusters and shade the ground,—incomparable food combination,—there is not even a tradition.

In the Rio Grande country there is a scarlet morning-glory, about a thumb's breadth across, twining so delicately that, until in the dew-beam of morning you catch its bright blossoming, between the leaf blades, it would never be suspected, yet by all counting it must have been companion to the corn these two thousand years. So also with the blue butterflies and the yellow leaf-bird hopping in and out. But long before it came into our Southwest, the corn had established itself as the friend and the familiar of man. With what patience, equaled not even by the dog, it waited upon the tribes until they learned to defend it from the cut-worm and the crow! With what subtle sympathies men adjusted the grass of the gods to his own conditions of cold and altitude, short seasons and long, clay bottoms and caking sand! How he sang and danced to it until the power of in-knowing awaked in him to the possibilities of seed-saving and hybridization; by what reciprocal intention did it teach him to make pots for cooking, mills for grinding and bins for storage! You can no more separate the American from the influence of the corn, than from the influence of his own wife. No, not even the white American, who, thanklessly resting his own achievement on this unacknowledged foundation, tramples out the giver.

If ever I make Black Medicine for my own tribe, it will be for their forgetting of the long journey corn and the red man came together in order to secure to us the quick mastery of the American continent, for which we pridefully plume only ourselves.  But not quite—oh, never quite without some ironic back thrust of the Red Gods!  For, throughout the world, is not Corn-fed Pride the symbol of certain crass and self-praising qualities of the American people?

It goes on still and forever, this silent working together of man and the grass of the field.  Guayule, moving to make rubber as plentiful as it is indispensable to our culture, sotol with its fiber, osha with its healing, the light, springy wood of the sahuaro and the Joshua-tree, *hohoba, sangre de drago,* the enduring dye and incomparable honey pasture of the Rocky Mountain bee-weed.  Are they not all *teosinte*—god-given?  Go heedfully where you go, then, along the trail borders.  Break no bough needlessly, and uproot no seeming weed.  Who knows which of them awaits on the tardy opportunity which your indifference delays, of inestimable coöperation?

# MAKING THE SUN NOISE

# MAKING THE SUN NOISE

NOW and again, when the gray sea wool pads the streets of New York against the city's bludgeoning noises, suddenly the sea pack is pierced by eager, almost melodious whistles, that have, for me, a magical association. At the sound, the fog is streaked with tree boles disappearing upward in the dark of feathery boughs, under which the great bull elk are pealing. They will go on all day, about the time of the October running, like the steam-tugs whistling to each other in East River, when the clouds are low and no one disturbs them, love-call and challenge, high and silvery.

Or, toward morning, when sleep lightens a little under the lifting weight of darkness, the squeal of a steam-cock will turn mellow in the moonlight, and I think that the racoons have come back to my melon patch. Along the edge of sleep, I can hear them quite distinctly, quarreling over the rinds I left for them under the window of my wickiup. A whole family would come, parents and three little ones, and one or two others that I supposed might be the young of last year. Half an hour earlier, I heard them up the cañada, calling softly to the rendezvous, but when they arrived, how still they could be, and how merry! chasing and tagging one another in the intervals in which their elders, reaching far into the hollowed rind, would scoop out a handful of juicy pulp for each in turn. Occasionally one would be bunted quite over. Then the soft whimpers and giggles, and the admonitory squeaks! In the morning nothing left but a rind scooped paper thin; not a seed nor a dropped morsel on the clean sand, patted over as with the prints of a child's slender hand.

The last time I saw marks like that was in the riverbottom below San Juan pueblo, while we waited for the dancers of the Swift-coming Rain to come out of the kiva. But the only place in New York that I have the feeling that goes with night-seeking food and frolic, is down at the bottom of Manhattan Island. There, the interlacing ties and pillars of the "El" make a streaked, woodsy shadow in the summer moonlight. Just ahead of me, once, I saw a quite ordinary Eastside young man, as he struck across it, fall unconsciously into the bearing of night walkers, assimilating themselves to the checkered forest path. Between his shoulders, *I* knew, by the way he carried them, the creepy, prideful thrill left over from the time when you had not to see or hear your enemy to know that he was about.

It is only when they come back to you stripped to

the midrib by recollection, that you realize that hunting experiences, whether they are rationalized as an interest in nature or in science, are valued for the hunting thrill, access to older and older layers of experience in which there was no time but Now, when we were incapable of sin and our mistakes were never thrown up to us.  Then we still knew the beast for our brother, not forgetting that we once spoke with him after the animal kind, and yet hunted him, as in the endless transmutations of nature it was permitted that Life should assume the deer to be food for us.  Therefore since the best thing we get out of any study of animal life is the feel of it, expect nothing from me that could be done better for you by the zoölogist.  What I would do, if I could, would be to stir you to saving what is left of our wild life, by which richly we may renew ourselves in the animal experience, beginning as among our Ancients hunting begins, with a prayer, while to killing ensues the ritualistic pacification of Life, fleeing from the stiffening form.  "O our brothers of the wilderness, for our necessities we are about to kill you.  We hope that you will understand, and that there may be peace between your spirit and our spirit!"

This was said to the buffalo when, as Miera y Pacheco found them, they ranged as far south as Saydegil, or, as Zebulon Pike reported, along the head waters of the Rio Grande.  For the great bear there was not only propitiatory prayer, but sacrifice. Think how the first man, when he had first separated a buffalo from his breath, must have feared him, roaming the viewless fields of air, as to this day the *chiffonetti* sees him in the White Buffalo Dance at the Rio Grande pueblos, motionless on all the hills, heads lowered to the sacred earth medicine. For to the Indian the animals are nearer to gods than men, being more mysterious, and in that time which is accessible to us now only in dreams, had speech with them. There was a man at Halona told me how his father's father and two others penned an old bull in a corner somewhere about the Sierra Zuñi, and in the last, desperate, eye-to-eye moment, as they made propitiatory smoke before the killing stroke, the old bull spoke to them.

"I am old," he said, "and not much good to you. Let me live out my life, and when you are in need of help, I will befriend you."

 Standing aside while the buffalo chief trotted to safety, the three hunters had deep, breath-taking communion with the magic might of buffalo. At that time to have good hunting medicine was as much a man's business as to learn how to plant an arrow completely out of sight, end to end in the quarry.

It is difficult to those who see animals only in the zoo, to get back to that primitive sense of their mysteriousness, but there is a singular feeling of presence that persists in places where they were once most at home.

Often on the vast, pale stretches above the Mogollon Rim, where the country rock is so thinly surfaced that nothing grows but this "hardtack" of gallita grass, you can see its surfaces move in a racing pattern, far off, under the feet of the ghostly bands of pronghorns, of which there are still some fragmentary living herds to be found in the feeding-grounds protected by forest reservations. Just to see a pronghorn, you would know him for a frequenter of the dry-grass country, by the dark bridle about the face and throat, which betrays his kinship to the goat, so much creature of a particular environment that still old-timers describe any open, self-colored grass and cholla region as "antelope country," though there was never the flash of a white rump signaling the flight of scattered bands across its haunted spaces. Pronghorn does will even drop their young in the tall grass in preference to other cover, where only the swooping eagle finds them, for the fawns are scentless, and, so, comparatively safe from prowlers. But if they hear, far down the wind, the sharp, barking *kau! kau!* of the mothers, they cower like young quail. For the pronghorn will make a fighting stand against the eagle, against even the gray lobos of the cattle country.

The pronghorns have disappeared faster than the deer because of the very qualities that should have made us keep them, their gentleness, their childlike, bright fixity of curiosity, their capacity for enlivening the great empty *abras* with their swift, scudding beauty of flight. The deer linger, not being grass-lovers, and able to hide themselves in the tall chaparral.

Over on Kaibab, north of the Grand Cañon, are the largest herds of blacktail left anywhere in the world. During the day, they lie close at the heads of ravines or in the bottoms of narrow cañons, or under cedar clumps in pockets of the broken, earth-altar steps of the mesas. Better, they love the ledge in the warm sun, with a precipice below and a rounded slope above, and low wind-breaks of the pine, whose needles muffle their tread as they steal to the feeding-grounds along the forest borders. But the still hunter must not trust too much to the soft footage, for the great mule ears of the blacktail are as sensitive as the aërial to vibrations ever so slightly differentiated from the forest sounds. Even though you come in time to see the grass blades rising, warm where he has lain, you will not hear him go, nor see the gray shape slide past gray rocks, nor the stir of branched antlers in the antlered brush.

On Kaibab, where they have not been hunted much, bands of blacktail can be found in the dark of the moon, feeding late into foggy mornings, or early evening, around the edges of minute flowery meadows, where the buck-brush and the scrub oaks venture out from under the pines.   Once bedded, however, they are difficult to arouse before feeding-time, though they can be occasionally discovered, making restless little noises toward the end of the afternoon.   If they range anywhere in the vicinity of planted fields, they are likely to be found toward morning, when the crasser appetite is appeased, cropping at the ripening side of grapes, just one selective bite, ruining the bunch, or at apples reddening on the lowest bough.   Startled at such mischief, they go bounding prodigiously on all four feet at once, sure-footed as a mountain sheep, and wary as an antelope.

West of Kanab and on, west and south, to the California mountains, especially around San Jacinto and San Bernardino, it is still possible, if you know where to look, to see the blacktail feeding by moonlight on the rich browse; light-stepping; curved antlers carried on a massive neck and small, graceful head; the steel-tendoned legs ready, at the slightest shift of the great ears which give it the common name of mule-deer, to go bounding up the rocky stairs into the tall coverts of ceanothus, rippling with the light under side of leaves in the wind, like the wind on the sea. But, even in such places, you must have Good Medicine to see deer at night and at the same time not expose yourself to the Uinipin, haunting the high country north and west of the great bend of the Colorado.   All Paiutes, and I think all Utes also, fear the Uinipin, so that in

night camps you can hear them, waking, begin to sing
crooningly, one, and then another waked by him and
joining in, a charm song, I suppose, until the fear
that walks in darkness is sung away.

The blacktail have a tendency to collect in vast herds
about the turn of the seasons, and to migrate, so that
the oldest ways about the country north of Mogollon
are likely to be deer traces, down along the Chama,
down from the Chaco to strike the Jemez River and so
to the *plan del Rio Grande.* Many of the Navajo
trails, probably the crossing of the Grand Cañon
known as El Vado de los Padres, are blacktail routes
to the favored grazing-grounds, already worn white
when our Ancients found them.

The whitetail deer, carrying that appendage aloft in
flight, like a banner, was never so plentiful in the arid
regions, but may be found still in the White Mountain
Apache country, and in the cane-brake along the Colorado delta. Here, it goes by long, springy bounds,
three or four in clusters separated by one high and
curved like the flight of a bird. I have not heard men
who hunt it, speak of the whitetail deer with such regard for the sportsmanly occasion it affords, as they
speak of the crafty blacktail. Yet in the delta flats it
is crafty enough, slinking and slinking, making a
subtle pattern of its tracks over the crust, through
which at any moment the hunter's own weight may let
him down into the illimitable mire of new-made river-
bottoms.

Whitetail are at all times deer of the cienagas and the brush lands, and in forest country tend to keep the easy habit of the cane-brake, as though they still wore the covert of the brush.  Once I saw an old whitetail buck lounging through the wood, moving softly in the shadow and automatically falling asleep for a moment or two in every warm patch of sun.  But for seeing things like that, you have either to have Good Medicine, or much training in "deer-walking," feeling the ground under your foot before letting it bear your weight, and sustaining the push of the covert with such delicate measure that never a bough flies back nor twig scrapes with betraying noises.  There is also a deer song of the Navajo, having in its rhythm something of the delicate-stepping, noble grace of all deer, and the respect for them engendered by the myths of how the great Deer-Soul first assumed this form for the feeding of man, his children:

> From the Black Mountain
>   Comes the deer to my singing. . . .
> Quarry mine, blessed am I
> In the luck of the chase
>   Comes the deer to my singing.

No Indian, hunting, ever looks for particular deer, featuring themselves in the landscape, but low on the ground for deer "sign."  In a restricted, rough mountain region in northwestern New Mexico and northeastern Arizona, he still looks for wapiti.  This round-horned elk is the deer for stateliness, for trophies and hunts royal. Here still, when the dark hillsides are patterned gold by the aspens, the great bulls may be heard challenging, thick-necked, swaggering as they gather their harems, especially threatening to the spike bulls hanging on the outskirts of the band. Such wished-for sights are rather to be heard of than witnessed, though there are old men among the Jicarilla Apache who remember the elk dancing at the licks. In the days of our Ancients, wapiti went through this country in great bands, black for numbers, and had their regular traces to the salt licks, wide as country roads. All animal trails can be distinguished from man trails by their fashion of running clear and well defined for considerable intervals, and then abruptly vanishing.

Wherever there are deer, there is also mokiách, the puma, hunting-god of the Keres. On the potreros of the Rio Grande, between the Rito de los Frijoles and the cañada of Cochití, there are still shrines to him, crouching figures carved in the country rock, still visited with oblations. At the hunting-dances, sometimes, you can also hear the "spirit roar" that frightens the quarry out of its power of fleeing. But if you hear the reaching cry of mokiách himself, at night on the potreros,—not the high, whining love-call, but the hunting-cry, when Lord Puma lifts himself from the broken-backed quarry, to "make the sun noise,"—you will hear just at the end of it, a curious throaty catch,

*Ai . . . i . . . i . ha!* which is the beginning of all laughter. For who laughs, except when the occasion is translated, in some deep self of himself, into a flash of triumph? So the horse laughed, *Ha, ha!* amid the trumpets; and no other animal that I know except kin and clan of the puma. The dog, having come to his estate through servility, never laughs, though I have known him capable of joyous, sycophantic yelps on being noticed; also sheep-dogs, on being praised, make distinct facial motions that, with their masters, pass for smiles.

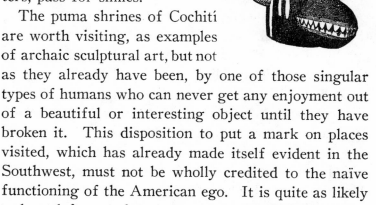

The puma shrines of Cochití are worth visiting, as examples of archaic sculptural art, but not as they already have been, by one of those singular types of humans who can never get any enjoyment out of a beautiful or interesting object until they have broken it. This disposition to put a mark on places visited, which has already made itself evident in the Southwest, must not be wholly credited to the naïve functioning of the American ego. It is quite as likely to be a left-over from puma nature within us, since Mokiách, the lord Puma himself, when he has killed and eaten, covers his kill and marks it. Then woe be to the beast that eats of it!

So he marks his favorite lounging-tree, choicely selected, where the leafage is a screen between him and the observer, but not between him and the sun. The great bear, too, makes long, drawing scrapes across the tree boles, sharpening his claws perhaps, but also reaching high, resenting, if one can believe the literary interpreters of bears, and taking as a challenge, any mark put higher. Now and then, from seldom-visited mountains, the "sign" of grizzly bear is reported. In the Navajo and Ute country, one is occasionally killed, always with propitiatory rites to mitigate the sacrilege of such taking off, which even the great bear whose den is corona in the northern heavens, out of which he annually issues to ramp across the sky, might resent. In the spring, when the first thunder is heard, they say at Zuñi, "Ah, ha! the great bear is stretching out his first leg." By mid-April he fills the Middle Heaven with his rumbling.

Of little black bears, there are enough to make it a not too unusual occurrence, in remote school districts, for teachers to write and say that the children on the way home yesterday saw a bear, and will not be at school again until something has been done about it. Along toward October, black bears come down from the summer ranges to the piedmont, to fatten on the piñon-nuts, literally tearing a tree to pieces to get at the globose, friable cones. Large bears will also earn the enmity of cattle-owners, carrying off calves and young colts. Juan Alguacil told me that when he was

goat-herding somewhere in the neighborhood of Inscription Rock, a bear walked out of the piñon scrub,
cuffed two of his goats to death, quite gently, and
dragged them off, together, Juan holding back his
dogs with one hand and crossing himself with the
other, thankful that it was goats only that were
wanted.

No bear, so far as I know, has had a price set upon
his head, as has that limping lobo in the Kaibab country; for there are still true wolves hereabout, though,
from the paucity of wolf myths in Pueblo lore, I suspect them as late comers, drawn there since colts and
young heifers came into the country with Oñate.
Wolves, too, are markers of their ranges, for the flesh-
eaters have their special territories, of which possession is the law, and infringements punishable with
death. The scope of such range is usually restricted
to the distance competently traveled on a full stomach,
and covers at least one
drinking-place. The lobos
have smelling-posts, which
they visit to pick up the
latest news; though *what*
that news may be, has not
yet been translated.

These are the great
beasts which, though they
cost us something in beef

and grass, we must afford to keep for the need, the inestimable need of children to have a portion of the world not wholly made up of asphalt and radio and flat shadows on a screen. What measure, after all, shall we have of man, when all the great beasts are gone, and all the early men? Already we are disposed to draw from sick dregs of the neuropathic clinic our concept of Man Beginning; but man, as I find him at the Back of Beyond of our Ancients, had something in him of the quality with which we endow the deific concept, knew what the buffalo thought in his heart, and how to find his mate as the bird finds it. I knew a man, once, who had a tamed she bear, that he used to take with him, camping in the mountains, chaining her comfortably to a tree at night. And always, in the season, the mate duly visited her, once, he told me, having back-tracked the buck bear to the point where his traces began to show intention, from beyond the mountain crest, twenty miles away. I know of no fallacy which the West blows away more completely than that one which fears to find man separated from God because proved a brother to the beast.

Of all the smaller stock of bobcats, lynxes, foxes, racoons, there is no immediate danger of extinction. There are too many places in the Southwest where man will never be able to establish himself, to fear its becoming man-infested to an injurious degree. Though the beaver in the mountain go too fast, being insufficiently protected by our appreciation, and having coats that ladies still covet.   The presence of the lesser beasties, adds a puckish charm, the faun charm, to the less-frequented wilds, even when it involves a certain amount of human discretion.   Last Moon of Yellow Flowers, lingering on Tummomoc to note the rise or quiescence of growing smells after the sun goes down, there drifted across the field of our headlight, a furry, fairy shape, its foot-high banner glistening, Christmas white, utterly lovely and unfamiliar of its kind, which was scarcely noted until a glimpse of short, soot-black legs moving it about, and a sooty nose directing it, warned us to back softly, and hope it had business of its own from which it might not be easily distracted.

The arid stretches have their own lovers, of which the most mysterious is the kangaroo-rat, about which everything has been written except why he prefers to have his house under the inedible creosote bush; where he drinks, if ever; and where and by what lonely moonlit way he finds his mate, never domiciled in his own roomy galleries.

The pine woods have Neatoma the "pack-rat," around whom folklore of our own gathers.   Yearly, in the White Mountain country, the Apaches ship car-loads of pine nuts thieved largely from the curious, rubbishy heaps of the pack-rat, for the building of which he will thieve as many of man's possessions as can be dragged to it, old boots, tin cans, whatever glitters or piles up conveniently. The man in that country who cannot tell you a good pack-rat story is no native, but a tenderfoot. For no man has ever really entered into the heart of any country until he has adopted or made up myths about its familiar objects.

In beginning with the pack-rat, making itself a friendly nuisance about his shack, man is following an older procedure than he knows. Primitive man notices as a child notices, a pictured world upon a flat horizon. Whatever detaches itself, pricks itself first upon his attention; the great beasts he fears or feeds upon, the tree from which he takes his bow, though not necessarily the tree that shades his house. What interests him makes his world. Every tribe of the southwest has a name for the soot-black beetle scurrying before his foot, and endows him with a share in tribal myth, all out of proportion to his importance in the natural scene. It was little Ishits, who was entrusted with the bag of stars when the tribes came up from the Four Womb Worlds through a hole in the ground, but instead of placing them regularly about, where they would do the most good, Ishits allowed them to escape skyward like a swarm of flies. It is for this reason, as the hour approaches when the stars come out to mock him with their disorder, that little Ishits may be found shamefacedly sticking up his hinder parts as he hides his head in the sand. And with what agony, when there is a shooting star, he must hear the children shouting derisively his name!

Once you understand this principle of detachment, as distinguishing the things that first, beyond his needs, pricked themselves on man's attention, you begin to observe it still at work in us.  It is, indeed, a perilous adventure to begin naming the world of created things, if at the same time you are obliged to keep them in relation to the whole.  But the thing that of its own motion severs us from that responsibility—do we not take to it with glad relapse into infantile relief? Especially little black-beetle phrases scurrying across the front of things ("Yes, we have no bananas!"), owing their power of acceptance to their having strictly nothing to do with anything else.

Thus the coyote detached itself from the wolf kind, to follow the better hunter, and feed on the leavings of his kill.  Any day in this country you may see him trotting out of gun-range, of which he probably has a more accurate notion than you have; any night, hear him mourning his lost wolfhood or deriding his superior, man, as drunken men in their cups alternately bemoan and mock their condition.  Of myths about the coyote, there are nine times as many as about the lordly buffalo whom men followed.  He is the cat'spaw, the Charley Chaplin of pueblo folklore, the biter bitten, the butt of utterly primitive jokes such as I suspect may actually have been played in the time when there was no wall between the thinking of man and the other animals other than the insurmountable wall between the dull and the clever.

Animals more powerful than man, and all of them more mysterious, were thought of as being nearer to the gods than men. They were prayed to and propitiated as intercessors. In their sportsmanly code it is a crime to take the quarry without allowing it every opportunity to escape by its natural powers, and in most tribes boys are not permitted the use of the bow until they have run down small game and taken it with their hands.

The notice of birds by the aboriginal mind travels a curiously intricate path, taking value from association with the mysterious formless powers, as the eagle with the Thunder, twin dwellers of the upper air.

Thus eagles' plumes and bluebirds' feathers become emblems of skyey approval. Eagle down is the sign of man's secret godward aspiration, and the milky way a drift of snowy feathers where the lesser gods make prayer plumes for the elder. By association with the water-holes where they resort to feed fat on the small rodents coming to drink, snakes become water symbols, and the plumed serpent, wriggling like the lightning against the curtain of the dark cloud, the patron of the Water-Sources. There are, however, not nearly so many thick rattlers at the water-holes to-day as when our Ancients named them guar-

dians of the springs.   Often the snake-dancers of
Hopi have to make up the kiva's quota with harmless
gopher-snakes, and striped frequenters of the melon
fields.

I am Indian enough, I hope, not to miss the birds
that are place marks; shrill, chittering Texas night-
hawks above the water holes, jewel-green humming-
birds that haunt the hundred-belled yucca bocata.
Also Indian enough to leave nameless and unnoticed a
hundred singers, to observe the elf owl in the sahuaro,
drawing its spread wing like a lady's fan, for protective cover before topaz glittering eyes. . . . Witch,
O witch . . .!

> With this raven's plume,
> With this owl's feather
> I will make Black Prayers for her
> Who takes my man from me. . . .
> With this owl's plume
> With this raven's feather!

Now and then you find a horned lark, which, like
the lark that Shelley heard, rises as it sings, treasured
in a cage at the pueblo, for which the children gather
grasshoppers, threading them on grass stems.   But
for the most part it is the literary interest which is
served by birds, man making them to stand for his
thought in upper airy reaches of his mind, long before
he had any other use for those he could not use for
food.   So because the track of the road-runner's feet
turns two ways, he ties the shining feathers on the

cradle board to confuse the evil spirits coming to trouble the child's mind, as the four-toed sign of the cross protects from harm.

Anybody who cared for birds for their own sake, however, would find all that his liking needs in the crested ranges of the Mogollon Rim, which is the farthest north for tropic birds, and farthest south for birds of the arctic in their yearly migrations. In the Chiricahuas there is a thick-billed parrot with splashes of poppy red upon his wings, and little green macaws, whose feathers make the knot like a sprouting corn hill, tied in the dark locks of the corn-dancers, talking to themselves among the yellow pines. Or in the Alpine island tops of sacred mountains with the whistling marmot and the rabbit-eared coney, one discovers the snowy ptarmigan turning rock-moss color to protect its rock-speckled eggs, lacking all other cover between them and the sky. Between seasons, great fleets of water-fowl sail the wind rivers above the Colorado draw, or gather along the estuary, waiting for the ebb to uncover springs of sweet water among the reedy dunes, and pelicans perform their stately dance along the medanos, clotted with satin shiny clumps of *rosas San Juan*. Once the sandhill crane could be heard whooping by unfrequented watercourses, but I doubt you will hear that bugling call anywhere now except among the ghost-invoking cries of the Navajo fire-dancers, crying "Come, Come,

Come!" Thus I might name a hundred species from the broad-tailed humming-birds, droning like bees about the holy peaks of San Francisco Mountains, to the hermit thrush singing at evening on steep, dark-forested slopes the sacrament of desire, only to find that for you, as for our Ancients, and Keats and Shelley, birds serve best when they serve as symbols for free roving, skyey thought.

All down the spurs of the Rockies, into Sonora, ranges the *cimarron,* the wild sheep, the furthest-drawn of all wild life that comes to its journey's end here, having come, if books are to be believed, from the Altai Mountains of central Asia, delicate-footed, smoky rock-gray, and horned as spirits of the ancient rocks should be. These are best to be seen about the timber line and above it, or occasionally heard on sunny afternoons as a faint *tap-tapping* of some old ram, lightening his horns by battening them against the mountain wall. So free, so much the familiar of the hoary, holy peaks they are, that one wonders how it is the fancy of the myth-makers passed them over, and made the horse stand next to the eagle in imagery.

That means horse stories also, for it was here, at the end of the Spanish journey, that the horse began to go wild, probably even in Coronado's time, and the great caballadas which the range men brought in for the annual *conducta,* became the ramudas of the later cow-punchers.

The medicine of these "long-tailed elk" belongs first to the Navajo, who sees the day rising as a turquoise-colored stallion "making the sun noise" as he comes from the sacred east.

The Turquoise Horse of Johano-ai. . . .

> There, on precious hides outspread, standeth he,
> Dust of glittering grains, there spurneth he,
> How joyous his neigh!

Mine to me, also, is the medicine of the turquoise Horse.

We had gone into the Ute country, but west of it, somewhere about opposite the Land of Standing Rocks, and camped there on a high sandstone boss, overlooking a great open bolson hollowing toward one of those flat flood plains called Dancing-places of the Sun, and my bed was so placed that I could see, at the first blue gleam of the Turquoise Horse in the east, the wild stallions lead out their mares to drink at the cloud pools. Here the table-lands run high, and an eddy of the wind river, pushed out by the immense spurs of the Colorado Front, brings great caballadas of gray-backed clouds stooping to the headlands. Below the island buttes, they doze or sway slightly, like moored boats in a fairway, until with the first, false dawn they move stealthily back into the wind stream, leaving behind them, where they rested, in pits and hollows of the surface rock, a glimmering residue,

leaden at first, winking silver as the sun pierces the
rifts of the continental wall.   If I could find me a
painter to paint me that! the buttes, earth shadowed,
the long gleams of the shafted light, and the wild
horses, mane and tail tossed by the young wind, coming
to the cloud pools to drink.

Once a band of mares came alone, sniffed, and
wheeled about the cupped granite bosses of the lower
mesa, refusing the glimmering drink with impatient,
reproachful whinnies and flickings of long tails.
Suddenly out of the shadow raced their stallion,
dolphin-colored, with a dappled neck; sniffed once, and
turning, neighed and shouldered them into a huddled
silence, away from what, from my camp, I supposed
must be a tainted drink.   Round the pitted rocks with
their thin glimmer of water, the stallion wheeled and
raced, with loud, screaming neighs.   Suddenly, up
came the sun, as it does in that country, with the effect
of booming sound, and a sensible burst of warmth.
Back to the pools the mares came trooping, not drinking at first, but waiting as farm horses at a watering-
trough, when, with delicate, tentative sniffs, one and
another muzzle went down. . . . Not till I lifted the
thin ice rim from the camp water-pail did I realize
that they had been waiting for the ice that forms
over the cloud pools in the dead end of the night, to
melt.   So then, and this could not have been the first
time that he had done it, the patriarch stallion had

called the sun to that office. And what would the sun be to him but a larger stallion ranging the blue field of the skies, brought forth by his prayer from behind the fencing mountains?

This is Good Medicine. They that make the sun noise shall not fail of the sun's full recompense.

# THE SAINTS IN NEW MEXICO

# THE SAINTS IN NEW MEXICO

B ROTHER David, in the *convento* fronting the
Old Santa Fé Trail just before it takes the
last turn that brings it to La Fonda, is of the opinion
that the saints had it in mind to make themselves at
home in New Mexico as long ago as 1287, when saints
were made as fast as millionaires in war-time. That
was at Florence, when the Franciscan Order was
young, filled with the Wine of the Spirit, the art of
painting reawakening under the hand of Giovanni
Cimabue. To one of the Brown-gowns, Cimabue
gave two paintings of the Annunciation, which in due
process came to hang in the oldest American church
of San Miguel, across the river from *La Villa Real
de la Santa Fé de San Francisco.* This was the district known as the barrio of Analco, which Oñate
built for the Tlascalans who came with him as en-
listed men and camp helpers, up from Old Mexico.
Any Corpus Christi Day you may recognize typical
Aztec heads, bared to the Host, by the slightly nar-
rowed foreheads and the great height above the ears
and the thatch of soot-black, upstanding hair.

As to the authenticity of the pictures, I am no
judge of such matters, though, like Brother David, a

good believer. They are, at any rate, of the early Florentine period, and hang on either side of the altar at San Miguel, in which company may also be found the holy archangel Michael, patron of the foundation, copy of an original by Raphael, and a copy of Da Vinci's "Ecce Homo." One of the Cimabues, if you accept Brother David's identification, has holes in it, souvenir of one of the various rebellions of *los Indios* against the invading religious.

For further evidence of what the saints were thinking in their hearts long before they put it into the heart of Christopher Columbus to break a sea trail toward the west, there hangs also, at San Miguel, the most mellow and musically toned bell in the world, which is thought to have been made in Spain in 1336, out of the gold and silver ornaments vowed by a forgotten Christian city to San José for help afforded in one of their victorious encounters with the Moors. It is supposed to have been brought to New Mexico by a scion of that Nicholas Ortiz called Niño Ladron de Guevara, because of a city he stole from the Moors, for his king. Ortiz came to New Mexico with De Vargas to the reconquest, in 1692, and if you ask what he would be doing with a seven-hundred-and-eighty-pound bell in his baggage, on a military expedition into a revolting province a month's journey from anywhere, with virtually no roads and only wooden-wheeled ox-carts to travel on them, I would answer that that is precisely the sort of baggage that one of our old American families of New Mexico would think indispensable to bring.    Especially if he were of the sort to whom stealing cities was all in the days' work.    Surely the saints, who choose by the inner quality, would have had none but those who were already good Americans in their hearts.

In one of these same solid-wheeled carretas rode Our Lady, la Conquistadora, for whom Don Diego built booths at his resting-places, at the last of which, before his triumphant engagement with the Indians who had established themselves in the *villa real,* rises the chapel called the Rosario.    For, said Don Diego to the reconquered and reordered settlement, a Lady has come among you and must be properly housed.

What I can't understand is, why, once having had that lovely and gracious Lady for our helper, we ever let her go out of our lives.    There are so many things one would rather ask help for from a woman.    I always feel a sense of personal loss as Our Lady of Victory goes by in her yearly procession from the parish church to the Rosario chapel, preceded by the crucifer in purple and white, acolytes in white and red, and the long lines of black-shawled women and bareheaded, singing men.    After a week she comes back, refurbished, and for days, after her passing, the streets of Santa Fé have a warm, sweet smell from the flower petals scattered by white-veiled girls

walking backward before the blue-and-gold platform on which la Conquistadora is carried.

This would be the second Sunday after Trinity, which is the next after Corpus Christi. Once you have seen Jose Sena marshaling that solemn procession along the streets marked by freshly planted evergreens, with its nearing and departing rhythm of the *Salve Maria,* you have the key to much in our English-speaking life that is mortifying and confusing. For what do our Kiwanis and Ku-Kluxers seek, with their made-up school-boy titles and their pillow-cases, but to recapture the lost art of expressing dramatically the fundamental life relations which, here in our Southwest, flow naturally into forms born of the great age of Dante and Lope de Vega? Take up your station near one of the private altars set at the turns of the route, under canopies of Spanish shawls and priceless Navajo serapes, with heirloom altar-cloths and silver candlesticks. From here you see the long procession come and go between the gardens, brown gowns of the Franciscans, black rebozos of the matrons, white veils of young communicants, and reverent, hatless men.  Sometimes the archbishop himself treads resplendently the soft, thick dust.  But you will not need to wait until you see the twinkle of the monstrance in the sun nor the puffs of incense smoke, to know when the Host approaches; you will know it by the bowing of the double line of spectators, like wheat going down and recovering in a summer wind.

There used to be a beautiful procession of Our Lady of Guadalupe at Taos, but it was successfully done away with, as the passion-play of the *Penitentes* is being destroyed, by a few English-speaking Americans who have insisted on their constitutional right to keep their hats on in the faces of others seriously occupied with the observance of a faith not their own. Beauty and bad manners quickly part company.  At Santa Fé, however, we still keep up the *luminare,* little fires and low along the streets in honor of Her who made the roses bloom for Juan Diego on the bare rocks of Old Mexico.

One must begin with these things, if one is to understand the New Mexico of the Sangre de Cristo and the Rio Grande country.  Unraveling backward from the saints, in whom the submerged culture of the Spanish-speaking makes a point of contact for what most people forget about it, we find that it began as an overflow from the most vital phase of Spanish culture, that reach of years between the sixteen and the seventeen hundreds, called *siglo de oro*. This was the century of gold that produced the revolt of letters against a slavish classicism, in which Castilian replaced Latin as the language of belles-lettres, when the king wrote comedies and the people took the same interest in literature that they took in bull-fights.

It was in this century that the idea that history should concern itself with all manifestations of human life, was born, and science made a symbolic turn by accepting the Copernican theory that the sun is the center of our planetary system. It was the century whose beginning marked the height of the Spanish novel in "Don Quixote"; in which Velasquez set the high mark of Spanish painting and Juan de Herrera achieved the Escorial. In that *siglo de oro,* Lope de Vega wrote his thousand comedies, and Pedro Calderón his religious plays. Lope de Rueda regenerated the Spanish theater, introducing music between the acts, and sometimes into the acts, by which door grand opera came through. It was about the time that Don Diego de Vargas Zapata Lujan Ponce de Leon and the thief of Guevara were plodding north with Our Lady in a covered wagon from Chihuahua, that the guitar definitely replaced the viola as the popular instrument of Spain, and more than likely the gray coyote mocked its strumming from the camps along the Jornada del Muerto. Since at that time the

SAINTS DO NOT STAY LONG IN ANY COUNTRY WHERE THERE IS NOT SOME SAINTLINESS OF HEART

319

passion for novel-reading had, in the mother country, become almost a disease, the young *capitans* of De Vargas would have carried immortal pages stowed in their saddle-bags. For a long time there was a trickle of resplendent literature over the way that they had come, along with church bells, Spanish shawls, and carved tortoise-shell combs.

So Brother David might be right, and the "Annunciation" of San Miguel is a Cimabue. I wish somebody with authority would look at these fast-vanishing *santos* of New Mexico. . . . There is a lovely Santa Rosalia at Isleta which incites me to covetousness. And there was a carved virgin at Zuñi, wonder-working, but a tourist stole her—may he drown in the black Lake of Tears! At Chimayó, when the custodian's back is turned, lift up the Victorian draperies of the saints, and discover rich bits of Spanish lacquer reminding you of the hoop-skirted ladies Velasquez used to paint. In the museum at Santa Fé, there is a little Virgin with a dove,—there she stays until I can build a proper house for her,—surrounded with a wreath of cherubs, which has been painted over in plain green and blue and red of a later day. But in the *Penitente* chapel, from which, in consideration of much-needed repairs upon the roof, the brothers consented that she should come into my keeping, there was not wanting evidence that underneath this gaudy modern wear, there is sixteenth-century blue and gilt and crimson. Better than these survivals, I confess that I love the painted presentments that came straight out of the *paisano's* heart in the days when boards to paint them on had to be laboriously whittled out with a knife. I am also partial to the marvelous punched-tin candelabra and picture-frames that were first made in Chihuahua in imitation of soft native-silver altar furniture which the descendants of conquistadores melted down into ingots, for nothing intrigues me more than the way in which art patterns come lifting to the surface of mixed blood-streams, and art feeling reëxpresses itself in foreign material.

This is a singing land. Any aboriginal can make a song for you out of the material his life provides, so that the saints suffered no lack in the decay, outside of formal church worship, of the suave Gregorian intervals to which they made their *entrada*. Neither did the social life of these earliest American families suffer any loss in the ballades and arias which belonged to the *siglo de oro*. What they brought was not songs but capacity for song-making, so that among innumerable collected New Mexican folk songs, few bear any Spanish traces other than the small change of melodic phrases and the sensuous feeling which runs ever with Spanish blood. The words and the rhythms run with the land, the labored pace of the ox-team, the jogging horse-trot of the days when a long journey was beguiled by guitar-playing while the *atajo* picked its way and the peaked sombrero made a half-moon of shadow on the singer's upturned face, the rapid round of the ponies treading out the wheat, and the swing of the waltz, which did not come in until emperors went out. Over at Ranchos de Taos, along the loma and even nearer to the *villa real,* still, the young people dance to *coplas* composed for the occasion with all the air of improvisation, but doubtless long incubated in the poet's inner self, to be brought forth with premeditated flourishes; young, simple couplets of compliment and lawful love. Salute your partner:

> Doña, hear me,
> Say not that which me disheartens.

Up the middle, hands across, and swing the lady.

> De las estrellas del cielo
> Tango que bajarte dos,
> Una para saludarte,
> Y otro para dacite adios.

Then suddenly, in the midst of such simple entertainment, a jet from that concealed fountain of desire at the heart of the Spanish-speaking, breaking up in passages of unpremeditated force and beauty, dying in its own depths as a fountain drops to its source again.

It is chiefly at occasions of profounder import, such

as weddings, funerals, and *velorios,* that one best
takes the measure of the singing gift of New Mexico.
A *velorio* is a party to the saints, vowed, perhaps,
after special assistance in your personal affairs or as
a pledge for recovery from illness.  The long *sala,* as
long as the builder's purse and as wide as the nearest
attainable cottonwood vigas, is cleared, a table set out
like an altar with white sheets and covers of drawn-
work and that special wheel-lace of which the art is
still preserved in the outlying districts, and with all
the neighborhood *santos,* Mary in her blue and white,
Our Lady of Guadalupe with her crown awry and
half her rays missing, Jesus in a long red mantle, or
San Francisco,—at Cochití, I saw him once in a pink
cotton kimono,—battered and featureless with age
but precious as the vessel by which the sought-for help
has come, set forth with tinsel gilt and tissue-paper
roses.  Then a row of candles is stuck across the floor
in front of the altar, and the *velorio* begins.

It opens with a hymn, "Gozos al Glorioso San Antonio de Padua," perhaps, or that lovely hymn to the
Trinity beginning:

> Lord God, with all sweet singing
> Praise Thee the great cherubim,
> The angels and the seraphim,
> Saying, Holy, Holy, Holy!

Between the hymns, prayers are recited, and sometimes short meditations on the virtues are read.

Dark, Madonna-eyed mothers bring their young broods, and kneeling, small heads stair-stepping all in a row, recite the *Corazon de Jesús*. Next them kneels some bearded, unkempt man, a returned convict, a half-simple goatherd, or some far-derived aristocrat of the conquest. It is all one in the presence of the saints. Between prayers there is gossip and a taste of good food, enchiladas, tamales, and little fried cakes eaten with thick hot chocolate.

The most important person at either a *velorio* or a funeral is the *cantador,* more than likely he who leads the singing for the local chapter of *Los Hermanos Penitentes*. In the remoter communities the dead are attended all through the night by song, laid out in state in the *sala* as the saints are, as though, by the mere act of death, already assoiled of the body's stain. The words of these funeral chants come out of well-thumbed books of almost indecipherable script, but the music is of the country and hints at all its many derivations. Now it intones and hums in monkish monotones, or clears to pure Gregorian intervals, again it surprisingly turns off to recognizable phrases of Indian dance songs or wails like the *alabados* of the whipping processions of the *Penitentes*. If the dead shall have been a member of that order, the body will be taken, for a midnight interval, to the morada. Nothing that I know of human occasions is at once so weird and yet so touching as the slow march of the brethren back with the body, to the measure of the hymn called "The Dawn of the Morning."

Angel de me guardia, noble compañia,
Dareme gracias, Ave Maria!

After the funeral come the visits of consolation; black, all black, deep-fringed shawls and black sombreros. Poor is he who has not a *sombrero negro* laid away for such occasions, or who knows not how to make consolation take the dignity of a ceremonial.

Weddings, too! Scarcely a grandmother but has laid way, with a shorn curl, a dead baby's shoe, and such humble treasures of the heart, the marriage letter which her lover wrote to her parents, asking for her hand, and had presented by his own most creditable relative. And where should she keep it but in the wedding chest, hand-carved, in which the prospective bridegroom presented her with the wedding-dress and such other items of feminine adornment as his purse afforded, a high comb, a fan, a long-fringed embroidered shawl, or cloth of his own dyeing. The custom of marriage letters wanes, but there are *placitas* still where the village letter-writer prides himself, such is the felicity of his phrasing, upon never having a marriage letter from his pen rejected. In those neighborhoods, also, you are likely to find the forty-stanza song of "Advice to the Newly Wed," the peculiar possession of the local musician, who hands it on as the tribal bard transferred the tribal lay to a successor of his own choosing.

Nothing is more endearing than the scrupulous regard for the sole possession of æsthetic property of this character, in the little towns of New Mexico. I recall, in one of the *placitas* where I used to visit, a man who had served a term in the *penitenciario,* and had made a song of it, which it was always a point of politeness to ask him to sing on every social occasion where he was present. And unless somebody has remembered it by accident, I have the only other record, which was given me under promise that I would not myself go about entertaining company singing, "When I was in the penitentiary, how long, long the day!"—which I am not in the least likely to do.

The "Entriega de Novios" I had from Miguel Salazar, at Arroyo Seco, under the same primitive copyright which refrains from robbing the unfortunate of what is perhaps his sole claim to distinction. For, by common consent, songs of this communal character are the possession of the blind. So with the music of the *baile,* viola, violin, and guitar, or occasionally the flute. You see them go about led by the seeing, from *placita* to *placita,* making sweet sound out of darkness, shapes that might have come out of the pages of Cervantes, kept secure in their contribution to the community, often their sole sustenance, by a courtesy surpassing the reach of our most efficient institutions.

Sometimes in the twilight along the loma, when the lights begin to come out, and the sound of the night-jar is shaken in the clear obscure of the twilight, you may hear a blind man strumming softly while he sings a sick child asleep:

> Pajaro coo, coo, coo,
> Pobrecito animalito,
> Tiene hambre tecolotito,
> Coo, coo, coo!

Or, as he hears young lovers pass, he swings softly into "Lupita," to the measures of which we danced on Armistice Day in the plaza of Santa Fé, almost an official New Mexican melody so nearly does its stirring but sensuous movement keep to the rhythm of Spanish-speaking life along the Rio Grande.

It is a rhythm, if you insist on explicitness, which has not yet lost the sense of right- and left-handedness, of male and female, all the plain distinctions with which life marked us before we gave ourselves to the god of machines. Something of the native gesture is already lost, though still you may find in some half-hidden hamlet, in the mountains called Blood of Christ, a dyer at work over his tubs under a poplar tree, or speeding the shuttle of a loom, or perhaps a woman skilled in the making of feather flowers, pure white, or deep wine-red shading to purple at the heart, after a fashion older than the conquest. At almost all the outlying villages the wheat is still threshed on the communal threshing-floor by trotting ponies, or occasionally by flocks of piebald goats driven in from the prados, with many *holas!* and much cracking of whips. Basketful by basketful, it is cradled and lifted, falling in a golden rain, winnowed by the women, and at last, before it goes to the water-mill, washed and picked over by hand. The resultant grist is a pure wheat meal, yellowish and of incomparable flavor. At Truchas I saw the women making fine white flour against a saint's day, by many siftings and resiftings, as it must have been done these two hundred years. Always and everywhere bread is baked in the conical, outdoor ovens, little turtle-shaped loaves to go into the herder's wallet with round, pale, leathery goats'-milk cheeses, and make the chief item of his diet.

The whole material means of life is of incredible simplicity in the *placitas* and lomas and cienaguillas of New Mexico: brown beans with *chile,* whole-wheat loaves, or tortillas of corn meal, squashes and melons, and a fine pervasive flavor of garlic over all. When meat-hunger must be satisfied, some one kills a goat or a calf, of which every family has its share; also there are rabbits, venison, and bear-meat, brought down by the wood-cutters in their turn. Coffee is the prevailing drink, and a little wine, not bad of its kind, grown in sunny nooks from grape stock that came over with the Brown-gowns, all the way from the vineyards of Spain. For gala occasions delicious little balloon-shaped *sopaipas* with chocolate, which is made thick here, as in Old Mexico. But if you give your cook leave, she will unfold a variety of toothsome combinations of these simple elements that will intrigue as much as it surprises.

This would be on the eve of the Day of the Patron, more especially on the day of Our Lady of Guadalupe, on the twelfth of December, which is the very day of her appearing to Juan Diego as he was hurrying down from Tepeyac, crowned, as you may see her in many a presentment of wood or paint, surrounded with rays of living light, with somewhere a rose tucked in, in memory of those she caused John Jim to pluck from the bare, winter rocks of Guadalupe. There is a special devotion to Our Lady of Guadalupe in the lomas and llanos of New Mexico, as who should not have, who has plucked there the rose of mystical delight from its vast, stony spaces. There is also a charming little play of the Miraculous Appearance, which can be seen in many a swept *placita,* as well as in the Saint Francis auditorium of Santa Fé.

It is the celebration of Guadalupe Day which brings the sheep-herders in from the mountains. Any time after the end of October, before the money-yellow leaves of the aspen have begun to fall, then snows come trailing across the upper valleys. Then the flocks, following an instinct so old that it is almost the only instinct sheep have left to them for taking their own course, the flocks begin to seek the lower levels. Night by night, on up to All Souls Day, you can watch the rings of herders' fires closing in on the settlements. Mornings, when the frost jewels the flocks, all the herder's skill is required to keep them from crowding down too fast upon the winter pastures, which must last them until the rise of the creeks, in the spring thaw. Crowded into the narrow cañons, they feed with a tearing sound on the sagebrush and buckthorn, and are occasionally picked up by bears fattening for their winter sleep.

About this time, the heavy strings of scarlet pepper that have hung drying on the south wall of every house, visible for miles in the landscape, are taken down, and quantities of them are ground into fine dust, that, simmered gently in grease with the right amount of garlic, constitutes the *chile,* inevitable accompaniment of every New Mexican dish. The onion and garlic crops are neatly braided by their tops into long strands, to hang close under the rafters all winter, disseminating that pervasive ghost of smell that haunts all such houses long after the vigas have fallen in and the walls are mudded back into the earth.

Between All Souls Day and Guadalupe, if there is a hot spring in the vicinity, will take place the semiannual wash.  Twice a year, family and neighborhood groups repair, for two or three days, to the spring, with all the season's wear to be soused in the comfortable *agua caliente,* which at Taos is pale green and radiant like liquid moonlight.  The women stand knee-deep in the water with a liberal froth of pounded amole root, and the children as well as the bright-barred blankets are put to soak, emerging happy and clean past believing.  No doubt something of their original state of mischief is soaked out of them, for about this time elders begin to hint of the necessity of flawless conduct antecedent to the Kiss of *Niño Dios.*  It is on the eve of the Good Night, *la vespera de la Nochebuena,* that the little Manuels, Pedros, Consuelos, and Carmencitas go forward on their knees, to kiss the Christ Child lying in its manger between the mimic oxen and the angels, whispering to it their dearest wish.  And if you have been good, say, since Guadalupe Day, your wish is sure to be granted.

But it is advisable, if the wish is very urgent, to confide it also to some sympathizing relative.  For did not Pedro Jose-Maria Archuleta, aged seven and a half, tell me that though he had not let it be known to any one besides his soldier brother, who was in France and so had to be told by letter, which his sister kindly wrote for him, that he greatly desired a toy cannon from the *tienda* at Ranchos de Taos, he did truly discover said cannon on the window-sill by his bed, on awaking Christmas morning?

But long before *la Nochebuena,* the flocks will have come down to the mesas in the neighborhood of the herder's home. Since he may himself be one of the important actors, who so well fitted for it, in the miracle-play of "Los Pastores."

No doubt the original play came into the country with the Franciscans, but it has undergone so many local variations and adaptations that, as it is still performed, it may fairly be called native. Many well-thumbed manuscripts of it have been collected, but you may also find it passed from generation to generation by memory, fathers committing their parts to sons, along with the traditional shepherd's scrip and staff, or the black-and-gilt or white-and-gilt costume of angel or devil. There used to be another local drama in a more modern manner, "Los Comanchos," or, as it is sometimes called, after its chief actor, "Quernaverde," at the period toward the close of the seventeen hundreds, when the fierce Comanche harried the towns of the Rio Grande. It is still possible to find old men remembering how they played *Quernaverde* himself, able to repeat perfectly the lines of the original; but I have never been privileged to see such a performance.

It is not altogether, I think, the religious interests which holds "Los Pastores" in remembrance. These are a shepherd people, and there is great likeness of the country roundabout to the land of the *Nacimiento,* the Borning.  There are great peaks here, like Horeb and Carmel, divided by dry gashes, and a river burrowing its way south through a rift deep and rugged as the rift of Jordan.  By the time the flocks come in to winter in the valleys, glory as of flaming swords; sacramental purple, hyacinth, lilac, and lavender, making holy with their twilight changes the circling mountains of the Sangre de Cristo.

The play of "Los Pastores" bears traces of its origin in the intertwined episodes of conflict between the Powers of Light and Darkness as represented by *Lucifer* and *The Angel,* couched in literary language, directed to the local great families, and the more colloquial and clowning, and devotional, shepherd intervals.  The properties are of the simplest, the artifices all those which with great solemnity have been heralded recently as new stage-craft; costumes symbolic rather than realistic, actors brought up through the audience, simple open mechanisms, such as the letting down of the *Archangel Michael* by a rope from the rafters, and the star of Bethlehem, an oil lantern pulled visibly along on another rope in front of the approaching shepherds.  Should a hitch occur in any of these arrangements, the audience assists audibly with practical suggestions, falling instantly reverential again as the play goes forward.  The gracious gift of sympathy, which informs all the manners and customs of the Spanish-speaking, makes inimitable actors of them, so that if you never before believed the myth of the Borning, and in spite of knowing that by midday to-morrow the *Archangel* will be playing *correr del gallo* and the head shepherd may be drunk, you believe in it, at least for *la vespera de la Noche-buena.*

After the play, which may take place in the street before the houses of the chief citizens, especially before the house of the resident padre, if there be one, or in the schoolhouse or the church comes the Kiss of *Niño Dios.* Sometimes the *Nacimiento* is a part of the play. Mary and Joseph are represented by living persons, naïvely surrounded by toy oxen and asses, with a cradled and rosy *Niño.* It may be placed on a platform at the other end of the room from the stage, which is the scene of the shepherd's camp, and the audience obligingly turns around when the shepherds reach the *"portal de Belen."*

If there is a church in the village, the *Nacimiento* will be set out in the corner at the right of the high altar, and will be as handsome and as near life-size as the means of the community permit. You come through the soft dark to the church, magnificently lit. For when your own home boasts no more than a single cheap kerosene lamp, half a hundred candles is magnificent indeed. And if you happen to be in one of the towns of the original Spanish foundation, the church itself is of proportions and of a style of decoration as grandiose as the *siglo de oro.* You come in full of excited wonder, hearing the small, ancient melodeon droning in its corner, and the altar boys moving about among the candles, doing their Christian best not to be too much puffed up by their office. In front of the twinkling altar you kneel, repeating as many of the prayers as your excitement may have allowed you to remember, and with each prayer you edge a little nearer on your knees to the happy child in its manger. It holds out its hands, it veritably smiles. So, at least, amid the quaver of the candle-light it seems. And by that time you may be so rapt in wonder that your mother has to nudge you when your turn comes to lean over and bestow the whispered wish and the reverent kiss on *Niño Dios.*

When there is no play, or between the play and the midnight mass, the whole village gathers at the most popular *tienda,* tall Dons whose aristocratic heads are ringed wtih the shining crease where the heavy sombrero has rested, ancient Doñas, black-shawled, who otherwise, except to go to church, may not move ten steps from their own doorways in the course of the whole year, sheep-owners picking up a few stout fellows for the spring shearing.

Nothing happens, and everything. Young people

meet for the first time, or come to an understanding under the very eyes of the duenna. Gossip is whispered, infirmities inquired after, information exchanged as to far summer pastures and the unexpected appearance of poison-weed in los cienagas.

The store is packed, the air is thick with cigarette smoke, the whole assemblage is decorous and happy. Thus the time passes until the bell from the church announces the hour of the midnight mass.

If there happens to be an Indian pueblo in the vicinity, the community gathers there, not always at the exact midnight hour, for the Keres obstinately hold that nobody can be properly born except at a certain juncture of the stars to which the dead hour of the night is not propitious. At the pueblo, while they wait for the stars to declare the hour of the Borning, the matachine is often performed.

They do it best at Cochiti. So far as its origin has been uncovered, the matachine is an ancient Mexican dance-drama, which, after the conquistadores, in the interest of one-hundred-percent Españolization forbid the production of native drama, was given a mocking Christian dress. In some districts it seems to have been assimilated to a medieval play of the soul's adventure, under which waggish, phallic by-play has been insinuated. In the glancing light of the bonfires of *Nochebuena* it is still resplendent, stirring forgotten motions of man's mind.

After the mass, Our Lady is led forth under a

canopy, to circle the little town between the *luminare*.
The *tombes* sound, the children, clutching made-in-
Germany toys to their breasts, in childish ecstasy
beat out the ancient dance steps in the dust. Amid
singing, the four *fiscales* fire off their guns, some
enterprising youth, newly home from government
board-school, lets off a packet of fire-crackers. Gro-
tesque figures enact a pantomime of assault and
defeat about the smiling Virgin; circling and dancing
away into the shadows, symbols of a receding pagan
faith. All done and over, the householder, retiring,
hangs a lantern over his door, lest One looking for a
room to be born in should find all doors closed, as once
in Bethlehem.

For I have written thus far in vain if you do not
begin to understand that New Mexico is still a place
in which the miraculous may happen. All myth, all
miracle, is in the beginning a notice of a Borning in
the deep self; new ideas, new concepts of spiritual
reality making their way to expression in whatever
stuff is current in the mind of the locality. That this
thin stream of the *siglo de oro,* which poured out here,
began at once to give rise to appearances, miraculous
healings, to local songs and drama such as the yearly
passion play of the penitentes, is evidence of the
sensitiveness of spirit which made possible such presentments of spiritual reaction.

At Isleta, Juan de Padilla, first Franciscan martyr,

is said to rise in his coffin as an augury of good years, by people who no more doubted it than they doubted the recurrence of wet years and dry. Of how Padre Padilla got from Kansas, where he was killed, to Isleta, below the villa of the Duke of Albuquerque, it has somehow not occurred to the Isletaños to inquire, a small matter indeed, to one who has veritably seen the hollowed cottonwood tree, with its desiccated figure in serge gown and dark beard, coming up through the soil that enclosed it.

There is at Chimayó a sand spring of such healing properties that a *sanctuario,* loveliest of the privately owned chapels of Rio Arriba, has been built over it, out of the contributions of grateful visitors. Pilgrimages to it occur regularly, and a tea made of the sand is held sovereign for all ailments. A pinch of it also will, if thrown into the fire, stop the highest wind in no longer time than it takes for smoke to reach the chimney-top.

Not that I have seen this myself, but I have seen the new shoes of little Santiago at Chimayó, who runs about at night on helpful errands at such a rate that new shoes become necessary from time to time. Santiago came in also with Oñate, and was seen riding his white horse at the pageant which celebrated the founding of his first capital at Yunque-Yunque. At Acoma, you may, if you have good friends there, see him blessing the mares on his day, in one of those inimitable plays of fancy which we sedulously import from Europe in the East, while the Indian Bureau is as sedulously destroying native examples of it in the West.  He rode hard, did Santiago, in all the little chapels of his westward journey's ending, during the years of the late war, holding with great gallantry banners of red and white and blue, shouting, "God and St. James for the United States!" for the sake of scions of old American families out of the prados and *placitas* of New Mexico.  Almost nobody remembers that New Mexico was among the first to fill its quota of volunteers, but you will see by the flag that he still carries, that Santiago does not forget.  Neither do the young men.  I recall asking one whom I met walking the Trail of the Blood, on Good Friday, after the Armistice, how he liked France. "Not so very well," he replied, and then, faintly frowning, with that look of puzzled pain which has made me ashamed since 1917 to look young men in the face, "Now that I 'm back, I don't like the United States so well, either."

And that was the first time I had ever heard one of his breed voicing the question which must lie forever back of their dark, handsome eyes, as to the validity of the easy contempt in which we have until now held the culture and capacity of this people.  I should feel more ashamed of it myself if I had not come to realize that where the blood-stream is vigorous, it is only the form of culture that disappears. The capacity lies fallow and rises again, as I expect to see it rise here, on this ground, within a generation or two in forms of music and dramatic and pictorial art of a quality which takes its savor from the land. The sand spring boils up no more at Chimayó; there is, in fact, only a scooped hole to show where it was, but the spirit of a race waits on its appointed time.

In the meantime the tradition of an older, more colorful life in New Mexico, under the surface of Spanish-speaking society, goes on unsuspected by the rest of us. There is a whole pharmacopœia of native remedies, most of which are *por el estomago* and have little value except that of comforting aromatic drafts. There is a still longer list of *remedios* for the soul, such, for instance, as the crossed pins under the hem of her skirt which a maiden going to meet a youth makes as a protection against too ardent addresses, and the invaluable advice of such wise saws as "When the moon is growing, sap is flowing, cut no crop then." Neither drink water at the dead hour of night, when all water goes dead, lest the drinker die also; nor spit in the fire, for fire is the eye of God. Such straws lie lightly on the surface of that life, to show the way the current eddies and widens in a back-water which will give an unexpected volume to the stream that is ready to swell the power of the Southwest the moment we give it free access into ours.

Under the picturesque surface, there is a rich detritus of household reminiscence of the great days of the Spanish occupation. Thus you hear how the great-grandfather of your informant served his year for the lovely daughter of the *rico* of Rio Arriba, going down with her father on the annual *conducta* to Chihuahua, in the days when the service of a young man to an elder was almost as much of a hat-in-hand performance as that of a courtier to a prince; thus proving his business capacity by filling a handsome marriage chest, and then going to fight the Apaches de Navajo for the sake of the Indian slave-girl that custom required him to present to the daughter of a *rico* to be her personal attendant. Failing in any of these performances, he was "given the squashes." You hear of how young sons and daughters went with vast cavalcades of stage-coaches and peons and armed escorts a six-weeks journey to Leavenworth, where the railroad ended, on their way to school, and were met, returning, with a like magnificence. You hear of the wedding of the Lunas and Oteros, rich and powerful families with estates divided by the Rio Grande about where the present towns of Los Lunas and Tomé now stand. You hear of the beauty of the bride of fifteen, of the trousseau made in Philadelphia and freighted across the plains, of the wagon-loads of provisions for the wedding festival, which lasted two weeks, and of how the bride was ferried over the Rio Grande, which then lacked a bridge, in a flower-garlanded boat, to the carriage with outriders which carried her to her new home. Still you may be shown pieces of the solid-silver dinner service which was the natural possession of a *muy rico* of those days, old shawls, stiff with incomparable embroidery, and intricate linked ornaments of pearl and gold. You hear how wandering players drifted up the Rio Grande, performing in the villas,—there were but three at that time, Villa Real of Santa Fé, with Santa Cruz in Rio Arriba and Albuquerque in the Rio Abajo,—and at the haciendas before the thousands of peons and the numerous close-knit families of the haciendaros. It was the fashion for the players to single out the handsomest woman in the audience for their carefully prepared compliments, for which it was equally the fashion for her escort to reward them with flung gold, so that it was an expensive business to appear at the play as an avowed admirer of so lovely a lady as Eloisa Luna Otero, who was, and remained, not only the most beautiful of the *señoras y señoritas* of the player's song, but, until her death, the most powerful lady of New Mexico.

There were other ladies of whom you may hear almost as much, though not in the same breath. There was Señora Doña Gertrudes Barcelo, born of the *gentes principales,* but also born a gambler, who came out of Taos with an American lover and set up as *banquir* at the then fashionable and not yet wholly disreputable game of four-card monte at La Villa Real, as Santa Fé continued to be called for some time after the whole of New Spain forsook all royalty forever.  Doña Gertrudes is also celebrated for having the most costly funeral, with a bill duly made out by the bishop, who claimed eight hundred dollars for his services and fifty dollars for every time the coffin was set down on the way to the grave.

All New Mexico is marked by the little crosses of such estancias, and by the shapes of them, pecked into the rock or painted bright, hopeful blue, or ornately cut and wreathed, you know much more of the neighborhood, of its origin as a pueblo, a villa, or the original house cluster of a hacienda, than I have time to tell you.

You may visit the saints still, in New Mexico, on their days; San Felipe, San Estévan, San Ildefonso, San Hieronimo.  Wherever there is a patron, there is a festival, with the patron carried in procession around the plaza, to be domiciled for the day in a booth of green boughs set forth with all the pueblo holds of preciousness, vases of flowers, candlesticks, silk kerchiefs, rare old serapes and homespun cotton mantles such as the Hopi make, embroidered with emblems of the earth and the fructifying powers.

To the patron belongs the place of honor, but the whole family of Blessed Personages will often be given an outing under the aspen boughs, with seats for the *principales* along the sides of the booth, and a low altar where the fruits of the earth are laid, and bas-

kets of bread and cakes to be blessed for the chief meal of the fiesta which takes place after the religious ceremonies and before such other distractions as races, *correr del gallo,* and dances older than the oldest saint in Christendom. Gentle and lovely festivals, marred only by rude tourists who insist on crowding between the patron and the races in his honor, and young, short-haired, cigarette-smoking females in riding-breeches, incredibly shocking to the mingled native strains.

If you should happen to be on Acoma at the feast of St. Stephen, or any other occasion, do not go away without looking at the picture of St. Joseph which the King of Spain gave to Fray Ramirez in 1629, who in turn gave it to the Acomas to be their defense against smallpox, drought, Apaches, and smut in the corn, which was so envied them by the pueblo of Laguna that their fiscales, failing to gain possession of the miraculous painting in any other way, broke in and stole it, and so kept it, under guard night and day, for fifty years. At the end of that time, both pueblos having beggared themselves at lawsuits, the painting was finally awarded to the original owners, and such was the joy of St. Joseph at learning, as he miraculously did, of the court decision, that the *fiscales* of Acoma, coming to fetch him home, found him leaning against a mesquite-tree, half-way. Or at Sia, look for the nub of the cross set up there by De Vargas in 1694; or at Trampas—but why should I tag with curiosities a life which depends upon more than its possessions for dignity and worth?

Saints do not stay long in any country where there is not some saintliness of heart.

It was Don Juan de Oñate who brought the blessed St. Francis into the country as his patron, and though somehow his name has passed from many places which once bore it, I think the Franciscan spirit yet makes its Western journey's end in the hearts of the Spanish-speaking, for there is no people more graciously giving, and none that I ever heard of who sustain the lack of material prosperity with so happy a dignity. We who go about with a vast impedimenta of Things, clanking entrails of our Frankenstein culture, do not always count it a virtue to them. Neither shall we, as a people, pluck the flower of the culture still capable of flowering for all our trampling of it, until we have learned why, and this is the one place in the United States where that secret is still to be learned, Francis of Assisi called holy the kind of poverty which consists in being able to afford to do without.

# THE TRAIL OF THE BLOOD

# THE TRAIL OF THE BLOOD

D ON JUAN DE OÑATE, explorer, settler, and Adelantado of the province of Nueva Mexico, was also a devout man.

Faithful son of the church and member of the Third Order of St. Francis, he writes himself down as keeping Lent with his men after the fashion of the whipping brotherhoods.

Thus the furthest ripple of the spiritual intensity which showed itself first in whipping brotherhoods, flowered in the art of the *Cinquecento,* and bore the colonization of the Western hemisphere as its fruit, was absorbed into the Spanish-speaking settlements along the Rio Grande and its tributaries, to reappear as *Los Hermanos Penitentes,* whose annual penance ends in the realistic and sometimes fatal crucifixion of one of their number.

Every year about the time Arcturus leads the herdsmen over the eastern hills, and the willows redden along the stream-borders, you can hear in the neighborhood of the mud-walled towns the fall of the lash on bared backs, and the eery tootle of the flute as the *pitero* leads forth the procession from the local chapter-house. It is a heart- and ear-piercing tune the

349

flute plays, wailing through the quarter-notes of the native Indian scale to the breaking-point, and falling off to passages of plaintive sweetness in pure Gregorian intervals. Behind it the ghostly light of lanterns bobs level with the tops of the young sage, and the shadowy forms of men move in unison with the chant that is led by the *pitero* almost up to the door of heaven, and dropped into the very slough of human despair. If you are fortunate in your choice of location, and not too much of a bounder, you may be permitted to see the whole of a native American passion play beside which Oberammergau is a tourist's interval.

To understand how the practice of the Third Order has been reworked into an American community drama, one must realize the nature of the human material worked upon. Oñate not only brought with him the most exigent stuff of Spanish stock, Aguilars, Ortegas, de Herreras, Guiterres; he brought also a considerable company of old Mexican natives, chiefly Tlascalans, in whom, as well as in the native New Mexican stock absorbed by them to make the present Spanish-speaking population, there was a long-seasoned disposition to express man's own sense of his relation to the Saving Powers by dramatic mimesis. Later there came Chaves, Armijos, Vigils, Lunas, Oteros, continuing the rich strain that produced in old Spain the magnificently theatric era of

Lope de Vega. If anything of the mother country's abundant creative energy spilled over to the colonies, it was bound to be dramatic in quality, as whatever they absorbed from the Pueblos was mimetic in form —Deer Dance and Corn Dance and Race of the Swift-coming Rain. With every contributory strain of Indian blood came memories of whipping rites, of fastings and of gashings and expiation by the maddening prick of the cactus thorn.

Items of this sort emerge obscurely between the record of Oñate and September of 1794, at which date, by a report made by Father Bernal to Governor Chacon, the order of *Los Hermanos Penitentes* is shown to have been in existence for some time. Then no more mention until 1886, when the French Bishop of Santa Fé is discovered issuing an order forbidding the performance of mass in the penitente chapels.

From this we understand that in the interim the drama that the dark-whites of the Southwest had made for themselves had become more sacredly familiar than the formal observances of the church. It was perhaps not wholly because they had made it for themselves that still, in the Rio Grande villages and in the flat lands about Las Vegas, north across the Colorado boundary and south into Old Mexico, a narrow space, you find the tall, gaunt crosses of the *Calvarios,* and every season when the wild plums whiten the creek-borders, out of the squat, shuttered chapter-houses hear the rise and fall of the blood-soaked *disciplinas.*

The morada, or chapter-house, identified among the other flat-topped buildings by its cupola and the cross over the door, exists wherever there is a brother-hood. Always there are two rooms, one of which is a chapel, the other housing the implements of the order. Occasionally there is a third, serving as office and club-room for the members. There is never more than a single entrance to the morada.

Straight away from it leads the *Rastro de la Sangre* to the stark-lifted arms of the cross on the nearest hill, the *Calvario.* In the more accessible, tourist-tormented settlements, both chapter-house and *Calvario* will be secret, removed from observation; but in the older communities you will find them placed in the same relation to the community life as the kiva to the pueblo. At Trampas the brotherhood occupies a room in the loft of the church, its walls spattered with the blood of generations of scourgings. At Abiquiu the children play under the *Calvario,* and the women gossip as they linger there over the drawing of water. That the true evaluation of *Los Hermanos Penitentes* in the life of the people should have been persistently missed by most writers about it is perhaps due to our inherent American disposition to look upon every sort of social differentiation as a "sight," to be gaped at and judged for its quality of diversion rather than to be understood.  It is always so much easier to dispose of phenomena like the penitente crucifixions in the current Freudian phrases than to penetrate far enough below the surface of history and our common nature to discover that the morada is an instinctive reversion to the council lodge and the kiva, the self-established pivot of community relations.  Something of the cult and something of the clan shows in its organization, which is without central government, the good of the order being maintained by occasional conferences of the local *hermanos mayores,* the elder brothers, presiding over the local chapters.

Of the historic progressions by which the Third Order has become a fraternal benefit society, incorporated under the laws of New Mexico as provided for all such organizations, little is recorded, but much may be inferred from the social background of the people among whom it is still cherished.

Not originally a secret society, it became so first under the moral necessity of protecting its penitents from spiritual pride by concealing their identity under the black bag which is still worn by *flagelantes* in all public processions.  Finally it was driven to conceal itself from the deeply rooted ill breeding of the American public, which, not to emulate, constrains me to set down here far less than I know of what goes on in the moradas and in the hearts of the penitentes. Besides the *hermano mayor,* there are three officers whose function is so public that to name them violates none of the secrecy under which the society still maintains itself, the *infermo,* who looks after the sick, the *resador,* who accompanies the penances of the members with the necessary prayers, and the *pitero,* whose flute leads forth the processions on the Trail of the Blood.

Of the times and occasions by which the flagellations of the Third Order passed into veritable crucifixions with nails, nothing is preserved. The modern substitution of cords, and the reduction of the time from the traditional three hours to forty-five minutes has taken place within the last quarter of a century. The change means less than might be supposed. It is necessary to recall here that death was not ordinarily supposed to ensue of the actual wounds of crucifixion, but, after two or three days, of loss of blood and starvation. Three years ago I saw a young man in khaki with wound stripes on his sleeve, following the *Rastro de la Sangre,* and I would have given much to know what he thought about it. Whether, for instance, he found the emotional phases which make war bearable, very different from the ecstasy that sustains the *Cristo* through his agony, whether indeed, the charm of war for men does not partly lie in its office of expiation.

Like every communal art, the New Mexican passion play is more or less shaped by its environment. The intensely dramatic landscape and the introverting effect of isolation have their part in it. For three centuries after Oñate, the distances of New Mexico were stupendous. Even in this day of high-powered motors the road about Abiquiu, Tierra Amarilla, and Picuris are difficult to negotiate. Always there were too few priests for the people. In Taos County, which is exactly the size of the State of Maryland, there are still only three parishes.

In the dark interval after the crass, new-made Republic of Mexico abolished the Franciscans, the only centers of organized faith for scores of settlements among the wild gorges of the Rio Grande and the plains of Las Vegas were the little chapels of the chapter-houses of *Los Hermanos Penitentes.*

Spanish-speaking New Mexico was never a reading community. Hardly yet does the power of print run to the well-swept *placitas,* and in the middle years of the nineteenth century that primer of Americanism, the mail-order catalogue, had not yet been invented. One source they had of art and drama and mystery, of spiritual energization and culture, the story, every detail of which had been worked into the fiber of their lives by the brown-skirted *frailes,* of the passion and death of Jesus. Not the social philosophy of Jesus as we modernly conceive it, not the esoteric teaching, but the drama of a dying and resurgent Saviour. Finding themselves in the dark of a social submergence lasting more than two generations, *Los Hermanos Penitentes* hugged their possession to their breasts and erected around it the shrine of their annual performance.

Special saints' days, the first and second days of May, and funerals of the brothers are observed ceremonially, but the avowed purpose of the penitentes is to keep alive the memory of the suffering and death of the Saviour. It begins with the first Friday in Lent, with the gathering of the *hermanos de luz,* the whole body of officers, at the morada. To them, singly and by twos and threes, the brothers assemble from the *placitas,* from low huts on the loma, from sheep camps and woodcutter's fires. There is a pungent smell of sage-brush in the air, the smell of the rain-freshened earth, and the evening star like a torch in the green streak of sky beyond the mountains.

The high windows of the morada, too high to afford any glimpse of what is going on within, are shut and barred.

From time to time the sound of singing can be heard, like bees droning within a hollow log. Late, usually about midnight, the first procession issues, making its way with the help of fitful lanterns and the feel of the ground underfoot, toward the *Calvario,* which is set on a low hill about half a mile from the morada. By the rise and fall of the lanterns and the intermittent droning, you make out that they are telling the stations of the cross. The squeal of the flute is high and keen, like the glimmer of the sky-line along the mountain-tops made audible.

These early demonstrations are all singing processions. As Lent advances, however, strange ripping sounds, intermittently in fives and threes, can be heard issuing from the moradas, and to the midnight processions will be added figures of men clad only in white-cotton drawers, naked to the waist, bare arms rising and falling as the *disciplinas* are laid on, first over one shoulder and then over the other. Later they may be seen drawing huge, unhewn crosses, staggering and falling, whipped to their feet again by the zealous *sangrador*. Often the crosses are so heavy that the bearer must be accompanied by a brother to ease the long beam to the ground when the penitente faints under it, lest it slip and crush him.

As the season progresses, the penitential passion rising with it, one is likely to meet anywhere in the deep lanes between the fields, or in the foot-trails of the wild, sharp gorges, the solitary penitent, dragging his bloody cross, or two or three making their way from morada to morada on their knees, accompanied by the *resador* reciting the prayers that make the office effective. On one such occasion, just at the edge of dusk, I met one of these private processions headed by a youth carrying aloft, in an almost un-seeing mood of exaltation, a huge and pathetic effigy of the crucified, followed by the *resador*.

After him two men staggered under crosses, and a third, half naked like the others, clasped between his breast and arms, manacled at the wrists against any temptation to let it fall, a head of cholla, that wicked-est of barbed cacti. Around the heads of all of them were bound tight fillets of wild rose-brier, beaded with drops of blood. This was early in my acquaint-ance with the strange brotherhood, and I had been many times warned by my American friends against letting myself be seen in the neighborhood of their rites. But the procession had come upon me so sud-denly that there was no retreat, and by a swift reach of spirit, making myself one with them, I dropped on my knees on the moist earth between the budding thickets of the wild plums, offering with uplifted palms my sincere respect to the symbols of their faith. With only an instant's check and a side-glance, the procession swept by me, and the wailing lost itself in the immensity of the mountain shadow.

But with that brief moment on my knees all the sense of wild strangeness in the Lenten rites went from me. The shiver the sound of wailing flutes and the rattle of the thunder-twirler excited in me, break-ing the midnight, is the shiver of recognition of what my blood remembers. Whatever was brought to the surface of consciousness by that act must have been of perceptible quality, for never afterward, when I went among the penitentes alone, did I have anything but deeply recognizing glances that ended in my being admitted at last into several of the chapels, and in coming into possession of one of the ancient manuscript books of hymns, much thumbed and blood-spattered.  But lest I give a false impression of revealing mysteries, it must be said that the penitente hymns can be heard at any funeral watch night, and the prayers as they are read in procession, by any bystander who has the wit to understand the quaint, sixteenth-century Spanish in which they are sung.  It meant, my coming into touch with them in this fashion, that I was admitted to the community mind on this matter, and to the gossip of the wives and sisters of the brotherhood, who participate in many of the purely religious functions of the order.

The formal Easter drama begins on the evening of Holy Tuesday when the brothers, on entering the chapter-house, receive the "seal of obligation," the three gashes down and across, made by a flake of obsidian or broken glass, set just deep enough in its wooden handle to miss severing the muscles of the back.  After the seal, the penitent asks for and receives the three strokes in remembrance of the three meditations, of the passion of Our Lord, and according to his fortitude or the depth of his repentance, strokes for the five wounds, the seven last words, and, if he holds out, for the forty days.

Ash Wednesday is spent in prayers and confessions and private penances. Day and night the sound  of the steady blows of the *disciplinas* can be heard from the morada, drowned from time to time by the wailing anguish of the hymns.

Originally the *disciplina* seems to have been of ancient iron ring-work, such as may still be found occasionally in the moradas, but all that the modern spectator sees are the white whips braided of leaves of the yucca whose white bells swinging above the leaf cluster a little later in the season make incense of the air. By use of the leaf matter is stripped from the fibers, leaving the stinging flail to which in excess of fervor bits of metal are sometimes attached.

From hour to hour on Holy Thursday processions go out, to the *Calvario,* to the campo santo, or to neighboring moradas. Bareheaded and singing, they pass between the pale thickets of rabbit-brush and sage. Welcoming delegations come out to meet them, and after brief sessions of prayer inside the chapel, set them on their way. The singing is led by the *cantador,* proud of his office, and referring constantly to the well-thumbed note-book in which the *alabados* have been written by hand and spelled by ear from generation to generation.

Always the flute-player accompanies the official processions, and his wailing tune is punctured by the skirl of the *métraca,* the wooden rattle, the "bull roarer," the "thunder twirler," of which the bell that signals the elevation of the host is the last, most Christian reminder.

In this country the towns hug the skirts of the mountains.  Rounding the *prados* they spread from point to point of rising land, having always a friendly eye one upon the other, so that the flow of processions between the moradas takes on an effect of community pageant.  Gradually as Holy Week advances, the whole community is swept into the fervor of atonement.  Children leave their play to follow the master of novices, Raphael-eyed cherubs lifting their sweet trebles and altos, learning the stations of the cross as they plod back and forth between the morada and the *Calvario.*  In some such fashion all affairs are left for penitente week.  It is more than likely that the saints flock there at that season for the savor of willing sacrifice, as we go into the desert to see the palo-verde bloom.

The height of spiritual frenzy is reached by midnight of Holy Thursday, when the procession, led by the chosen *Cristo* of the year, with head veiled for humbleness, staggers forth from the morada, the hymns shrill with pain, the wet whips falling steadily, followed by that most desolating sound, the slither of the crosses in the dust. The direction of this midnight trail is never known to outsiders. Guards are stationed to prevent its being followed to its lonely destination in the hills. Forth in the midnight he goes, whipped by the *sangrador,* and back he comes in the dawning, dragging his heavy cross, often in a fainting condition and leaning upon the *compañeros.* Years when Easter comes while the ground is still frozen, the way of the cross can be tracked by blood from the torn feet of the penitentes.

For an hour or two the morada swallows up the weary group of *flagelantes.* Then, as the great red sun comes over the mountain and the friends and families of the penitentes begin to collect about the door to join in the morning procession to the campo santo, the keen flute and the skirling rattle call forth the still-fasting and only half-conscious brotherhood.

The blood is stiff upon the *disciplinas* that fall on flinching backs with the steady sound of rain; the heavy crosses rake the stony ground, the voices rise wavering and charged with homely, human passion.

> "Por el rastro de la sangre
> Que Jesu Cristo derrama,"

they sing.

> "By the trail of that dear blood
> Which by Jesus Christ was shed,"

and again, as they near the great cross standing sentinel among the village dead,

> "There is no one now
> Who is not worth something,
> Since now Christ is dead."

Drawing over my head the black shawl which is the universal outdoor wear of matrons in that country, to join the "women following afar off," my thoughts followed those who, down all history, have taken the Trail of the Blood to our ultimate gain in peace and spiritual insight.    There were women in that procession whose own sons had walked in another bloody trail that same year in France, and as we knelt among the little crosses painted heaven blue, as with eternal hope, I was thankful to be able to cry quietly with them behind my shawl, while the voices of the men rose piercingly:

> "The rose has dried,
> And the garden has withered!
> The common flower of the field,
> And my white lily,
> On the cross have found their fate.
> *Dios, tien piedad de mi!*
>
> My son is no more;
> The dear of my soul
> Has gone and forsaken me!
> *Dios, tien piedad de mi!"*

It is not until after this sunrise observance that the weary brothers break their fast with coarse food, and rest in preparation for the passion play, which formerly took place at the prescribed third hour, with faithful realistic detail. But in the early eighties the church instituted so active a protest against the traditional practice that it has been many years now since a veritable crucifixion with nails has taken place. In the remoter villages the *Cristo* is bound upon the cross with ropes so tightly drawn that the strongest man cannot safely endure it for more than about forty minutes. The body of the *Cristo* is covered with a sheet, and his head encased in the customary black bag to prevent recognition, and, as a protection from tourist curiosity, the elevation of the cross seldom takes place until after dusk.

At Talpa three years ago we saw the last stage that human experience travels on its way from being a propitiatory rite to legitimate dramatic art. Here an effigy was substituted for the living *Cristo,* and the involved emotional complex was released in dialogue and mimetic acts, restrained by the compass of attention of the audience. Talpa lies at the upper edge of the loma, where the *rillito* comes out between round, detrital hills, having Ranchos de Taos hidden in the cañon below it, and Fernandez de Taos in the fertile bolson toward the west. It looks across as the crow flies to Taos Pueblo, at the foot of Pueblo Mountain. In between, the fields were starting green, and the

AND THE FALL OF THE WHIPS LIKE RAIN

365

pink of peach orchards melted into the warm tones of adobe walls. Three moradas had turned out for the occasion, with their assembled women folk, and about the traditional hour began the stations of the cross.

In that clean, bright air, between the most majestic mountains, the black shawls of the elder women gave almost as insistent a note as the clear cerise and orange and green scarfs of the young girls. For an hour the shifting procession moved down the hollow of the valley and up the little hill of the *Calvario,* rising and falling in slow rhythm to the stations as they passed. *Cantador* and *resador* walked in grave responsibility at the head, close behind them the young scions of the blood of the conquistadores, with dark, handsome faces, simply serious and devout. Behind them young girls, black crape over their white communion dresses, carried on a platform the chief treasure of Talpa, Our Lady, also swathed in black, from whose outstretched waxen hand drooped one of the webby, wheel-lace handkerchiefs which are not made anywhere now in this country outside of the mud huts of New Mexico. Last of all, the brothers dragged the *carreta de muerte,* with its grinning image of the Angel of Death, arrow laid to bow in its skeleton hands. Formerly this carriage of death was the ancient New Mexican ox-cart, with solid rounds of cottonwood-tree for wheels, loaded with stones and

drawn with chains or horsehair ropes, which the penitentes took across their naked breasts, or, in excess of
contrition, their bare throats, and the Death was life-
size.   It is related in the annals of the brotherhood
that on one occasion the arrow was loosened by a
jolt, from the grinning angel, and found its mark
between the shoulders of a penitente.   But every
decade of penitente history shows a shrinkage in the
size and importance of the figure of Death.   On one
occasion I was offered one, about half life-size, most
horribly realistic, for a price, to add to my collection
of curiosities.

Meanwhile, as nearly the whole population of the
village surged down the valley toward the *Calvario,*
the older brothers had set up the three crosses a few
paces from the chapel door, and laid the implements
of the passion in order.

The effigy was brought forth in its blue-painted
casket, a most deplorable life-size figure, and with the
utmost reverence, as though it had been a beloved
body, affixed to the central cross.

As the procession returned from the *Calvario,* the
hymns changed from the wail of penance to the poignant note of human sorrow, and the drama of the
passion began.   They were all there, the historic char-
acters: the Roman centurion with his spear, the
Jewish constabulary, the three Marys with their lanterns, the soldiers that diced for the seamless robe.

This being a war year, and the passion of patriotism being scarcely less in New Mexico than the passion of penance, Caiaphas-Pontius Pilate, the two parts rolled in one, in his white robe, had mounted on the very tip on his high priest's hat, an American flag, which fluttered and flapped brightly amid the solemn scene.

All that could be heard, and understood, for the Spanish of Talpa is not the Spanish of the books, of the dialogue seemed superior in literary value to the Oberammergau drama. It had the true folk quality, and something of the rhythmic elegance of phrasing which characterizes as much as I have been privileged to hear of the ritual of the order. Until he comes unexpectedly upon something of this kind, the casual observer is likely to forget that the age that fed the cultural life of the Spanish colonies was the resplendent age of Spanish literature. But it will not be by me that the interest and charm of the American passion play will be handed over to an American public, still in that undeveloped stage in which appreciation too often takes the form of tearing a lovely thing to tatters. When I think of what American people do to much of the beauty and strangeness of which they find themselves possessed, I hope there is some truth in the gossip of mysterious disappearances and burials alive visited on the violators of the enjoined secrecy of the order. But my acquaintance with the friendly, simple folk among whom it flourishes gives little color to the hope.

The formal drama of crucifixion and laying in the tomb closes about the hour that the sudden glory of high altitudes pours about the mountains from the level sun.

Through its rose and lilac veils the penitentes return singly and in twos and threes to their homes, the goatherd beds the flock, lights come out in the huts along the loma, and the great day is over.

A few of the brothers will return to the morada after dark for the *tinieblas* commemorating the dreadful three hours of Jerusalem. There seems to be even among the celebrants some confusion of mind about this act of the drama, confounding it with the night of Holy Thursday, in which the disciples desert the Saviour one by one, and the bitter hour of betrayal closes the scene. Probably both the betrayal and the hours of darkness were once kept, but now the two scenes, by a device familiar to the drama, are telescoped and kept by choice usually on the night preceding the crucifixion. During this celebration the little chapel is dark, and there is great rattling of chains, roar of the thunder-twirler, shrieks of devils in hell and gibbering ghosts. I have had men tell me with rueful laughter, that they can remember as boys being half scared out of their wits by the too realistic performance of the *tinieblas*.

For the ordinary sight-seer the business of *Los Hermanos Penitentes* ends here, and gives rise to the erroneous impression that its sole function is of emotional release. In the spirit of our own worship of dead levelness, which we are pleased to call consistency, we are even led to speak contemptuously of a religious experience that runs to a yearly climax with the recurrent rhythms of the earth. But the work of the order in the lives of its members is no more over with the annual flagellations than the work of nature is over with the resurgent glory of the spring.

The chapel of the morada is open on Lady days, on days of the local saints, and on all Christian festivals. In communities where there is no resident priest, it becomes the repository of the village *santos*. From it they are carried to houses of sickness and mourning, and the body of Christ is borne about the fields on Corpus Christi Day. The ritual of the order gives the touch of divine consolation to funerals in lonely neighborhoods, which may not be visited by the priestly office oftener than once in the year, and the *infermo* is the recognized source of neighborhood relief in sickness and affliction.

In the dark period after the removal of the Franciscans, prolonged into the first thirty or forty years of the rule of the invading *Americanos,* when civil processes were all in the hands of interests alien, or even hostile, to the natives, many matters which might otherwise have been brought to the courts were settled by the local *hermano mayor*. Gossiping in the

twilight with the wives and mothers of the brotherhood, one hears how Tomacito was made to pay for
the damages his cow committed against the corn of
Pablito, of how Ascencio was required to withdraw
his membership from his own morada to one six miles
distant because of a too conspicuous interest in the
wife of Bartolomé, and how at Questa, after the visit
of the national representative of the Anti-Tuberculosis
campaign, a penalty of two strokes with the *disciplina*
was prescribed for spitting on the floor.   One Assumption day at Fernandez de Taos I was a party to the
visit of Our Lady from the morada there to one at
Prado, newly established and not yet furnished.

Forth she went in the morning with garments rev-
erently kissed by the escorting brothers, and back she
came in the twilight in a new silk gown bestowed by
the women of Prado.

A happy custom this, of visiting with the blessed
dead, for my part more improving than the inanities
of the ouija-board.

There was a time, beginning in that dark period to
which I have referred, and after lines of political
cleavage between the native New Mexicans and the
invasive Americans sharply showed, when the order
became the instrument of political intrigue, but that
is passing with the growth of mutual understanding
and the advance of the English press.   Everywhere
among the more foreseeing of the present population

there is an increasing appreciation of the social value of an organization which shows itself possessed of the seeds of self-help and the vital spark of community spirit. A year or two ago, on the day of the Assumption of the Virgin, when I had gone into the little chapel at Fernandez de Taos to pray, with full courtesy of the brotherhood, a party of curiosity-mongers undertook rudely to force their way in after me, with the result that there were pistol-shots exchanged and a narrow escape from a tragedy. Promptly, however, on the part of the Protestant community, and on the part of the Taos Indians, on whose land the morada stood, there was a general rally in defense of the right and dignity of the order. For this is more than a question of the right of free worship. It is a question of our general attitude toward those native spiritual impulses out of which great national art must spring. It is because I am not able to think of *Los Hermanos Penitentes* in any more important connection than this, as often as Lent comes round and my mind goes visiting the high valleys of the Sangre de Cristo and the *placitas* of Abiquiu and Rinconada, I think also of the young soldiers walking in the Trail of the Blood with the stripe of their own wounds on their sleeves, and the little flag that flapped so gaily from Pontius Pilate's hat.

# SACRED MOUNTAINS

## SACRED MOUNTAINS

T O the Navajo, the mountain is God, pure and holy; Him they call Reared-within-the-Mountain. Yearly their young men go out from their hogans, singing, toward the source of their strength.

> Lo, yonder the holy place.
> Swift and far I journey,
> To life unending, and beyond it. . .
> To joy unchanging, and beyond it.
> Yea, swift and far I journey.

This is an immemorial use of mountains which does not wear out with using. So man felt God in the earth; lifted Him by the power of the up-thrust to a seat in the zenith, with the earth His altar; lifted Him to the vault above the Cherubim, where He still tarried for us long after the Tewa glimpsed Him as Opa, the Universe Man, the sum of everything that is. Here from the Sky of the World, where we lost Him, we lap back on the trail of the Navajo and know Him again as the sacred power of mountains.

Most sacred is the bulk of Tsotsil, blue as a summer rainstorm, where it watches, from its high and level plateau, the black caterpillar trains of the Santa Fé crawl across the cindery plain between the Rio Grande and the Rio Puerco.   This is a rim-rock mesa, red sandstone, topping the softer stuff and weathering in huge blocks like a ruined wall.   Like the teocalli of the Aztecs, it rises from the mesa platform, a pyramidal, solitary mass of broken cones, from whose top, streams cloud like smoke of accepted sacrifice, following the high wind river.   For a whole day's travel, east and west, it dominates the landscape to the north of the railway, a semicircular volcanic mass, having a secondary cone within, one clear creek, and a giant's tongue of black lava protruded down the shallow red sandstone cañon where the railway follows the old trail past Acoma to Zuñi.   Tsotsil, it is called by the Navajo, in reference to the lava tongue, and, ceremonially, Blue Turquoise Mountain, sacred world altar of the South.   But on the maps you will find it designated as Mt. Taylor.   It was so Lieutenant Simpson named it in 1826, after the President who sent him to learn the lie of the land, and incidentally rediscover the lost Inscription Rock.

It was from the Sierra Zuñi, that broad-backed, blue wooded range showing solidly upon the south, as Tsotsil slips behind you, that Simpson first sighted the holy mountain, which has hardly faded upon the eastern horizon before the dark triangular peak of Dokoslid begins to rise out of the west.   Dokoslid is its Navajo name, ceremonially Haliotos Mountain, colored like that shell their Ancients used to bring back from pilgrimages to the World-encompassing Water, to be the symbol of their ritualistic west. But the Spanish *frailes,* seeing it outstanding from the Coconino plateau as the gentle Francisco of Assisi in their faith, called it by his name, to be the mark from which to take the mind's measure of that country.

Now between these two points, Mt. Taylor and San Francisco Mountain, is about the same distance as between Buffalo and Chicago, and north of it almost as many miles more to the end of the Navajo country, wherein a man might go mad with terror of its vastness, had he not the friendly lift of mountains to give him that sense of mastery over the environment which is the first awakening of man to the presence of God within himself.

Three peaks, rammed shoulder to shoulder, make up the central mass, and behind them, visible between the open forests of yellow pine and the droves of round-backed, blind cones covered with tawny gallita grass, a chain of lesser peaks tails out to Sunset Mountain. The land lifts steadily here, from the basin of the Little Colorado to the Coconino plateau, which fills in the corner between the Grand Cañon and the wall-sided western end of the Mogollon.

From the car windows, Sunset crater comes first into sight, cup-shaped, black from the base, but overlaid along its rim with red cinders yellowing toward the top, so that it glows forever, even under winter snows, with the color of its ancient fires. Between Sunset and San Francisco, there is a more recent cone, older than the Navajo, no doubt, but looking so new that the only man I have met who has ventured down its black throat, told me that so freshly cooled it seemed, he feared almost to set foot in it. San Francisco itself is old enough to grow forests, to drip with cool springs, to keep in its shadowed recesses virgin banks from snow's end to snow's beginning, and to nourish lovely Alpine meadows in its lap. Close under it, sits the town of Flagstaff, the first point of call between our earth and Mars.

It is not, however, to watch the stars go by that the Navajo goes up to Dokoslid. From salient peak to peak of its broken mass, he renews the sense of the familiar which makes a man at home. North by west, he looks across the motionless streak of the Grand Cañon, past Kaibab and Kanab, to the home of the Utes; straight north, beyond the shadow which is the cañon of the Coloradito, dropping in a thin wide veil into the abysmal depth by which it reaches the Colorado Grande, to the phantom shape of Navajo Mountain, from whose north wall springs mysteriously the flying arch of Rainbow Bridge. Hereabout the first man was made, the original Navajo man. This would have been between four and five hundred years ago, as the Navajos' chronology runs, before which time they had no history. North and east, the practised eye picks out, beyond the treeless basin of the Little Colorado, the painted rims of mesas going toward Oraibi and beyond it, drowned in a heat haze, till it touches the shadowy shape of Carrizal, out of which country came the Elder Brother of the Navajo, and beyond which rises the sacred mountain of the North, black Cannel-coal Mountain, color of the storm-clouds that descend upon it from the central knot of the Rockies.

Eastward, the view is cut off by the Sierra Zuñi, but beyond Mt. Taylor the land runs out, red and less red, into the white waste of the Mesa Fachada, called Saydegil, vast and untenanted and sacred as the sea, east by north to Pelado Peak, the Dawn-white Mountain of the east, White Bead mountain, white as wampum. These are the holy mountains of the Navajo, where dwell the Yei, from the peak of any one of which one or two of the others is always visible, shutting the tribe in a territory which would make three or four of our Eastern States, with a happy sense of home. Here the day comes up as a turquoise-colored horse, "making the sun noise," treading the sands, pale yellow and dazzling white as precious skins, drinking the dew.

It is only about the sacred precinct of San Francisco Mountains that this wished-for sight is to be seen. Mornings at the beginning of rains, when the cloud-rack has rested all night on the Coconino, leaving it white like hoar-frost, for the instant before the sun comes up like a thunder-burst the frost turns to dew that twinkles once, like the flash of inner light between two planes of consciousness, and vanishes. In winter, when the Coconino wood is streaked white with snow, the view toward the south is stretched out to the serrate ranges of the Mogollon Rim, flat against the sky-line like the blue and lilac mountains of a theater set.

From Bill Williams Mountain, it goes south with the Rio Verde to join the Salado, just beyond which rises, from the flat floor of the cactus country, Superstition Mountain, with the white dike across its brow marking the foam of the Flood. Once this, too, was Navajo country, probably about the end of the Greathouse period, when as nomadic clans the Navajo traded and perhaps raided Casa Grande and Los Muertos. Toward the east, the White Mountain group glitters silvery along the edge of peaks from which the Apache prays. On Mt. Thomas there is an old shrine, old as the ruins along the Mimbres River or the upper Gila.

Moving thus among the peaks of San Francisco Mountains, between the groves of spruce and royal pine, lucky to dream of, the consciousness of man extends itself, takes depth and height, color and shadow.

When the Navajo were waxing great in the land of their soul's choosing, the clans of the Hopi and

the Zuñi had sat down in the middle of it. South of
the Sierra Zuñi, but east of Zuñi River, as you go
from Tsotsil to Dokoslid, rises Toyoállanne, sacred
Corn Mountain for the Seven Cities that Coronado
came to find. It is called, also, Thunder Mountain,
a name preferred by the map-makers; flat-topped,
banded red and white, one of the many sandstone
islands among which Acoma and Inscription Rock
and the Enchanted Mesa and the Mount of the Beloved carry titles of romance. Here clouds rest, and
the priests of Zuñi go up to pray, and the sacred
societies dance themselves into harmony with the
Creative Powers. Around its broken cliffs are
shrines to the Twins of War and Wonder-working,
and here in a cleft of the living rock was discovered
the young god with the flute, beside a fountain, as
long ago as when men still believed that all the offices
of life were holy.

It must have been about that time that the women
of the Hopi towns began to visit the Mother Rock,
a huge altar lift of sunset-colored sandstone burning
into the jewel blue of the sky, where still they make
unblushingly the sign of life-renewal. Almost anywhere in high and solitary places, you may find signs
like this, or prayer plumes hidden in rock crevices,
laid up to Those Above. South, far south almost on
our southern border, the Papagos have their sacred
peak of Bobaquivari. Rising like the index finger of

a shut fist, it dominates all the intervening sierras as far as Rio Altar in Sonora. Near the foot of its northern face, there is a cave called Shuki, house of the Elder Brother, once the scene of impressive ceremonies, where now nothing is found besides a heap of rotting arrows. In a hollow of this seven-thousand-foot peak, whose name, Vavakolique, defines its shape, "pinched-in-below-the-middle," there is a pool of fresh water left from the deluge, finding its way down the perpendicular cliff to a natural *tinaja,* where it becomes the "lasting water," so coveted for the making of the sacred sahuaro wine that, still, about the beginning of the sahuaro harvest, long lines of Papago women may be seen making their way from Bobaquivari toward the hereditary orchards with great jars of *viikan shootak* carried in immemorial fashion on their heads.

Over in the Rio Grande country, as you come up out of the river gorge into the valley of Taos, you see Pueblo Mountain standing toward the north, with thin storms of rain enfilading among the cañons of Star Water and Pueblo Creek, and the dance of the Rainbow Boys in and out of the storm's blueness, . . . or suppose the rainbow comes forth, arching from foot to foot of Pueblo Mountain, moving as you move, while the Katchinas of the Middle Heaven water the pueblo fields, then you see how myths are made out of the stroke on stroke of beauty. Or should you be anywhere on the banded walls of the *plan del Zuñi,* and see the pointed-nosed winds go down the sandy streak by the river, raising banner trails of dust behind them, you would understand how it seemed to our Ancients that the Twin Brethren rode forth on snorting gray cayuses. Thus the function of mountains as makers of men's minds is clarified, lifting the earth processes, setting them upright as man is, to be apprehended in their entirety, issuing as myth, as drama, as philosophy.

In some such pattern of sacred mountains all the ancient worlds were mapped in the minds of men, Sinai and Olivet, Olympus and Ida and Pentelicus, . . . and yet not the lift of mastery which comes of knowing the world you live in, nor yet the stretching of man's mind to take in distance and detail, neither the pure air nor the accelerated pulse of altitude nor the quickened sense of beauty quite accounts to me for the universal habit of mankind of counting high places holy. Not unless we have gone completely astray on this business of holiness; not unless God *is* the mountain.

There is an effect of mountains on man as fear. I recall once, of a summer night, climbing the steep cumbre of one of the Rio Grande potreros, terrified to find the moon almost at my shoulder, a near and menacing object, mistress of hollow space from which, so

lightly poised it was, I might by ill-considered movement displace it dangerously. I should not, I know,
if I lived in that country, move about much at night
without first performing all known acts of propitiation.

But neither do men go to places they fear, if they
can help it. Yet all about the Tewa world the high
places where nobody need go except for such business, on Lake Peak, on the crest of Oku, sacred Tewa
turtle, and on the high peak of Jemez there are
shrines, centers of deep trails of many many moccasins. Also I find this strange, that the places where
the most shrines are known to be, such as the potreros
between Cochití and Shufine, west of the Rio Grande,
and the Small-house country on the upper Chama, are
the places in which people who know neither the
shrines nor the country find themselves walking with
the prick of expectancy between their shoulders, with
the stirring of some familiar unfamiliar sense. . . .
I remember, years ago at Paestum, arriving there too
late for the offices of the guide, and walking aimlessly
about in the twilight, being suddenly struck all over
with faint shivers of caution and a nameless excitement, which, as I stopped to taste, receded in fainter
shivers of regret. And the next morning the guide
pointing out that particular spot to me as the place of
the caves where wild animals were kept for the circus
—that sort of thing. But the people of Paestum, when
they had it, called the shivers Panic, and the people

of the potreros built shrines to the puma, hunting-god of the Keres.

A potrero is any naturally enclosed grazing-ground. Sheep-herders and cattlemen give that name to those singular lacunæ in the lava flows where water issues from under the black rock and grass abounds, and to the pastures at the bottom of box cañons. But the potreros of the Rio Grande are triangular fragments of bench lands lying between the *plan del Rio* and the foot of Jemez, running to elevations of from seven to eight thousand feet, fenced only by deep gashes in the volcanic tufa that lies like a blanket over all that region from Peña Blanca to Abiquiu. The bases of the triangles are against the wall of aërial blueness which shuts the western horizon from Santa Fé. Their apexes run out in pillars and battlements of the many-colored trap, around whose feet the river fawns. Across the table-like tops are spread more ruins than you will be able to find in all Europe.

What we felt there, may well be the residue of personality that man leaves in all places once frequented. What presences, then, have been among the mountain-tops to raise in us the response that is called holy! For to the aboriginal, to be holy is to be filled with strange, abundant life.

Not all mountains are so, though to me they all have personality as much as ever they have to the Navajo. Even the new mountains not yet worn down to the smoothed contours of maturity, that crop out of the scorched *abras* to the south of Mt. Taylor, west of the Rio Grande, mountains unnamed and never lived in, blind cinder-heaps, cupped craters, wedged-shaped dikes surviving the cleft sandstone walls that shaped them. Dead mountains, dead and dreaming. Mostly it is water they dream of, as women unfulfilled are said to dream of the sea. Any way you look, traveling across that country, the dream comes stealing. It comes flowing toward you like a river, down the road you travel, almost to the fore wheels of your car from under which it slips, to reappear as far behind you. Sometimes it lies like spilled quicksilver, cupped in the land's hollows; or spreads in one wide mirage like a lake on the surface of which the mountains float. Now and then a mountain fronts you, stark stone, uncomforted; but look behind you as you go and you see the dream creep back about its base. Toward evening, such mountains dream of fire, taking the light along their western faces, glowing with it as when they burst up molten from earth's core.

I knew a mountain once, over toward Lost Borders, which could both glow and pale, pale after the burning, like a lovely neglected woman who burned to no purpose, a dark mountain, whose bareness was like a pain. After some thousand years nothing grew there but sparse tufted grass, round-branched, rusted cacti, and the knee-high creosote. Occasionally, in hollows

ACROSS ITS BROW A WHITE STREAK OF THE FOAM OF THE FLOOD

387

where the seldom rains would catch, astragalus ripened a few papery pods, and slim spears of painted-cup. So dry it was, not even lizards darted, nor lichens grew upon the rocks. Then after several seasons of less frequent rains, a solitary rabbit found its way there. If by chance I saw it in my visits, I turned quickly and went another way; not for worlds would I have scared it from the mountain. And the second season after, I went there with a man of my acquaintance, and in my excitement to discover that the rabbit had found a mate, I cried out. Unhappily, the man was of the sort in whom a mountain wakes only the love of killing, and after he showed me the rabbits dangling bloody from his hand, I felt I could never go there again. But sometimes I have dreamed of it, and in my dream the mountain has a face, and on that face a look of hurt, intolerably familiar.

There is always something purposeful in the way a mountain changes with the changing light, as if from within. Going up from the valley of Jemez, between the Rio Puerco and the Rio Grande, there is a magic mountain, a rounded basalt head, probably an old volcanic plug from which time has eaten away the crater, Cerro de la Cabeza, which has the property of becoming air, pure and shadowless, hanging suspended between thin gildings of the morning sun, like the Curtain of the Doorway of the Dawn which was lifted by the Elder Brother when he came from Carrizal. Forty or fifty miles to the east, the peaks of Jemez are blown blue against the morning and the evening light, deep trumpet blueness, against which, if you should see it from the Sangre de Cristo side in the spring twilight, the tops of the potreros vibrate lilac and lavender, and the green of the piedmont passes into the luminous air in thin trebles of French horns. There must have been a time, for man, when the impact of the mountain on his sense was too direct for clear distinctions of seeing or hearing—oh, long before he was able to make poetry without melody, or to separate the singing and the verse from the motions of the self that made it. It comes back here for definite, memorable moments, as when, in the early winter months, the sunset light has a way of passing invisibly through space, to break on the first object it encounters, tree-tops or the clinkered crests of extinct craters, into a glory of gold and hyacinthine color. Thus the whole Sangre de Cristo fills with secret fire, rose flame, shadowed with violet, deepening at its base to the hue of the spirit's most poignant mystery . . . holy, holy, holy. . . .

The moment comes and goes. Not beauty only, for there is a special kind of beauty for every hour the mountain knows, beauty which man perceives without participating, beauty to which he feels himself a stranger. There is the beauty of the structureless gloom of gathering storms, beauty with terror of the milling maelstroms of the air, beauty edged with intolerable loneliness of the moon-bow flung on the fluffy, silver-flecked floor of cloud observed from peaks above the tree line. There is beauty of the mountain meadows, to which the response is a joyous sense of well-being, lakes like jade, jeweled with water-lilies, long bajadas thick with the plumes of bear-grass bowing like white ladies to the royal wind. From all these we come back, knowing that long before men set up an anthropomorphic deity there was a state, easily met among mountains, called holy, being whole with the experienceable universe.

Curiously, one of these moments of complete and happy abandonment to wholeness, comes, for me, with the birth, in the air before me, of the fragile, six-parted flowers of the snow. It is only at very high altitudes that it is possible to see snowflakes shaping level with your eyes, coming out of the thick grayness as a star comes out of the twilight. There is a falling flash that gathers whiteness as it falls, and suddenly on the black cloth of your coat you catch a cluster of stemless, feathery blooms that under your breath dissolve and regather, always six-sided but never twice the same. Snowflakes forming under such conditions are unusually large, probably because they cannot form at all except in the absence of all motion but their own. Those that come sliding down the long slopes of mountain being almost always clogged together, shattered in particles, or whipped by the wind into round, icy grains. Sometimes on the surface of heavy falls after warm days divided by cold nights, will be found a still more varied bloom of snow flowers in the form of hoar-frost, mingled with ice spicules which the Tewas call "seed-of-the-snow." It is, I think, of some such shape of matter is made the thin shell that far beyond the reach of man's highest flight of air, shuts in our world against the invasive universe. Well! What if science has not yet found it? Very clear spring and winter mornings, after long falls of snow or heavy rain, from heaven-reaching cumbres I have seen it, straining the blue out of the sun shafts, breaking and scattering them as heat and light. Now, I remember that when we were very young, the German housemaid used to bring us clear sugar eggs for Easter, with a peep-hole at one end, to an inclosed colored picture; so the earth ball within its shell might look, should there be seraph or any other creature to peep in.

Mountains are the only things we know to grow beautiful in aging. Young mountains are all terrible, hard from the moment they are cold, angular and graceless. There must be peaks of volcanic origin, in Arizona, which cannot be more than fifteen or twenty thousand years old. Not old enough to have anything growing on them but lichens of lovely rich colors and seaweed patterns. Ever since Mac, to whom this book is dedicated, told me that a lichen is the perfect coöperation of two living and unlike plant organisms, grown into one the better to compass the rock's devouring, I have been afraid of lichens; and the little stone crops and saxifrages that live in the crevices of the rocks, by their power of extracting sustenance from minerals, seem terrible in their frail prettiness, as to men must seem certain sorts of women.

South of Mt. Taylor, breaking along the mass of outpoured lava which you pass through and around on the way to Inscription Rock, there are craters of comparative newness, where the lava edges cut like glass and the strains and flaws of cooling look as if they had happened yesterday. There are cones too steep for climbing, and craters so deep that the Indians of that country used to drive mountain sheep into these gateless *encierros,* to kill them at their leisure. In one of these the Apaches, who claim the malpais immemorially, used to hide their women and their horses while the men went a-raiding. The whole of the lava flow, about the size of the State of Delaware, is unexplored except by the sheep-herders, who know of certain secret, well-watered meadows deep within the black rock, not possible to be reached except by goats and well-instructed herders. Here are said to be the sacred places of the Apache, still so sacred that I have heard that four men of their nation have joined the Navajo in whose reservation the

malpais lies, to see that they are kept unviolated.
Here, also, there are wonders, a lava bridge high
enough for an airplane to fly under, with pines growing on the arch, and ice caves, one of
them not so far from the road but
with intelligence you may find it,
which Evon Voght, the custodian of
Inscription Rock, discovered and
made accessible no longer ago than
last summer. In one of those curious sink-holes
which occur in lava flows, there is a cave, filled almost
to the top with stratified ice, where no ice forms now,
except thin coatings on the pools in exceptional win-
ters.   Since there was never any ice-age in this
Southwest, the presence of age-old ice-banks remains
one of the mountain's unfathomed mysteries.

There is a trail through the malpais, leading
directly from Zuñi to Acoma, still used by the Puebleños, which is thought to be the one by which
Alvarado with the embassy from Cicuyé found his
way, but not advisable for any but led horses.   There
are lost mines here, or stories of them, which amounts
to the same thing, for a lost mine ceases to inflate the
adventurous sense the moment it is found; but the
pathless terror of desertness will keep the malpais for
a long time, safe in its wildness.

For he who does not understand that the wildness
of mountains serves us far more than their tameness,
understands very little.   Slopes given to the plow may

serve us less than the vast, stony undulations that are patterned gray and green in the spring, and gray and gold in October, with the quaking aspens. All up the Sangre de Cristo, the pine and aspen patterns make a hieroglyph still undeciphered, except as you find the key to it in the script of pagan thinking, at the back of the mind of man. Once, walking at the head waters of the Rio Santa Fé, between the straight white aspen boles, with the sunlight shattered overhead by the glinting gold of the leaves, and a brown goatherd came by, white goats and black flecked with blue shadow; then I saw all the secrets of ancient Greece go by with them, like summer lightning, in a revealing flash. Once, riding over fresh fallen snow which had brought down with it and half buried fortunes of red-gold coin, I saw the Grail pass between the tall cross-bearers of the silver firs, the unattainable Cup of the soul's adventure. Painter, poet, who that come after me shall yet fix its unsubstantial quality! As for me, I make my prayer with the Navajos:

> Young man, Chieftain,
> Reared-within-the-Mountain,
>
> .   .   .   .   .   .   .
> In beauty may I walk. . . .
> On the trail of pollen may I walk,
> With dew about my feet may I walk,
> In old age wandering on a trail of beauty,
> Livingly, may I walk. . . .
> In beauty be it finished.

# RIO COLORADO

# RIO COLORADO

T HE first I knew of it was as a dim blue streak, shadow of a shadow, far east from the cinder-colored ranges of Lost Borders, its contours winding like a river, fixed in a motionless unreality. Above it fled a river of shimmering cloud between viewless shores of air, toward which our Paiute swamper, Tinnemaha, would look inquiringly whenever I asked him for a forecast of the weather. Not until, by that mysterious certainty Indians have of what is going on in you, he understood that I had recognized it as the Grand Cañon, did he tell me what the Paiutes believed of how it came to be just there, on the eastern rim of the country where their own borders ran out in unmapped desertness.

That was after Pamaquásh and Hínuno, the Divine Twins of the Paiutes, the paired upbuilding and down-pulling forces of nature, had come to the end of their long cycle of struggles for mastery of the earth, and Hínuno, the younger, had been banished by his brother to the unrained-on space beyond the borders. There for days they heard him raging, throwing great rocks about, splitting the mountains, till the earth roared and trembled. Then silence. "So," said Pamaquásh, "my brother is dead by this time"; and went to bury him. He found the country very much as you see it now, with the great gash of the Colorado ripped through it almost to the under-world. Also he found Hínuno, the mischief-maker, sleeping beside it, in the shade of his arrows, and to put an end to all this business of destruction, Pamaquásh changed him into the piñon pine, making food and shelter in what had been a foodless, shadeless reach of desolation. Afterward Pamaquásh became the wind; and when it blows, you may hear, through all that country, his brother the pine-tree alternately pleading with him and deriding.

A little later, between the pages of a book of early Spanish voyages, I saw the river, a greasy, glimmering streak below the lantern-shine of a tall-pooped caravel, as Don Francisco de Ulloa beat up the Sea of Cortés in 1536 in search of seven cities stuffed with gold. Cortés, the great captain, sent him, having pawned his wife's jewels for that last throw at fortune, so little of the wealth he had raked from the cities of Anahuac having stuck to his fingers. It was believed at that time that Las Californias were islands, upper and lower, peopled with Amazons and other fabulous creatures, and that by skirting the coast of the mainland, a port might be found to the country of the Seven Cities.

What Ulloa actually discovered was the sea "thick, black, and very muddy . . . all the land full of sand in

a great round compass, joining itself with the other
shore"; also the sea running with great rage into the
land and with such fury returning that the admiral
would not trust his ships upon it to explore an inlet,
surmised, rather than observed, to be the mouth of
some great river.  Doubling back about the peninsula
of Baja California, his ships slid down the vast slope of
the uncharted Pacific, and so no more of Ulloa.  No
more, also, of Cortés, who, broken by the failure of his
last fling at fortune, sailed east and dropped below
the horizon of death, leaving room for that Coronado
who, by the viceroy Mendoza, was sent overland in
search of the still fondly believed-in Seven Cities of
Cibola.  At the same time Mendoza sent Hernando de
Alarcón with three ships, to brave the great Colorado
bore, at which Ulloa balked, and coöperate with Coronado from the coast.  They were of good stuff, these
Spanish captains.  Against the advice of his pilots,
Alarcón made the inlet, and discovered "a mighty
river which ran with so great a fury of stream that we
could hardly sail against it."  Nevertheless he made
some distance up the river, partly by seamanship and
partly by that suave facility for seeming anything that
the occasion demands of them, which is the special
genius of the Spanish-speaking.

What he seemed to the Cócopahs, with his white skin
and shining armor and his moving water-house, was a
son of the Sún, which happy assumption Alarcón was

too polite to disappoint. As the sun-god the Cócopahs cheerfully towed him as far up the river, some say, as The Needles; at any rate, until other Indians were met who had had news of Coronado, already killing and pillaging in the pueblos, and opinion gained ground that the strangers, far from being children of the Sun, were Christians, and as such deserved execution.

Partly on this account and partly through the failure of Coronado to communicate with him within the specified time, Alarcón, after naming the river Good Guidance, buried letters at the foot of a tree, and sailed back, having discovered very little besides the fact that California is not an island. Of the two parties sent out to find him, the one under Melchior Diaz, from Culiacan, found the letters, also many Indians whom he described as "fit for nothing but to make Christians of them," which, judging by what Christians have made of Indians to-day, is faint praise indeed. Diaz rafted across the river, probably near Yuma, and from a habit the natives had of carrying fire about in rolls of cedar bark, named it Rio del Tizon, River of the Brand. In the meantime, Lopez de Cárdenas, proceeding westward at Coronado's command, twenty days from Tusayan, across a country elevated and full of low twisted pines, very cold and open toward the north, issued suddenly upon the most awesome of earth's evidences of the Left Hand of Power. But beyond stating that he found it impossible to cross, and that there was no gold in that country, Cárdenas wasted few words on the Grand Cañon. Nor did any one, until Juan de Oñate, as I have already described to you, skirted its southern course as far as the sea in the south, under the name of Rio Grande de Buena Esperanza.

Father Kino, whose work was among the Pimas and the Sobaipuris, called it, about the end of the seventeenth century, Rio de los Mártires, and it was not until the end of the era of the padres that we find Padre Garces, out of that same Mission of San Xavier del Bac that Eusebio Kino founded, furnishing authentic information about it as the Great Red River. Red it was, charged with the silt of a red north country, and as people saw it, not as highfaluting discoverers felt about it, so it was called.

Garces, whose soul is among the saints, whether or not his name will ever be, the Yumas killed; and it was Padre Escalante, setting out from Santa Fé with Miera y Pacheco, who followed it north to the old Ute ford which later became part of the Spanish Trail to Monterey as El Vado de los Padres. Escalante seems to have gone north of the crossing, past the clear-flowing Grand which has since been determined to be the main fork of the river, to the muddy, smoothly gliding Green. Somewhere in his wanderings he must have met Kaibab Paiutes who would have told him how Tavwots, the mighty hunter, had cut out the cañon as a trail to the under-world, so that a grieving chief of their people might visit his wife there, and know that she was contented; and how afterward Tavwots had led a river down that deep way lest the living be tempted to walk too often in the trail of the dead.

What one is struck with, however, in all these early accounts of the natives of the Colorado basin, is the lack of interest displayed by the discoverers in what the aborigines thought, and a profound concern with how they looked. Great of body they found them, strong and well made, and shockingly undressed. Padre Escalante, who added to the rosary of the river's names by referring to it frequently as Rio Cosnina, finds time to record that the women's clothing hardly covered "what one might see without danger"; and that gallant young Britisher who in 1826 strewed the estuary with names like Greenhithe and Howard's Reach, solemnly records that on entering a native dwelling he looked with anxiety among the furniture to discover something in the nature of a chemise that his hostess might put on, at least in his company. As for James Ohio Pattie, he seems to have given away practically his whole wardrobe in order to achieve a propriety that one might suppose would have long slipped from him as James Pursley reports the conventional sense of the value of gold did, between the Platte and the Rio Grande, so that he threw away what he had gathered.

Yet so it reads: Spanish priest, British naval officer
and American pioneer, who sailed uncharted seas, followed unmapped rivers to the bowels of the earth,
fought strange tribes, and beasts the ratio of whose
strength to the strength of man is as one to seven, all
ended by being embarrassed to the extent that they
thought it important to set down in their diaries, in
the presence of native women whose single garment
was something less than neck to ankles. All of which
leads one to wonder, first, if this is the sort of thing
that happens to the minds of all superior peoples to the
degree that they feel themselves superior, and secondly,
whether, as I have often suspected, female propriety
may not be wholly man's invention.

The Patties came in the middle twenties, heading
the incursion of trappers who in the blank forty-year
interval between them and the good days of the padres,
began to discover that the Rocky Mountains could be
more easily penetrated from the south than from the
north. From Santa Fé, James Ohio trapped west to
the Gila, first of all Americans to see the tall sahuaro,
the short-haired great-horned mountain sheep, the
wild pig called *javalina*.

He saw the Indians baking mescal, and the ruins
of the Great-house People, thick on the hot, salt
plain. But going north, he reports nothing of the
Grand Cañon except as "horrid mountains," an in-
superable barrier to the business of trapping beaver.
Men like these live as close to the earth as ground-

squirrels. The finding of food after fasting, the taking of a good catch of pelts, bloody escapes from Indians and bears; these are their memorable occasions. Although it seems certain that the Patties were the first Americans to follow the river north to its source in Wyoming and south to its delta in the racing gulf, scarcely one place that they touched is recognizable from their description of it.

The Patties followed the Green, which is longer than the main fork, looping north through Colorado into the Wind River range of Wyoming. It was between their two *pasears* that Lieutenant Hardy, R.N., sailed up the estuary. The year that they were in the south, Ashley of Missouri with two buffalo-hide coracles followed the Green, in the hope of restoring his fortunes by trapping, as far south as the Uintahs.

Between the Green and the Grand, which takes the east flow of Medicine Bow, where the Continental Divide swings in great sweeps down from the northeast as far as Rabbits Ears, sits the most massive and formidable company of mountain peaks in the Northern continent. From the vast curving amphitheaters of the Divide, enormous detached spurs lie out toward the Grand like separate ranges. All their lines are instinct with the power of the thrust that split and lifted them. Even their rammed shoulders clear the encumbering woods, and the snow-fields, glittering like molten silver over the chaotic drift of débris, skirt the upper reaches of summer green.

Anywhere along the Colorado Front, a score of peaks may be counted, clearing the thirteen-thousand-foot levels, bold, weather-beaten, sloping steeply to the west. Times they sit shining, appeased as elder gods, surrounded with soft seraglios of clouds. Then come great rages of the desire of mountains, and clouds cast out in tears of rain. One hears the downward swirl of rapid waters between the thunder and the torment of the great wind rivers. Far down, squeezed between walls of two thousand-foot cañons, foam the spurned waters.

Other times it pleases the mountains to clothe themselves with whiteness, wearing the wonder of the deep snow as a man sometimes wears the beauty of a virtuous wife. Then the warmth of the snow's clinging eats into the mountains' strength, until it comes crashing down in vast avalanches of débris. In this manner is accomplished the desire of mountains to be ground down into dust that shall be man.

Among the upper tributaries of the Grand, the water wears a hollow in the softer rock, affording lakes, stone-rimmed, amber and jade; then grassy willow flats, and as the water gets down and down, fir and yellow pine and free flowering meadows, between deep, wall-sided troughs. The Grand takes its explicit rise between Long's peak and Arapahoe, draining south along the Colorado Front. The Snake and Blue rivers draw north from Montezuma and Glacier Park. Powerful mountain streams, wedged between hard, high walls, pour in their ever-foaming waters. Troublesome, Two Elk, Weary Man's Creek—they take expressive names. About Three Rivers' Junction the mountains stand apart, divided by broad, massy table-lands. Here where the Blue and the Grand and the Muddy—which should be called Milky—rivers meet, the confluent passes through the cliff of Gore's Range and turns south. Sage-brush appears; valleys green with cottonwoods are molded in the softer stuff; red buttes stand up.

The Green, whose length stretches the Colorado to two thousand miles, leaves its cold lakes by swift plunges, cascades white as wool, falling three to four hundred feet to the mile. Early in its course the river issues from its mountain steep, to flow clear and un-ruffled between low red and umber-colored hills, flecked with the light green of cottonwoods or darker checkers of ranch fields. Banded, cone-shaped mountains crowd down to the river's bank, or, standing a little distance off, hold hands under the flat headlands.

It was hereabout that Powell started his expedition in 1871, the first to make successfully the entire length of the Grand Cañon. A little farther down, Ashley of Missouri, when the green of the cottonwoods was like thin smoke above a land red as the embers of its ancient fires, launched his bull-boats in the spring of 1825. Here the river goes deep and swift and stilly, between banks fringed with willow and box-elder and cottonwoods. Whitefish, or Colorado salmon, weighing twenty-five to thirty pounds, are caught. Across pale yellow sands, red buttes rear themselves from breast-shaped hills of detritus. Herds of spotted cattle and little fuzzy wild burros come down to the river to drink.

Then, suddenly, the Rio seems to stop dead at the foot of the Uintah Mountains, trending directly east and west across its course. It is not until the boats are fairly against the mountain that the river is seen to turn abruptly between the many-colored walls of Flaming Gorge. Straight-faced, painted cliffs, so high that their sides seem to lean together, run for incalculable stretches, coloring the close air with their bright reflections.

The going here is swift but not dangerous for the boats. Where the gorge recedes, rounding the Horseshoe turn, beaver make their home, and far-blown water-fowl come up from the gulf to breed. In the intervales between the series of wall-sided narrows, clear streams enter from the slopes of the Uintahs. Smoke-colored bighorn feed among the rainbow buttes. Where the walls close again, the tireless cliff-swallows build their colonies of frowzy nests. Kingfisher Cañon takes its name from the birds whose plumage tones with the shadowed water. It is not until the flaming sandstone walls of Red Cañon are reached that the rapids begin.

There was another voyager down these swift-running narrows, one William Manley, who deserves a larger mention. He had come in the glorious days of forty-nine, with an emigrant train, as far as the Continental Divide. There, faced with the prospect of wintering at Salt Lake among the Latter-Day Saints, who had none too saintly a disposition toward strangers not of their faith, he and six of his bull-whacking companions decided to boat down the Colorado—even at that date not certainly believed to reach the Pacific. It was now late summer and all the cottonwoods along the river burning gold as if for augury, when Manley and his men found an old ferry-boat on the river bank which they fitted out for the voyage, with a little bacon, a little flour, ammunition, and salt. What else they lacked, the expedition made up for in courage, for at that time as well as in Ashley's day, it was believed that a whirlpool called the Suck lurked somewhere in the Uintah narrows, and river tribes were known to be hostile. Nevertheless the bull-whackers turned in their whips, and trusted themselves upon the waters, racing and leaping, as Powell found thirty years afterward, like herds of startled deer through fallen timber.

Beyond Red Cañon lies Ashley's Falls, where the

trace of Ashley's inscription and the date was discovered by the Powell party; and beyond that, Brown's
Hole. The Hole was a famous rendezvous of the
trappers in old times. About here the hills stand off,
terraced, of smooth-faced, burnt red sandstone, having
the flats of the terraces clothed with the dark green of
cedar and pine. Even in these depleted days, Brown's
Hole—or, as you find it in recent maps, Brown's Park
—is the haunt of abundant game, though not as in the
days of Ashley and Manley, when great bands of antelope and deer served to make a figure for the leap of
dancing water. Otter and ocelot and beaver lurked
here, and the whole land is alive with the glitter of
salient peaks, silver-tipped with snow. Even through
the duskiest cañons goes the blue dart of the kingfisher,
and the song of the water-ouzel rising like bubbles in a
clear spring, and the crystal trickle of notes from the
cañon wren.

Below the park-like valley where the trappers slipped
their bales of pelts and refitted for new *pasears,* rises
the towering Gate of Lodore. This is more than the
beginning of the scarcely intermittent run of fierce
rapids and cruel, hidden rocks; it is the beginning of
that poverty of invention and the substitution of fancy
for imagination which has lined the whole of that
magnificent chain of mountain gorges with names that
seldom rise above the level of McGuffy's Fifth Reader.
They bring you down through Hell's Half Mile,

through Glen Cañon and Labyrinth and Desolation, past Gunnison's Crossing, on the old Mormon Trail, past the Uintah and the Yampa rivers, to the junction of the Green and the Grand. It was at Gunnison's Crossing that Manley, partly through misadventure and partly by persuasive warnings of friendly Indians, abandoned his ferry-boat and broke across country on foot to join the nearest emigrant trail.

There the little jinx who rode upon his shoulder contrived that he should be a member of the division which, seeking a cut-off to the San Joaquin Valley, passed through and all but perished in that ghastly waste which takes its name to this day from what befell them there, Death Valley. There is also a name and a date on one of the towering walls of Glen Cañon: D. Julien, who in 1836 reached so far in what—if you take the accompanying native pictograph into account —might have been a sail-boat. Of him nothing else is known.

Below the junction of the Grand and the Green, the augmented water pours down, a succession of rapids of great pitch and violence, over falls of sharp-cut rocks, and unbroken rushes between beachless shores of thousand-foot cliffs. Of the river here, you may read what is written by the Kolb brothers and Dellenbaugh and Powell, how there is a tilted range of many-tinted lamina at the mouth of Yampa, that is to say, Bear River; how the flood waters are often so charged

with the red sand of the Upper Country that fish are
smothered in their native element by the excess of sand
in their gills.  All this you read, along with how many
times the boat upset and with what hardihood the
one-armed veteran of Shiloh risked himself upon exploratory climbs, of which the going back was more
difficult than the going forward.

This is excellent matter for boys' minds to feed upon.
But for intimations of the future cradled in the country through which the river flows, you must depend
for the present upon what I depend upon—chance ex-
cursions, vistas snatched from mountain-tops, far-
carried gossip of the camp fire and the hogan.

Here the river runs through the long, bare, rolling
valley of the Uintah, home of the Utes, runneled and
gullied by local storms that move from centers of
dense darkness across the landscape, quivering with
the lightning, trailing long, lilac-tinted ropes of rain.
Across the vast, pale *abras,* awash with scattered
quicksilver of mirage, painted mountains swim in the
blue haze.

This is the Land of Standing Rocks.  White spires
top the square-sided cliffs, red like old blood, or choco-
late-colored, greenish gray like sage-brush after the
*torneo* has passed.  Ashley Valley is a Mormon para-
dise where the sound of dropping fruit is heard and
the bee-weed crowding the fences makes the roadsides
fragrant.

Beyond it are high, grassy intervals and wastes of

wind-sculptured sandstone rounded like the backs of prehistoric beasts come up out of the deep to feed.

All the rivers here are self-colored by the land, between thin ribbons of green. Indian writings are cut into the rocks, and in the very cañons of the Colorado, cliff dwellings with the ladders still hanging in place from their deserted balconies, snuggle into the *cuevas*. Back from the rivers arise the flat-topped, straight-faced remnants of an older land, bright-hued taluses sloping to the yellow sand. Old eagles nest hereabout. There was a Ute who came down to Tesuque in the winter of 1918 to be instructed in the Eagle Dance, who told me that his people had visited certain aeries for a known two hundred years, to gather the feathers that no man might mount on his war-bonnet until the council had well considered the deed a plume commemorated, and its worthiness.

The last series of gorges through which the river runs, below the gorges of the Green and Grand to the marble gate of Grand Cañon, is called Glen Cañon. Here the explorer who has safely cleared Cataract Cañon, flung down dark inclines and around fallen cliff-sides, huge as houses, with a raging sound and great tossings of the water's yellow mane, may find, in so far as terms of pleasantness may be used for the race of the Rio Colorado, comparatively pleasant going. Clear streams drop down past the *cuevas* in a silver rain, lining their courses with lace-work of

fragile ferns. Other times they come slipping through
the palisaded cliffs, bordered with beaver-meadows
where all the greenness and color of the West, which
waits invisibly on the flow of water as music waits in
the air on the vibration of the aërial, breaks into the
happiest expression; wild bloom and the footless, iridescent whir of the humming-bird between sky-reach-
ing walls.

At its extreme southern end, Glen Cañon widens to
receive the Paria, river and vale and headland, to which
Lee, the renegade Mormon who was charged with the
responsibility of the Mountain Meadow Massacre, fled
with the faithfulest of his wives. I knew one of the
men supposed to have dipped his hands in the blood of
those unfortunate emigrants; a tall, prophet-bearded,
fanatical-looking creature, all the furnishings of whose
house were so arranged that his back would be always
against a wall; who never stood in any company unless
the company was all in front of him; who never ate
or slept without his gun crooked in the hollow of his
arm. And I thought perhaps Lee welcomed the far-
riding figure of the law when at last it found him. Just
about here the Arizona state line crosses, and that
section of country lying between the Grand Cañon and
Utah and Nevada, was for long, because of its inac-
cessibility, a resort for wanted men.

Half-way between the juncture of the Green and
the Grand and the lowering gate of Marble Cañon, the

San Juan River makes its *entrada* from the east. Poured down in foaming rills from the south-facing slopes of the great granitic knot of the Colorado Rockies, the San Juan makes a slow curve south to gather in the sandstone cañons, in which rivers seldom run now except during rains. Here in Chaco, Mancos, Cañon de Chelly, Las Animas, rose the peak of pre-Columbian culture in the Southwest. All streams in this region turn into the San Juan basin, draining east as far as Mesa Fachada which the Navajo call Saydegil. It is all Navajo country hereabout, sage-brush and bunch-grass country, a land of seasonal rivers, and water-holes about which the peach-tree grows wild and is at home.

Back from the mouth of Aztec Creek, a matter of five or six miles, rises the dome of Navajo Mountain. Bold shadows on its jagged sides give it a phantom look. Down its south slope, facing the direction from which the nursing clouds are blown, runs a thin forest of low-branched cedar and pine. Bleak it looks, and pale, arising from a great sandstone platform, red- and orange-striped, rounded and nodular, as sandstone weathers. In a side cañon dropping down from its north slope, in a wilderness of boulders so formidable that I suppose I shall never be able to make my way there, stands the flying arch of Rainbow Bridge. I saw a shadow picture of it once, woven into a Navajo rug, through which humble medium its beauty and

proportions struck so fearsomely that nothing would
have persuaded me to set foot upon it. I quite understood what its discoverer told me of his Navajo guide
who would not pass under the arch because he had
forgotten the prayers appropriate to such passage.

El vado de los Padres, which Escalante found, is
just below Navajo Mountain. Just beyond it the river
plunges between the walls of a marble gorge that by
the rapid rise of the plateau on each side, is made to
seem as if it dropped suddenly into that under-world
to which its path was once supposed to be the trail.

Half-way down to the turn which sets the great
dragon cañon sprawling across the corner of Arizona,
the eastern wall gives way for the *entrada* of the
Little Colorado. It arrives from western New Mexico, from the Sierra Zuñi, having drawn in that silver
thread along whose course arises the Middle Ant-
heap of the World, fed also by small rivulets going
north from the rim of the Mogollon Mesa, and
the infrequent floods of Moencopie Wash. From
Winslow, north, it cuts behind the San Francisco
Mountains and skirts the Painted Desert on the
west.

This Coloradito is a true desert river, flowing wide
and shallowly, eating new courses in the treeless valleys
with every heavy rain, or scuttling under its own
sands in drought like a frightened *azotl*. Not until it
reaches the sandstone formation of the Coconino pla-

teau does it bite down to the level of the Colorado Grande.

The number of persons who can speak with personal knowledge of the river between the *entrada* of the Little Colorado and the lower end of Boulder Cañon may be counted on the fingers of one hand: Dellenbaugh, Stanton, the Kolb brothers; perhaps some others, men whose business is with areonoid and rod. From point to point of the plateau one sees how the river runs, sometimes between a sheer wall and a shallow bank of sand, with strips and splashes of greenness, but oftener at the bottom of a trough of detritus from which the striated cliffs rise sheer to the sky-line. In Marble Cañon it goes without shores, between straight-sided, gleaming walls; vermilion and ocher, blue and saffron, like the sections of petrified wood one smuggles out of Adamana.

On still days the air is shaken with the roaring sound of the water forced through the narrows, audible far back from the brink of the cañon. Where the walls recede, the river shows opaque and yellowish, like a celluloid river in a panorama, with faint flecks of light and motion, difficult to translate into the proper terms of raging rapids. Now and again it disappears in the black gash of the inner cañon toward Sipapu. That very point at the crossing of Bright Angel Trail is the Hole in the Ground out of which, in the Days of the New, the Hopi came. From Hermit Rim

THE RIO . . . OPAQUE AND YELLOWISH LIKE A CELLULOID RIVER
IN A PANORAMA

417

the river writhes like a snake that, raging desperately against the steady up-push of the land, has stuck its fangs into its own side. For this river that drains an area about equal to the Republic of France does not proceed after the manner of rivers, seeking the land's lowest place. Not, at least, after it strikes the Colorado plateau.

This is a vast orderly country once laid down on the denuded earth-core as sea-bottom, now lying through almost its whole extent, more than a mile above sea-level. By many steep bajadas or meandering lines of castellated cliffs, tracing the flexures and fractures of its structural swells, it is divided into subsidiary plateaus, having each its own special interest. It was laid down in thousand-foot bands of limestone and shale, red, ocherous, sea-gray, and green, and so remains, tilted slightly toward the axis of the up-thrust. West, it runs to the palisades of the Virgin River beyond which the California desert drops two to three thousand feet. East of the Grand Cañon the plateau tilts down to the foot of Echo Cliffs, breaking high and abruptly between Marble Cañon and Moencopie Wash. Across this series of tilted tablelands, all the while that it was being slowly pushed skyward, the Rio Colorado cut its way.

Against the steady gnawing of the river, rose the land, as a log is pushed against a moving saw. Below the *entrada* of the Little Colorado, there must have

been times when the land rose faster than the river
could eat through the marble walls. Here the evidence
of its balked fury stuns appreciation. Beyond this
point, the river bends about the south front of Kaibab
plateau, rising almost half a mile above the Marble
Cañon country, which dips eastward here, and loses
itself under the painted mesas. West of Kaibab lies
Kanab; farthest west Shivwits, where the Shivwits
Paiutes still cling to their ancestral home. Between
them lie Shimuno and Uinkaret. These face you
darkly from the Coconino plateau which rims the
cañon on the south.

It is from Coconino that the cañon is best taken as a
spectacle. But not from any one point do you immediately come into relation with it. Go back among the
dark cedars and the widely spaced yellow pines until
your feet find by instinct the slightly sloping ground
that drops off suddenly into the abyss. Here you find
yourself at the head of one of the triangular bays
following the surface drainage inland to the farthest
point at which it can gather erosive force. So now
you perceive the structure of the Grand Cañon to be
that of a true valley, kept narrow and straight-sided
by the stubborn nature of its walls. Over toward
Bright Angel, where the material is softer, it makes
a gentler slope, or gets down from Kanab and Shi-
miuno by broken stairs and vast amphitheaters facing
the lowest land.

The thing to marvel at about the Grand Cañon, is that man should find it so in his nature to be astounded by the thousand-foot reach of a valley wall only when it happens to be arranged vertically in space. The towhee, the junco, and the piñonero flit ceaselessly over the rim and back again. The whisk-tailed squirrels are no more fearful of falling into that awful gulf than you are of dropping into interplanetary space. You wonder why we so constantly adjure childhood to be "too big to be afraid," when it is evidently a much happier state to be too small to be. The cedar and the white-fringed mountain mahogany go over, seeking down sheer walls and along the many-hued talus their familiar levels. On the Tonto plateau they give place to sage-brush, and next to the feather-foliaged greasewood. Far down on the hot zone of the lowest cañon levels, the yuccas and agaves consort with the dust-colored cat-claw and the cacti. On the north rim, where living streams come down the rocky stairs, they bring with them all the bloom and the bird song whose succession makes the charm of long mountain slopes. Caught all at once in this vertical sweep, it fixes forever the standard of comparison for men whose constant measure is of up-and-downness.

There must be something in this way of seeing things that is native to the deepest self of man, for once it is seen, there is no way afterward of not seeing it. Any time now,—and sometimes whether I will or no,—by a mere turn of attention, over the shoulder of my mind, as it were, I see it there . . . as I loved most to see it, . . . the noiseless dance of island towers, advancing, retreating; . . . cliffs burning red from within; the magical, shifty shadows, the vast down-throw of Kaibab, grape-colored, with a bloom on it of refracted light, . . . the twin, ember-glowing towers between which in the last day all the Navajos will come riding, riding down to Sipapu; old chiefs and older, he who broke the Chaco towns, lance-armed raiders, shield on elbow from the Shiprock region, fierce rene-gades from El Bosque Redondo, brass-buttoned cav-alry scouts, wound-striped khaki from Château-Thierry, . . . riding, riding, red fire in the west and shadows blue as morning.

But be careful whom you ask to point the place out to you, lest you be answered by one of the silly names cut out of a mythological dictionary and shaken in a hat before they were applied to the Grand Cañon for the benefit of that astonishing number of Americans who can never see anything unless it is supposed to look like something else. It is only from the north rim, however,—from Marble Cañon or from Kanab far-thest west,—that you understand why the long, flat silhouette of Kaibab should be called Mountain Lying Down, as it stoops to the hidden river. There is no use trying to improve on Indian names, really!

Kaibab is manured by the snow. Sacred spruces

grow there, and firs, well spaced, and plumy-yellow pines. Under them blacktail, streaking back their antlers, in the largest herds in the world; mokiách, the cougar, hunts the blacktail, and cattlemen hunt the last of the lobos. On Shimuno are ruins, mysterious, the extreme western reach of the stone-town builders. Across Kanab range dark cedars, mountain mahogany and the tree that was the younger brother of Pamaquásh. Low-lying Shivwits is gray with sage-brush and varnished creosote. All the vertical faces of the cliffs and the wide grassy flats are self-colored by the underlying formation, which is here chiefly vermilion limestone with thin beds of sea-colored shale.

Between Kanab and Uinkaret, cluster the cinder-streaked cones from which lava once flowed down the river gorge until it was cooled and checked by the racing water. Between these and the mass of San Francisco Mountain, blue against the south, and east and west between the Little Colorado and the Virgin rivers, lies all the splendor of the Left Hand of God.

Is the impulse which most people confess to, on first seeing the Grand Cañon, to cast themselves into its dim violet depths, confidently as a bird launches itself from a mountain-top upon the air, a reawakened pulse of surety we once had of its being as good a thing and as joyous to go down with the Left Hand as to go up with the Right? It is at any rate, here, a magnificent thing.

The sage-brush-covered platform which you see

from El Tovar, called Tonto plateau, is actually the
surface of that scoured granite core on which the
whole of Kaibab foundation was laid.    It is a matter
of three hours or less to go down to it, and so on down
into the V-shaped, inner cañon which the river has
cut in the most ancient rock.

There you see the frothy yellow flood making hidden bars of sand and spewing them forth in boiling
fountains of fury, like a man ridding himself of nursed,
secret grudges in spouts of temper.    But you will do
better in the way of understanding what the Left Hand
is about, if you stay on the rim and study the river of
clouds to which you are made privy on Kaibab and Coconino.    They come up burdened and shepherdless
from the delta until they strike the lift of desert-heated
air above Yuma and the Salada plains.    They lift
great glittering sails from the Pacific, defiling between the pillars of San Jacinto and San Bernardino.

Up and up they climb the viewless stairs, growing
diaphanous until at last they have hid themselves in
the deeps of the middle heavens.    About the intervening peaks you see them glimmer into visibility and disappear, as though mountains had the power some
people claim to exercise over the passing dead, of
compelling them to materialize.

Going north to find the Colorado Front, that will
release them into rain again, they are caught in the
eddies that play about the Grand Cañon.    Here acres

of naked rock give back the sun with such intensity it burns the hand to touch, and the middle depth of the gorge is blue with the quiver of heat-waves, rising. Then the cold air from Kaibab comes sliding down the russet-hued slope, and in the currents thus set in motion, whole flocks of dove-breasted clouds are netted. Sometimes they are packed close from rim to rim and in the whirl of hot and cold, struggle woundedly between the walls. Then the lightning bounds back and back from sheer rock surfaces, and the thunder loses itself in its own echo.

After such intervals, sometimes, the upper levels will be fleecy soft with snow, through which, far down, you can see the dust-colored cat-claw and the hot banks on which the gila monster sprawls; for never, never do the clouds get down to the river except they have been to the mountain and resolved themselves in rain. On that business almost any day you will see them feeling their way cautiously among the rock towers, or catch them of early mornings resting just under the Rim, behind some tall potrero.

I recall catching a flock of them there one morning, wing-folded under Yavapi Point, as I came in from watching a gibbous moon walking the Rim cautiously like a pregnant woman. I had walked too far, watching the moonlight drip down salient ledges, and the tops of the potreros swim into view out of abysmal darkness like young worlds appearing, so that moonset found me where I though it safest to wait until the

dawn came up, as it does in the Navajo country, a turquoise horse, neighing joyously.

So as I passed Yavapi, I saw the cloud flock sleeping, as I have seen seal sleep with their noses resting
on a point of rock, swaying with the sea's motion.
More lightly still the clouds slept, until, as if my step
had startled them, they began to scatter and rise, feeling for the wind's way, taking hands when they had
found it, curling up and over the rim.   Almost immediately I heard, far below, the soft *hee-haw* of the little
wild burros, long-eared like rabbits, rabbit-colored,
coming to drink of the dew, in the pits of the rocks
where the clouds had rested.   It was almost at this
same place that I saw on another occasion the dim face
of Rainbow Boy, behind the cloud-film in the rainbow
halo.   I am not sure that the other tourists saw anything but the changing configuration of the cliff
through the cloud-drift, but that was their misfortune.
It is only as they please that Those Above show themselves in the rainbow, which when the sun is low is
perfectly round here, or the moonbow, faint and fluc-
tuating on the level floor of cloud below the cañon
rim.

Below Havasu, where the fig and the vine go wild
and the tribe takes its name from the sky-colored
pools below the cascades, People of the Blue Water,
the cañon walls draw together; down where the river
foams and gurgles, the sun never reaches.   Here the
gorge is partly choked with lava, and the black rock

clinks when struck, like metal.   In the tributary cañons civet-cat and ocelot prowl, and otter fish in the clearing flood.   There are beaver on those infrequent streams, but the lack of trees to gnaw keeps them out of the dark, beachless stretches.

Beyond the *entrada* of the Virgin River from the north, the Colorado turns and widens, the hills stand back.   This is the site of the projected dam which, with a system of control dams at points farther up, all the way to Wyoming, will convert the river's fury into terms of power.   Below the turns the gorges are of diminished splendor, as the plateau breaks down by less and less steep bajadas to the level of the Mojave Desert.   Here it goes with a steady, wide surge over hard bottom.   Beyond Black Cañon and Pyramid and Bill Williams, the desert pushes up close along the river.   The last of the cinder cones, streaked with white and vermilion ash, and the black lava masses are left behind.   Here the mesquite and the creosote line the sandy washes, the ocotilla shakes its scarlet-tipped thyrses against the black rock, and the flat branchlets of the prickly-pear are lined with rose and white and saffron-colored flames.

At Mohave City the river issues between sandy flats under a wide sky in which the blue holds on until well past midnight, and the planets are white lamps swinging free in a twilight space.   Below the Santa Fé railroad crossing, The Needles, fawn-colored, splintered pinnacles, stand off to the east, and the *carrizales* begin. About Bill Williams Fork there are many colored walls, and then the long, winding slide to where the river turns about the point of Chocolate Mountains, turns again along a line of black, barren *picachos* and receives the Rio Gila.

Between Bill Williams and the Gila, the river seems to flow as Alarcón, being towed up it by the worshipful Cócopahs as a son of the Sun, observed, on a raised way of its own making, built up of enormous deposits of silt in its retarded course. To the west the land falls away in a glimmering desert basin, the Salton Sink, the logical continuation northward of the California Gulf. There must have been a time when Lower California was the island Alarcón expected to find, with the sea tides racing between San Jacinto and San Bernardino. Then the mountains lifted both together, and set back the sea-race toward the south. At that time the *entrada* of the Rio Colorado must have been about where Yuma is now, until by the steady pouring of its sands, it built a bar across the head of the estuary toward Cócopah Mountains, and cut off the Salton basin. Not all at once, nor permanently. Century by century the wilful river would break back into the inland sea, flooding and filling, until, in turn, the lake water cut the bar and mingled with the gulf again.

The last time it did that was four hundred years ago, and the last time it tried, was in the first decade of this century, when it had man to reckon with. In modern times there have been long intervals when the bottom of the Salton Sea lay as the Americans, looking for a transcontinental pass through the coastal mountains, found it in 1855: an interminable, low-lying, white desert, stretching from the pass of San Gorgonio in the direction of the California Gulf. It was after this discovery that we bought from Old Mexico the strip of country lying along the southern border of Arizona, known as the Gadsden Purchase.

The term Salton Sea applies only to the recent over-flow, which by no means covered the old lake bed, called after the tribes of that region, Lake Coahuila; but the whole of that lacustrine area, as outlined by the ancient beach lines and terraces and the bordering detrital slopes of the mountains, is best known as the Colorado Desert, El Desierte del rio Colorado. The Salton area is a spoon-shaped basin between the Santa Rosa and the Chuckwalla Mountains, pointed toward the gate-heads of San Jacinto and San Bernardino. By our modern method of recognizing localities by the impermanent works of man in them, the whole region is perhaps best located by such names as Indio, Imperial, Calexico, and Mexicali, for it goes down properly across the border along the Cócopahs, into the unmapped delta.

Forget now, if you know, how our border runs here. Forget if you can that shortsighted instinct of ours for the thing that promises most for the moment to the interested parties, which we call our Business Sense, by which our border was run in the worst possible place for the future that the land and river promised. It should have dropped from Nogales along the Sonoran crest to Guaymas and taken in the whole of Baja California, and might once or twice, in spite of initial error, have been laid there had it not been

for our characteristic tendency to label as impractical any project which knows intimately, looks far, and feels profoundly. But there, at least, the land lies, one vast alluvial plain and delta, hot under the sun, cooled by vast rushes of wind up from the gulf or down from the Pacific across the pass of San Gorgonio, watered by the perpetual race of mountain-seeking cloud-drift. And fertile! After the subsidence of spring floods, the gentle Yuma pokes a hole with his toe in the freshly deposited silt, drops a corn there, presses it in with the ball of his foot, and goes fishing until harvest. In the mountains of San Jacinto, passing south, gold is found; there a kunzite, garnet, and beryl, rose pink or diamond white.

The Gila comes in from the east, wide and slow and intermittent as the seasons run. It drains from the south slope of the Mogollon Rim, east by the Mimbres of New Mexico, north by the Salado to the White Mountains and by the Rio Verde to Bill Williams Mountain and the southern slope of that divide of which the north slope provides the blue water of the Havasupai. From the south the San Pedro River reaches the goal in good seasons, and the Santa Cruz, passing Tucson. Opposite Maricopa Point, where the Gila turns south around Gila Mountains, it receives the Hassyampa. This is a river inconsiderable except that its waters have a virtue by which, after having drunk them, you see the world all rainbow-colored, as all poets and most Arizonians see it.

These things are important; they come down with the river as the silt comes, and enrich the human history enacted there. All this color, the splendor of mountains and the broad lift of the mesas, the river's mighty rages, the drama of the Grand Cañon, the tribal legends, the wild asses drinking at the cloud pools, the cities of our Ancients—these come down to

the habitable lands and spread something as precious
to the culture that arises there as the alluvium of the
delta. Never to the deltas of the Nile or the Ganges,
never to Tigris and Euphrates, came a richer residuum
of the things that make great and powerful cultures.
Powerful, I mean, in their capacity to affect the
history of all culture.

Out of one of the great racial strains, rearing out
of history as the massive range of the Colorado Front
lifts from the continental axis, a human stream pours
into that country. Thin trickles of it show in Ashley
and Green valleys, along the tributaries of the San
Juan and the little Colorado; along the Gila and the
Salado are widening pools of it. About the upper
end of the Coahuila, above the Salton Sink, where the
old beach lines are still traced by the windrows of
spiny shrubs and salt-bush, there is an overflow from
the fat coastal valleys. Beyond these, the delta waits
the turning of the power of descending waters into the
invisible push of electric currents.

Ever since the chains of islands lying south of San
Jacinto were lifted and bound into a peninsula, the
delta has been a-building. In the equinoxes, *el burro
grande,* the great Colorado bore, comes tearing up the
estuary, with such force that only a short time ago the
*Topolobampo,* a thirty-six-ton steamer, was capsized
by it, with great loss of life.

The sound of *el burro grande* over the waters is like

the roll of young thunder. The land hereabouts is low-lying, reedy; vast *carrizales,* half submerged, alternating with flats of cottonwood and willow; lost sloughs beginning and ending nowhere in particular. Lions range in the canebrake, lynx and ocelot and droves of wild pig; beaver along the fresh-water dikes, deer that the cougar lies in wait for, and coyotes that follow the cougar for the sake of the offal he leaves from his kill. Out of the dikes and the hidden back-waters, innumerable water-birds rise with the crackle and roar of artillery.

Across all these the river finds its secret, sullen way. Now and then the cut banks of sandy loam between which it flows, cleave in huge cakes, and the river takes them gulpingly. Below the intake of the Imperial Canal, it works south until the edge of the Sonora mesa turns it west toward the back-water called Volcano Lake, where a season or two ago a wooden barrow-way was all that kept the river flood from rolling back into the new vineyards of its ancient inland sea. Beyond here are the geysers of boiling mud and the steam-pots which Melchior Diaz found. But before that the Cócopahs had made use of them as an ordeal against witchcraft. Let a tribesman but be suspected, and in he went; and as evidence of the correctness of Cócopah judgment, it is reported that none ever cleared himself by coming up again. Beyond Volcano Lake the main course of the river still bears the name of

that estimable young lieutenant of the British Royal
Navy who first mapped it, and was so disturbed over
the paucity of chemises among the native ladies.

Beyond the southern spur of Cócopah Mountains
the Rio Colorado meets the rush of blue water making
toward its ancient islets, and sets it back by the very
force of its opposing tides.   Where the red flood is
jammed back against the delta, it lets go its load of silt
in great shoals.   Where the tide reeves them out again,
the dust of granite mountains is distributed along the
sea-bottom, and raises the shore-line century by
century.

But who shall say, when they have made it the foundation of cities and rich orchards, from what mountain, by what deep-driven tributary, any more than
they shall say of the culture there in another hundred
years, what strains, American or Spanish or Amerind,
went to its making?

HASTA MAÑANA

# HASTA MAÑANA

MAN is not himself only, not solely a variation of his racial type in the pattern of his immediate experience. He is all that he sees; all that flows to him from a thousand sources, half noted, or noted not at all except by some sense that lies too deep for naming. He is the land, the lift of its mountain lines, the reach of its valleys; his is the rhythm of its seasonal processions, the involution and variation of its vegetal patterns. If there is in the country of his abiding, no more than a single refluent color, such as the veiled green of sage-brush or the splendid wine of sunset spilled along the Sangre de Cristo, he takes it in and gives it forth again in directions and occasions least suspected by himself, as a manner, as music, as a prevailing tone of thought, as the line of his rooftree, the pattern of his personal adornment.

Whatever this sense, always at work in man as the wheel is at work in the mill-race, taking up and turning into power the stuff of his sensory contacts, it works so deeply in him that often the only notice of its perpetual activity is a profound content in the presence of the thing it most works upon. He is aware of a steady purr in the midriff of his being, which, if he is an American, comes to the surface in such half articulate exhalations as "Gosh, but this a great country!"

To feel thus about your home-land is a sign that the mysterious quality of race is at work in you. For new races are not made new out of the dust as the first man was. They are made out of old races by reactions to new environment. Race is the pattern of established adjustments between the within and the without of man. Where two or three racial strains are run together, as coöperative adventurers in the new scene, or as conqueror grafting himself upon an earlier arrival, the land is the determining factor in the new design. By land, I mean all those things common to a given region, such as have been lightly or deeply touched upon in this book: the flow of prevailing winds, the succession of vegetal cover, the legend of ancient life; and the scene, above everything the magnificently shaped and colored scene. Operating subtly below all other types of adjustive experience, these are the things most quickly and surely passed from generation to generation, marked, in the face of all the daunting or neglectful things a land can do to its human inhabitants, by that purr of inward content, the index of race beginning.

Here between the Rio Colorado and the Rio Grande, between the Colorado plateau and the deserts of Sonora and Chihuahua, it begins under such conditions as have always patterned the great cultures of the past, great, I mean, in their capacity to affect world culture and human history. In Greece, in Rome, in England, world power began with aboriginal cultures of sufficient rootage to have already given rise to adequate symbols, in art and social forms, of their assimilation to the land, upon which were engrafted later, invasive types, superior at least in their capacity to interrupt with determining force, the indigenous patterns. So, in our Southwest, we began with an aboriginal top-soil culture, rich in the florescence of assimilation, to which was added the overflow from the golden century of Spain, melting and mixing with the native strain to the point of producing a distinctive if not final pattern before it received its second contribution from the American East.

If I say that this American contribution is prevailingly Nordic, it is not because I commit myself to the swelling myth about a Nordic race, but because the term, for the moment, stands as the index of an accepted type. It is a type that, when its early representatives reached the land of its journey's ending across the incredible adventure of the Santa Fé Trail, was already established in a sense of race, a sense, at least, of reliance upon some deeply fleshed sinew of a common adaptive experience. It knew what it wanted, and moved instinctively by the shortest cuts to a generically Western accomplishment.

Your true man of race is always instinctive. It is only hybrids and the half-assimilated who rationalize and codify and suffer under the necessity of explaining themselves. For the first hundred years, not many Americans reached the Southwest who were not already partly assimilated to it, by their natures. It is, in fact, hardly three quarters of a century since the flag of American federation was raised in the plaza of Santa Fé. And already the land bites sharply into the deep self of the people who live upon it.

The first evidence of cultural evolution is the voiceless rhythm of acceptance . . . land . . . my land! . . . between which and the beginning of cultural expression lies a period, sometimes prolonged for generations, depending on the realization and general adoption of native symbols for experiences intimate and peculiar to that land. The profoundest implications of human experience are never stated rationally, never with explicitness, but indirectly in what we agree to call art forms, rhythms, festivals, designs, melodies, objective symbolic substitutions.

The business of assembling such a set of symbols for the expression of its deeper reactions is, to a people newly come to a country, likely to be a long one, complicated as it is by the absorbing preoccupation of getting a living. There are many provinces in the United States in which there is as yet scarcely more than the first letter of the alphabet of such expression. These are places where there was never sufficient aboriginal life to interpret the land's primary reactions, or such aboriginals as were found, were too quickly and completely exterminated. Along our eastern coast often the invasive culture is edged with a complex which bolsters itself against implications of inferiority by a stubborn insensibility to the aboriginal contribution. As if a tree should prove itself more a tree by declining to be nourished by the humus laid down on the bare sand by the grass and the brier! Yet, oddly, it is from just the generation that has declined the ten-thousand-year-old alphabet ready to his hand, that the fiercest diatribes against our American lack of adequate spiritual exchange proceeds.

Before there can be any nationally releasing expression, there must be a widely accepted set of releasing symbols. Such symbols must be generic, image and superscription of the land's true regnancy. We can no more produce, in any section of the United States, a quick and characteristic culture with the worn currency of classicism and Christianity, than we can do business with the coinage of imperial Rome.

Here in the Southwest, and up along the western coast, where our blood-stream reaches its New-World journey's ending, it finds itself possessed with no effort, along with beauty and food- and power-producing natural resources, of a competent alphabet of cultural expression. Thus it gains so enormously over all other sections, where such notation is still to be produced, that one confidently predicts the rise there, within appreciable time, of the *next* great and fructifying world culture.

It draws, this land of prophecy, from more than the region herein described, from all up the California coast to San Francisco, between the sea and the Sierras, from districts east of the Rio Grande toward Texas, from Chihuahua and Sonora of the South. But by virtue of its acceptance and use of aboriginal material as a medium of spiritual expression, it takes its dominant note from the place of the Sacred Mountains, from the place of our Ancients, the home of the Guardian of the Water Sources. Takes it, in point of time just so much in advance of other American provinces as goes to the development in them, of similar indigenous mediums of cultural expression.

Three strains of comparative purity lie here in absorbing contact, the Indian, the Spanish, and the so-called Nordic-American, for by distance, by terror of vastness and raw surfaces, the more timorous, least adaptive elements of our population are strained out. Of these three the Spanish serves chiefly to mollify temperamentally the aboriginal strain, so that in New Mexico and Arizona we approach nearest, in the New World, to the cultural beginnings which produced the glory that was Greece, the energetic blond engrafture on a dark, earth-nurtured race, in a land whose beauty takes the breath like pain.

Elsewhere in the United States the same, or nearly the same, elements will undoubtedly rise to high levels of cultural attainment; perhaps next in the river and forest country north of San Francisco, spreading into Canada of the west coast. There rather than in the wheat country cut by the Canadian boundary, because on the coast the aboriginal root is ablest to take the graft. But here, centered economically about the *plan del Rio Colorado,* out of that top-soil that I have rendered as faithfully as is in me, look to see the fountain rise to world levels within the time of your children's children.

If you are of the temperament which takes as much pleasure in the spring showing of your garden, as in the summer's full florescence, go look about Santa Fé, or at Phœnix, Arizona, where the young shoot is in tender leaf. Look for native festivals, look for signs on garages and shops, signs of the stepped horizon, the altar-line of the mesas, signs of the four great winds of the world, of the fructifying cloud,— at San Felipe you will find it on the baptismal font,— signs of the plumed serpent, Guardian of the Water Sources, acceptable local symbols of wide-spread service and increase. Look for a Thunderbird Tourist Service. What more competent embodiment of the spirit of service, in a land where for ten thousand years it has been looked for from the corn rows, augury of a fruitful season, the dark-bodied, dun-feathered cloud of the summer rain, wing stretched from mountain to mountain, with arrows of the lightning in its claws.

Would you go with me if I asked you, to ancient Greece to see the Kouroi dance about the infant Jove? Go with me to Prescott instead, and I will show you the like of what has not happened for three thousand years.

Two or three years ago, at Prescott, certain of their young men thought it would be good fun to recapture for a summer's entertainment a dance of the Moquis, which the Bumbeltonion Indian Bureau cheats us and stultifies itself to suppress, a dance for the propitiation of the Sky Powers toward the food-bearing earth. And in the midst of their dancing, more colorful and more stirring than any Russian folk-jig imported at vast expense by some foreignly derived art patron in New York, the men of Prescott were pierced through with understanding. The earth spirit took them, and what was begun as a light adventure became a serious pursuit. Did you think, then, that it is only in MacDougal Street that art renews itself? Go to Prescott, to the dance of the Smokis. Go to Santa Fé, on the anniversary of the *entrada* on Don Diego de Vargas, or to Gallup, at the focus of desert enchantment, a little later, to see the

Indians themselves dancing, with all its subtlest implications, the intimate drama of the relation of race to environment.

Go even if you are susceptible to no more than the charm of strangeness, of unusual color and the inspiriting stir of native rhythms. As entertainment the Gallup and Santa Fé festivals outclass the unoriginal antics of modern stage dancing by as much as in recreational values they surpass them. But if you care for Art Becoming, if you are curious about the ultimate American expression in dance and drama, you cannot afford to miss them. Not at least until you have been to the Holy Mountain and learned what the young men of that country know so instinctively that they do not know that what goes on in them is the beat of the pulse of race-beginning.

What I have drawn for you here is the ground plan on which the rising curve of that pulse is plotted. The index of its highest peak awaits like the fulfilment of prophecy, *hasta mañana,* . . . "until to-morrow"!

# QUOTATIONS

447

## Chapter XII

Siglo de oro.
*The golden age.*

Por el estomago.
*For the stomach.*

La villa real de la Santa Fé de San Francisco.
*The royal city of the holy faith of San Francisco.*

### The Dawn of the Morning

Angel de me guardia, noble compania . . .
*Angel of my protection, noble assembly* . . .

Darame gracias, Ave Maria.
*Give me thy grace, Ave Marie.*

### Coplas

De las estrellas del cielo tango que bajarte dos.
*From the stars of the heaven I will bring down two.*

Una para saludarte, y otro para dacite adios.
*One to salute you, and the other to give you adieu.*

### Tecolito

*Pajaro, coo, coo, coo, etc.*

Little bird, coo, coo, coo.
Poor little, dear little animal,
Are you hungry, little owlet?
Coo, coo, coo!

Entriegas de Novios.
*Advice to the newly wed.*

La vespera de la buena noche.
*The evening of the good night: (Christmas night).*

### Chapter XIV

Dios tien piedad de me!
*God take pity on me!*

### Chapter XV

El desierto del rio Colorado.
*The desert of the Colorado River.*

# GLOSSARY

## RULES FOR PRONOUNCING SPANISH WORDS

In Spanish, every vowel has its full value, as follows:

a — ă............................as in *father*
e — ā............................as in *ale*
i — ē............................as in *eve*
o — ō............................as in *old*
u — ōō..........................as in *food*
y — ēē..........................as in *eel*
ay — ī..........................as in *ice*
ey — ā..........................as in *ale*

Consonants are sounded as in English, with the exception of the following:

c — before a, o, u..................as in *cake*
c — before e, i.....................th, as in *thin*
g — before a, o, u.................as in *go*
g — before e, i....................as in *gin*
gu — before a, o...................as in *guava*
gu — before e, i...................as in *get*
h................................always silent
j — guttural h.....................as in *hid*
ll — l'y...........................as in *William*
ñ — ny............................as in *canyon*
q — k.............................as in *key*
y — as a consonant................as in *year*
z — th............................as in *mother*
**rr** is distinctly rolled
**s** is sharply hissed

## ACCENTS

Spanish words ending in a vowel are accented on the next to the last syllable, except as otherwise noted.

Spanish words ending in a consonant are accented on the last syllable, except as otherwise noted.

Indian words are usually spelled and pronounced as Spanish, though this does not always render the exact sounds, which are impossible to represent in English phonetics. Wherever the pronunciation differs from the Spanish, it is marked as in the Century Dictionary.

Most Indian words are accented equally on all syllables, in which case there will be no accent mark.

A′bi-qui-u, a town in New Mexico; a former Tewa pueblo.

A-bo′, a ruined Piros pueblo east of the Rio Grande, New Mexico.

a′bra, wide-open valley.

a-ce′qui-a, irrigating ditch.

a-ce′qui-a ma′dre, mother ditch.

A′co-ma, from Ákome, people of the white rock; a Keres pueblo, New Mexico.

a-de-lan-ta′do, forerunner, chief officer in a new land.

a-do′be, clay for building.

a-ga′ve, any variety of the century plant.

A′gu-a Cal-i-en′te, hot-water spring.

a-gu-ar-di-en′te, ardent water, brandy.

A′ha-yu-ta, one of the Twins of War and Chance.

A′jo, Papago town, Arizona.

Ak′im-ult O-o′tam," River people," Pimas.

a-la-ba′dos, hymns.

A-la-mi′llo, little cottonwood; town on the Rio Grande, New Mexico.

al-cal′de, mayor, head man of a Spanish town; also place name.

al-fil-e-ri′a, stick pin, shape of seed pods.

Al-go-do′nes, cotton fields; place name.

al-gua-cil′, constable.

Al-i-hi-hi-a′ni, place where the children were buried; Papago shrine.

Al-ma-den′, mines; place name.

Al-o′sa-ka, mythical Hopi personage.

Al-tar′, altar; river and town in Papagueria.

a-mo′le, yucca soap-root.

A′na-huac, Mexican home of Aztecs.

an-te in-su-la, before the island.

An-ti′lla, the Antilles.

A-pa′che, the enemy; numerous tribes of Athapascan stock.

A-pa′ches de Na-va-jo′, Apaches of the planted fields; old name for Navajo tribes.

A-rap′a-hoe, traders; plains tribe; also place name.

A-ri-va′ca, ruined Arizona mission.

A-ri-zo′nac, small springs; original of Arizona.

arr-i-er′os, muleteers.

ar-roy′o, channel of a stream.

Ar-roy′o Cha′co, cañon of Chaco Creek, northwestern New Mexico.

Ar-roy′o Hon′do, deep arroyo.

a-ta′jo, mule-pack train.

au′to, an edict, a personal statement.

au′to de fe′, punishment for heresy.

A-wan′yu, plumed serpent deity.

A-wa′to-bi, place of the bows; extinct Hopi pueblo.

Az′tec, tribe of Mexico.

a-zo′tl, whip lash, lizard.

Az-tlan′, place of herons.

bai′le, ball, dance.

ba′ja, lower.

**ba-ja′da,** down throw of a hill, steep slope.

**ban′ca,** bench.

**ban-quir′,** dealer in four-card monte.

**bar-ran′ca,** high bank, escarpment.

**bar′ri-o,** ward, precinct.

**ba-ta-mo′te,** a shrub frequenting stream beds.

**ba′ta vo′ta,** water shield; Hopi original of above.

**bay-et′a,** red baize used for lining Spanish cloaks.

**Be-len′,** Bethlehem; town on Rio Grande.

**Ber-na-li′llo,** little Bernard, town on Rio Grande.

**bis-na′ga,** barrel cactus.

**Bo-ba-qui′va-ri,** pinched in below the middle; Papago mountain.

**bol-son′,** basin.

**Bo-qui′llo,** little mouth; mountain pass in Mexico.

**bo-re′go,** sheep-herder.

**Bos′que Re-don′do,** round woods; former Navajo reservation.

**bra′vo,** valiant.

**bur′ro-bur′ro,** anything out of the ordinary.

**bur′ro gran′de, el,** the Colorado bore.

**ca-ba-lla′da,** drove of horses.

**ca-ba-ller′o,** horseman, gentleman.

**ca-ba′llo,** horse.

**cache** (cash), hiding-place.

**ca-ci′que,** head priest.

**ca-la-ba′za,** squash, calabash; place name.

**Cal-va′ri-o,** Calvary.

**ca-mi′no re-al′,** king's highway.

**cam′po san′to,** camp of the saints; cemetery.

**Cañon de Chelly** (can-yon′ de Shay), among the cliffs; Spanish corruption of Navajo Tségi.

**can-ta-dor′,** song leader.

**cap-i-tan′,** captain, chief.

**car-re′ta,** cart.

**car-re′ta de mu-er′te,** death-cart.

**car-ri-zal′, car-ri-za′les,** from carrizo, reed-grass; place names.

**Ca′sa Rin-con-a′da,** house in the corner.

**ca-si′ta,** little house.

**Cay-mun-ge′, Cu-ya-mun′ge,** extinct Tewa pueblo; also town near Santa Fé.

**cay′use,** Indian pony.

**Cer′ro de Ca-be′za,** head-shaped hill.

**Cer′ro de Mon-te-zu′ma,** Hill of Montezuma.

**Cha′co,** white; cañon and ruins in northwestern New Mexico.

**Cha-la′cas,** one of the Aztec tribes.

**Cha′ma,** red; river and district.

**Cha-mi′ta,** little Chama.

**cha-par-ral′,** brush.

**char′co,** pond.

**Chet-tro Ket-tle,** House of the Winds; Chaco ruin.

**chif-o-net′ti,** sacred clown, representing spirits of ancestors.

**Chi-hua′hua,** province, city, and trail of Mexico.

**chi′le,** red pepper.

**Chi-li-li′,** ruined Piros pueblos, New Mexico.

**Chi-may-o′,** town, New Mexico.

**Chin-lee′,** creek in Navajo country.

**Chi-ri-ca′hua,** wild turkey; also Apache tribe; place name.

**cho′lla (cho′ya),** a round-branched cactus.

**cho-lli-tal′ (cho-yi-tal′),** where cholla grows.

**Chuck-wal′la,** large lizard; mountains.

**Chu-pa-de′ro,** cattle tick; mountains.

**Ci′bo-la or Shi′vo-la,** mythical treasure country; sun cities of Zuñi.

ci'bo-la, the buffalo.

ci-bo-ller'o, buffalo-hunter.

Ci-cu-ye', old name of Pecos.

ci-en'a-ga, swamp, wet meadow.

ci-en-a-gui'lla, little swampy place.

Co-a-hui'la, tribes; mountains and lake in California.

Co-ba'bi, Papago village, Arizona.

Co-chi-te'ños, inhabitants of Cochití.

Co-chi-ti', Keres pueblo on Rio Grande.

co-ci-ne'ra, cook.

Co-co-ni'no, plateau south of Grand Cañon.

Co'co-pahs, Division of Yuma Indians. Also place name.

Co-fi-ti-chi'que, Indian town on Savannah River. Visited by De Soto.

Co-lo-ra-di'to, little Colorado; river.

Co-lo-ra'do, ruddy, reddish.

Co-lo-ra'do Chi-qui'to, little Colorado; river.

co-man-dan'te, commander.

Co-mo-ba'bi, Papago village, Arizona.

com-pa-ñer'os, companions.

Com-pos-te'la, town in old Mexico.

con'chos, shells; shell-shaped ornaments.

con-duc'ta, official trade caravan.

con-quis-ta-do'res, conquerors in a new country.

con'tra yer'ba, counteracting herb.

con-ven'to, monastery.

co'plas, couplets.

Cor-di-ller'a, stringtown; string of mountains.

Cor'do-ba, town in New Mexico.

cor-on'a de Je-sús (hesús), crown of Jesus, thorn-bush.

cor-re-dor' del çam-in'o, runner of the road, chaparral cock.

cor-rer'del ga'llo, cock race.

Cos-ni'na, early name for Colorado River; same as Coconino.

Cos-ti'lla, the rib; river and town in New Mexico.

Cru-za'dos, cross-bearers; unidentified tribe.

cu-ev'as, shallow caves.

Cu-le'bra, winding; river and mountains, New Mexico.

Cu-li-a-can', San Miguel de Culican in Mexico.

cum'bre, crest.

dis-ci-pli'na, penitente whip.

Do-ko-slid, Navajo name for Mt. Taylor.

Do-min-gue'ños, inhabitants of Santa Domingo pueblo.

Don, sir; used with first name only.

Do'ña, lady; used with first name only.

El Guer'o, the blond.

El Mor'ro, the castle.

El Pa'so del Nor'te, the pass of the north, on the Rio Grande.

El Va'do de los Pad'res, the crossing of the fathers; on Colorado River.

en-cer'ro, shut-in place.

en-chi-la'das, corn cakes with chile sauce.

en-tra'da, entry, mouth of a river.

Es-pa-ño'la, Spanish town.

Es-tan'ci-a, station; also place name.

Fer-nan'dez de Ta'os (towse), town in New Mexico.

frai'le, Spanish monk.

Fray, brother.

Fray Cris-to-bal', Brother Christopher; hills along the Rio Grande.

Gal-is-te'o, river and town near Santa Fé, N. M.

Ga-lli'nas, hens; common place name in New Mexico.

ga-lli'ta, hard-tack; coarse grass.

gam-bu-ci'nos, prospectors, pocket hunters.

gar-am-bo'ya, flamboyant bush.

gen'tes prin-ci-pal'es, principal families.

Gi'la (he'la), river and mountains in Arizona.

grin'go, Yankee.

Guad-a-lu'pe, city of old Mexico.

Guay'mas, Mexican port on gulf of California.

guay-u'le, rubber-producing weed in Arizona.

ha-ci-en'da, country estate.

ha-ci-en-de'ro, country gentleman.

Ha'lo-na, ant-heap, Zuñi pueblo.

Has-sy-yam'pa, in one dialect "small rocks," in another "sacred bear"; river.

Ha-va-su, blue water.

Ha-va-su-pai', people of the blue water; cataract Cañon of the Colorado.

Ha'wi-kuh, ruined Zuñi pueblo first visited by Spaniards.

Her-man'os de luz, brothers of light; officers of penitente society.

Hi'nu-no, Paiute mythical personage.

hod'den-tin, sacred pollen.

ho-gan', Navajo hut.

ho-ho'ba, rejuvenator.

Ho'ho-kum, the unknown; prehistoric people of Casa Grande, Arizona.

ho-la', hello.

Ho'pi-tu shi'nu-mu, peaceful people; the Hopi.

Hual-a-pai, or Walapai, pine-tree people; Yuman tribe on the middle Colorado.

Hun'go Pa'vi, crooked nose; ruined Chaco pueblo.

In'di-o, Indian.

in-fer'mo, one who has care of the sick.

in-for-ma-ci-on'es, public records.

Is-le'ta, islet; Tigua pueblo on Rio Grande.

Is-le'ta del Sur, islet of the south; Tigua pueblo near El Paso.

ja-cal', square brush hut.

ja-va-li'na, wild pig.

Je'mez, river and pueblo, New Mexico.

Jo-han-o-ai', mythical Navajo personage.

Jor-na'da del Di-ab'lo, devil's journey; in Papago country, Arizona.

Jor-na'da del Mu-er'to, dead men's journey; between El Paso and Soccoro.

Juar'ez, Mexican city across from El Paso.

Kai'bab, mountain lying down; north of Grand Cañon.

Ka-le-o-ta'ka, mythical Hopi personage.

Ka-nab', plateau north of Grand Cañon.

Kas-kas'ki-a, former Indian tribe and town in Illinois.

Ka-tchi'nas, masked impersonators of the gods.

Ke'res, linguistic group of Cochití, Santo Domingo, San Felipe, Santa Ana, Sia, Laguna, and Acoma pueblos in New Mexico.

Kin Bin-i-o'la, House of the Rains; Chaco ruin, New Mexico.

Kin Kli-zhin, House of the Winds; Chaco ruin, New Mexico.

ki'si, booth where the snakes are kept for the Hopi Snake Dance.

ki'va, ceremonial chamber of the Pueblos.

Ko-shar'e, delight-makers, ceremonial clowns.

**Ko'ye-mi-shi,** mud-heads; Zuñi mythical personages.

**Ku-ko-mal'ik,** Papago village, Arizona.

**La Ba-ja'da,** steep slope between Santa Fé and Albuquerque.

**La Ca-ña'da,** cañon-like, place name.

**La Con-quis-ta-do'ra,** Our Lady Conqueror.

**LaFon'da,** the bottom, end of the trail.

**La-gu'na,** lake; one of the Keres pueblos, New Mexico.

**Las An'i-mas,** the souls; river and ruins.

**La-va'ca,** the cow; river, tributary to Rio Grande.

**lo'bo,** wolf.

**Los Co-man'chos,** the Comanches.

**Los Her-man'os Pen-i-ten'tes,** the Penitent Brothers.

**Los In'di-os,** the Indians.

**Los La-dron'es,** the robbers; mountains, New Mexico.

**Los Lu'nas,** the Luna estates.

**Los Muer'tos,** city of the dead, Arizona.

**Los Pas-tor'es,** the shepherds, a miracle play.

**Los Piñ'os,** the pine-trees; place name.

**lu-mi-na'ri-a,** bonfires.

**lla'no,** flat land, plain; also place name.

**ma-che'te,** native Mexican knife.

**Ma-da-le'na,** Magdalene Mountains, New Mexico.

**ma-guey',** the century plant.

**Man'cos,** left-handed; river of New Mexico.

**man'os,** hand-stone for grinding.

**Man-zan'o,** apple; one of the cities that died.

**Man-zan'os,** apples; mountain range east of Rio Grande, New Mexico.

**Ma-ri-co'pa,** an Arizona tribe.

**Mar'sat To-ja-pik',** dry hot month; Papago.

**ma'ta-chi-ne,** Mexican dance-drama, danced at New Mexican pueblos.

**Mat'sa-le-ma,** one of the twin gods of war and chance.

**Mat'sa-ki,** salt city; ruined Zuñi pueblo.

**me'dan-os,** sand-dunes.

**me'sa,** table-land.

**Me'sa Fa-cha'da,** mesa with great frontage; same as Saydegil.

**Me'sa Ver'de,** green mesa in Colorado.

**Me-sa Ju-man'-os,** mesa named after Jumano Indians, east of Rio Grande.

**mes-cal',** stalk and leaf base of agave prepared for eating.

**Mes-cal-er'o A-pa-che,** mescal-eating Apaches, New Mexico.

**Me-si'ta de la Ta'pi-a,** little mesa of the rim rock.

**me-si'lla,** little mesa; place name.

**mes-ti'zos,** half-breeds.

**me-ta'te,** milling-stone.

**me-tra'ca,** wooden rattle, bull roarer.

**Mim-bres,** willows; river in Arizona.

**Mis-hong'no-vi,** place of standing rock; Hopi pueblo.

**Mo'en-co-pi-e,** place of running water, Arizona.

**Mo-go-llon',** named after former Governor; mesa and mountain, Arizona.

**Mo-ja've,** three mountains; a Yuma tribe.

**mo'ki-ach,** Keres name for the puma.

**Mon-te-zu'ma,** chief of Aztec tribes; common place name.

**Mo'qui,** another name of Hopi.

**mo-ra'da,** lodge, chapter-house of penitentes.

**Mu-y ri'co,** very rich man.

**Na-ci-mi-en'to,** the Nativity.

**Na'hua-tl,** linguistic group of central Mexico; the Aztecs.

**Nau-fra'gi-os y Jor-na'da,** voyages and journey (of Cabeza de Vaca).

**Na-va-hu',** place of planted fields; Tewa ruin near Santa Fé.

**Na'va-jo,** people of the planted fields.

**ni-ñi'to,** infant.

**Ni'ño Di'os,** Christ child.

**No-che-bu-en'a,** the good night, Christmas.

**No-gal'es,** walnuts; town on Mexican-Arizona border.

**no-pal',** prickly-pear cactus.

**o-co-ti'lla,** little torch cactus.

**O'jo Cal-i-en'te,** hot spring.

**o-jo gi-gan'te,** giant's eye; spring.

**O'ku,** Turtle Mountain.

**o'lla,** water-jar.

**O-rai'bi,** place of the rock; Hopi pueblo.

**Or'gan-os,** organ-pipe mountains.

**os'ha,** wild angelica root.

**O-to-wi,** Tigua ruin.

**Pad'res,** Franciscan fathers.

**Pa-go'sa Pi-e'dra,** district of southern Colorado.

**pai-san'os,** country people.

**Pai'ute,** Utes of the small streams, widely distributed tribe.

**pa'ja-ra,** bird.

**pa-ja-ri'ta,** little bird.

**Pa-ja-ri'tan,** pertaining to Pajarita plateau.

**Pa-lo'ma,** dove; common place name.

**pa'lo ver'de,** green tree.

**Pa-ma-quash',** tall fellow; mythical Paiute hero.

**Pan-tak',** place where the coyote stayed; Papago camp.

**Pa-pa-gue-ri'a,** Papago land.

**Pa'pa-go,** modern form of above.

**Pa'pa O-o'tam,** people of the bean.

**Pa-ri'a,** the outcast, Colorado River intervale.

**pa-se-ar',** foot journey.

**pa'ti-o,** inclosed space between rooms.

**Paw-nee',** plains tribe; name from horn-shaped head-dress.

**Pe'cos,** abandoned pueblo; also river.

**Pe-der-nal',** flint mountain, New Mexico.

**Pe'ña Blan'ca,** white rock.

**Pe'ña Hue'ca,** notched, or spindle mountain.

**Pe-nas'co,** rocky.

**Pe-ñas'co Blan-co,** white rocky.

**pe-ni-ten-ci-ar'i-o,** penitentiary.

**pe-ñol',** great rock.

**pi-ca'cho,** awl-shaped peak.

**Pi-cu-ris',** Tanoan pueblo, New Mexico.

**Pi'ma,** or **Pi'mo,** "don't know"; Gila River Indians.

**Pi-me-ri'a Al'ta,** upper Pima country.

**Pi-ni-ni-can'gwi,** popcorn meal mesa neck; Pajaritan ruin.

**pi-ñon',** edible pine-nut tree.

**pi-ñon-er'o,** jay bird.

**pin'to,** spotted.

**Pi'ros,** nearly extinct tribe of lower Rio Grande Valley.

**pi-ta-hay'a,** cactus fruit.

**pi-te'ro,** flute-player.

**pla-ci'ta,** little place, hamlet.

**plan del Rio,** river plain.

**play'a,** beach, land smoothed by water.

**pla'za,** open ground between houses; public square.

**Po-se-un'ge,** a ruined pueblo near Chama; Poseyemo's birthplace.

**Po-shu-ouin'ge,** ruin near Abiquiu.

**Po-joa-que (po-hwa'kee),** Tewa pueblo, near Española, N. M.

**Po-joa-que'ños,** inhabitants of the above.

**Po-se-ye'mo,** or **Po-se-ue've,** Tewa culture hero.

**po-tre'ro,** colt pasture, any naturally fenced pasture.

**Po-tre'ro de las Va'cas,** potrero of the cows.

**pra'do,** meadow; also place name.

**pre-gon-er'o,** town crier.

**prin-ci-pal'es,** chief citizens.

**Pue-ble'ños,** inhabitants of the Indian towns of New Mexico and Arizona.

**pue'blo,** town.

**Pue'blo Bo-ni'to,** pretty town; one of the Chaco ruins.

**Pue'blo Pin-ta'do,** striped, or painted pueblo.

**Pu-ye',** ancient cliff city near Española, N. M.

**Qua-rai',** ruined Tigua pueblo, Estancia Valley, N. M.

**Quer-na-ver'de,** green horn; famous Comanche warrior.

**Ques'ta,** the quest; New Mexican town.

**Ques'ta la Osh'a,** medicine quest; one of the Culebra peaks.

**Qui-to-vac',** Papago village.

**Qui-to-va-qui'ta,** Papago village.

**Qui-vi'ra,** fabled treasure country.

**ra-ma'da,** shelter of boughs.

**ra-mu'da,** string of wild horses.

**ran'cho,** farm.

**ran-cher'o,** farmer.

**Ran'chos de Ta'os (towse),** farming settlement near Taos, N. M.

**Ran'chos de tem-po-ral'es,** ranches of the rainstorms; summer residences of the pueblo Indians.

**Ran'cho Te-jon',** badger ranch.

**Ra-ton',** wild rat; place name.

**re-me'di-os,** remedies.

**ri'co,** rich man.

**ri-lli'to,** brook.

**rin-con',** corner; place name.

**rin-con-ad'a,** place in the corner; common place name.

**ri'o,** river.

**Rio Ar-ri'ba,** upper river district.

**Rio A-ba'ja,** lower river district.

**Rio Bra'vo,** strong river; early name for Rio Grande.

**Rio Cha'ma,** red river.

**Rio Chi-qui'to,** little river.

**Rio Co-lo-ra'do,** ruddy river.

**Rio Con'chos,** shell river.

**Rio de Li'no,** river of flax.

**Rio de los Mar-tir'es,** river of the martyrs; early name for Colorado River.

**Rio del Ti-zon',** river of the fine brand; early name for Colorado River.

**Rio Grande de Bue'na Es-per-an'za,** great river of good hope; early name for Colorado River.

**Rio Gran'de del Nor'te,** great river of the north.

**Rio Man'cos,** left-hand river.

**Rio Puer'co,** dirty river.

**Rio Pie'dra,** stone river.

**Rio Ver'de,** green river.

**ri'to,** creek.

**Ri'to de los Fri-jo'les,** bean creek.

**Ro'bles,** oaks.

**ro'sa San Juan (hwan),** rose of St. John; Mexican primrose.

**Ro-sa'rio,** rosary.

**ru-ral'es,** country people.

**sa-hua'ro,** giant cactus.

**sa'la,** parlor.

**Sa-la'da, -do,** salty; common place name.

**Sa-li'nas,** salt lakes.

**Sal-ton',** leaping-place (grasshopper).

**San Ber-nar-di'no,** St. Bernard Mountain, California.

**Sanc-tu-ar'i-o,** sanctuary.

**San-di'a,** watermelon; mountain and pueblo.

**San Fe-li'pe,** St. Philip, Keres pueblo.

**San Gab-ri-el',** old name for capital of New Mexico.

**San Gor-go'ni-o,** pass leading into California from Arizona.

**sangra-dor',** officer in penitente society.

**San-gre de Cris-to,** Blood of Christ; mountain.

**san-gre de dra-go,** dragon's blood.

**San Il-de-fon'so,** Tewa pueblo.

**San Ja-cin'to,** Mountain in California.

**San Mar-ci-al',** town on Rio Grande.

**San Ma-te'o,** St. Matthew mountain, otherwise Mt. Taylor.

**San Mi-guel' de Cu-li-a-can',** town in Mexico.

**San'ta An'a,** St. Ann. Keres pueblo.

**San'ta Cla'ra,** Tewa pueblo.

**San'ta Cruz,** holy cross; river and town; New Mexico.

**San'ta Ro-sa,** chief Papago town, Arizona.

**San'ta Ro-sa-li'a,** old Spanish painting at Isleta.

**San'to Do-min'go,** St. Dominick; Keres pueblo.

**san'tos,** saints.

**San Xa'vi-er del Bac,** St. Xavier by the water; Papago mission near Tucson.

**Say-de-gil',** Navajo name for Mesa Fachada.

**Se-ka'la K'a-am'ja,** the deathless one, Apache myth.

**Sen-a-cu',** former Piros pueblo, now town on Rio Grande.

**Se-vi-lli'ta,** little Seville; town on Rio Grande.

**sha'man,** wise man.

**Shi-po'lo-vi,** mosquito place; Hopi pueblo.

**Shiv'wits,** small Paiute tribe north of Grand Cañon.

**Shi'wi-na,** Zuñi.

**Shong-o'po-vi,** place of grass; Hopi pueblo.

**Shu-fi-ne',** dark obsidian flakes; ruined cliff city near Española.

**Shu-ki',** home of Papago deity.

**Shu'mi-no,** mesa north of Grand Cañon.

**Si'a,** Keres pueblo on Jemez River.

**Sich-o'mo-vi,** wild currant place; Hopi pueblo.

**Si-er'ra,** saw-tooth mountain crest.

**Si-er'ra Blan'ca,** white mountain.

**Si-er'ra de la Es-pu'ma,** mountain of the foam.

**Si-er'ra Mad're,** mother mountain.

**Si-er'ra Zu'ñi,** Zuñi Mountain.

**si-es'ta,** midday rest.

**Si-kul'hi-matk,** place where the water goes around, water-shed; Papago town.

**Si-pa-pu',** mist-encompassed place; under-world of the Pueblos.

**sit'itch,** small parrot.

**So-bai-pu'ris,** Indians formerly about Tucson, Arizona.

**So-cor'ro,** New Mexican pueblo and town; from Our Lady of Succor.

**som-bre'ro,** hat.

**som-bre'ro ne'gro,** black hat.

**So-no-it'a,** former Jesuit mission, Arizona.

**so-pa-i'pas,** crullers.

**so-tol',** bear's-grass, any grass substitute for fiber.

**so-we'sa,** tree cactus of Mexico.

**staves of San Juan,** hollyhocks.

**Ta-bi-ra',** former Piros pueblo of New Mexico.

**Ta-ji'que,** former Tigua pueblo of New Mexico.

**Tal-la-has'see,** old town, Seminole settlement, Florida.

**Tal'pa,** knob, hamlet near Taos, New Mexico.

**ta-mal'es,** cakes of meat, corn meal and chile, cooked in corn husks.

**Ta'os (towse),** Tigua pueblo, New Mexico.

**Ta-ra-hu-mar'acs,** Indians of Sierra Madre, Mexico.

**Tav-wots',** the rabbit, Ute, and Paiute hero.

**Tca-mah-heehe,** leader of the Snake Dance.

**tem-por-al'es,** rainstorms.

**Te-na-bo',** former pueblo, Estancia Valley, New Mexico.

**te'o-ca-lli,** god-house, Mexico.

**te'o-sin-te,** grass of the gods.

**Te-pey-ac',** Mexican town, scene of the miracle of Guadalupe.

**Te-su'que,** cottonwood grove; Tewa pueblo near Santa Fé.

**Te'wa,** linguistic group of Rio Grande pueblos.

**ti-en'da,** store.

**ti-er'ra,** earth.

**ti-er'ra A-ma-ri'lla,** yellow earth.

**Ti'gua,** one of the linguistic groups of Rio Grande pueblos.

**Ti-guex' (guesh),** Tigua town on the Rio Grande.

**ti-na'ja,** water-jar, tank.

**Ti-na'jas Al'tas,** high tanks.

**Tin-ne-ma-ha',** Paiute hero.

**ti'po-nis,** sacred objects, fetishes.

**ti-zon',** firebrand.

**Tjuk-son',** at the foot of the black hill; original of Tucson.

**Tlas-calans',** one of the tribes of Mexico.

**tom'be,** drum.

**Tom-pi'ros,** Indians of the Salinas.

**Ton'to,** stupid, Apache band.

**To-po'hua,** Papago town.

**tor-ne'o,** whirlwind.

**tor-ti'lla,** native corn cakes.

**To-yo-al'lan-ne, Towayal'la-ne,** corn mountain of the Zuñis.

**Tram'pas,** pitfall, bog; New Mexican town.

**Tru'chas,** trout; New Mexican town.

**Tsan-ka-wi',** place of round cactus, Pajaritan ruin.

**Tse'ghi,** place among the cliffs; otherwise Cañon de Chelly.

**Tshri'gi,** bird; Pajaritan ruin.

**Tsot'sil,** Navajo name for Mt. Taylor.

**Tu-bac',** Jesuit mission in Arizona.

**Tu-cum-ca'ri,** Jesuit mission in Arizona.

**Tum-mo-moc',** horned toad; hill near Tucson, Ariz.

**Tu-sa-yan',** national forest; Hopi country.

**Uh-an-am-i,** Mount of the beloved; cliffs near Zuñi.

**U-in'i-pin, U-in'i-puts,** mischievous sprites of the Utes and Paiutes.

**U-in'ka-ret,** where the pine grows; tribe and mountains.

**U-in'tah,** Paiute band and mountains.

**U-ta-va-o-kat',** inner bone month, middle of winter; Papago.

**Val'dez,** hamlet in New Mexico.

**Va'lle de Cor-a-zon'es,** valley of hearts, Mexico.

**Va-vo-ko-li'que,** Papago form of Bobaquivari.

**Ve'gas,** meadows; place name.

**Ve-lar'de,** the lookout; place name.

**ve-lo'ri-o,** song service in honor of a saint.

**vi'gas,** rafters of a house.

**vi-ik-an shoo-tak,** lasting water, Papago.

**vi'lla re-al',** royal city, official foundation.

**Wal-pi'**, the notch, Hopi pueblo.

**wick'i-up**, round hut of brush.

**wo-kon'da**, or *wakanda*, the essential spirit of things.

**Yam'pa**, in one dialect, bear; in another, plant; one of the divisions of the Utes.

**Ya'va-pai**, people of the sun; Mohava-Apaches in Arizona.

**ye'i**, Navajo divinities.

**yer'ba san'ta**, herb of the saints; mint.

**ye'so**, whitewash.

**Yu'ma**, Indians on lower Colorado.

**Yun'que-Yun'que**, early Tewa pueblo near San Juan.

**Zu'ñi**, pueblo and people of Shiwina, New Mexico.